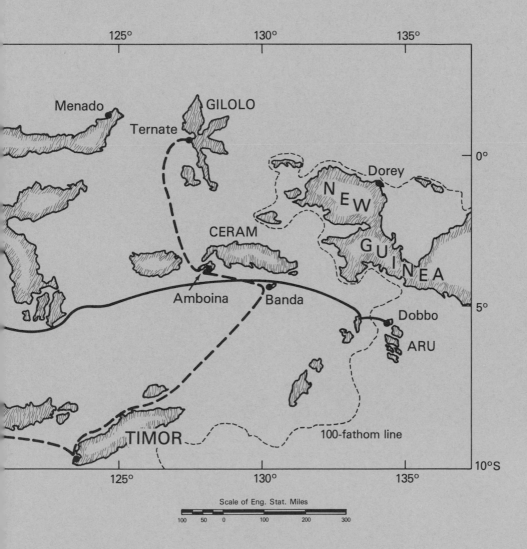

125°　　　　130°　　　　135°

Menado

GILOLO

Ternate

0°

Dorey

N E W

CERAM

G U I N E A

Amboina　　Banda

5°

Dobbo

ARU

TIMOR

100-fathom line

125°　　　　130°　　　　135°　　　10°S

Scale of Eng. Stat. Miles

100　50　0　　100　　200　　300

Just Before the Origin

JUST BEFORE
THE ORIGIN:
*Alfred Russel Wallace's
Theory of Evolution*

JOHN LANGDON BROOKS

New York   Columbia University Press   *1984*

Library of Congress Cataloging in Publication Data

Brooks, John Langdon, 1920–
Just before the origin.

Bibliography: p.
Includes index.
1. Wallace, Alfred Russel, 1823–1911.
2. Evolution—History.   3. Naturalists—England—
Biography.   I. Title.
QH31.W2B76   1983   575.01′62′0924   [B]   83-7710
ISBN 0-231-05676-1

Columbia University Press
New York   Guildford, Surrey

*Clothbound editions of Columbia University Press books are Smyth-sewn and
printed on permanent and durable acid-free paper.*

To
Yvette

CONTENTS

*PREFACE

The objective of this book is to reconstruct the stepwise elaboration of Alfred Wallace's ideas about the laws of organic change—what we now call evolution. This necessitated an examination of the experiential background for the concepts presented by Wallace in four major essays and several briefer statements on organic change written and published during his years (1848–1858) of collecting and studying natural history in tropical forests of the New and Old Worlds. His observations are revealed in a series of other scientific papers also published in British natural-history journals, in published and manuscript accounts of his travels, and in manuscript records of his collections. Because Wallace was surprisingly reticent about the circumstances of the formulation of most of his "pre-Darwinian" statements on organic change, these reconstructions are deductive and sometimes, of necessity, speculative.

Sufficient text of Wallace's important theoretical contributions is included to provide the reader with access to Wallace's ideas in the contexts in which he presented them in the pages of natural-history journals. I think that one of the reasons for the relative ignorance of Wallace's concepts has been their inaccessibility to most readers, scholars and lay people alike. Darwin's *Origin of Species,* on the other hand, has been in print since 1859 and available on most library shelves. One aim of this book is to bring Wallace's work out of its undeserved obscurity, so that the similar, but differing, formulations of these two great contemporary British naturalists of the last century can be compared.

One consequence of this study was the realization that a reexamination of the influence of Wallace's ideas on Darwin's own conception of organic change might shed further light on one of the crucial events in the history of thought about the world of life. Chapters 10 and 11 and the Epilogue are devoted to such a reexamination.

ACKNOWLEDGMENTS

The initial steps in this inquiry were facilitated by the excellent holdings of the Kline Science Library, Yale University, in nineteenth-century natural-history journals and books. It is a pleasure to acknowledge the help offered by the staff of the Kline Library, particularly that of John A. Harrison, Librarian, some fifteen years ago.

The consultation of European archival sources in 1967 was made possible by a grant (No. 4595) from the Penrose Fund of the American Philosophical Society. The Linnean Society of London provided access to its extensive collection of Wallace's manuscript materials. The assistance of that Society, and that of Th. O'Grady, then Executive Secretary, is gratefully acknowledged. Thanks are due M. J. Rowland, then Librarian at the British Museum (Natural History), and his Personal Assistant, Maria Skramovsky, who were most helpful in arranging for my examination and photocopying of the records of Wallace's collections in the Malay Archipelago.

Consultation of the Darwin Papers at the Cambridge University Library in 1967, and again in 1980, provided information of signal importance. I am most grateful for the assistance of many persons on both occasions. On my initial visit, Robert Stauffer of the University of Wisconsin helped set my course; through Daniel Merriman, Master of Davenport College, Yale, Sir Eric Ashby, Master of Clare College, Cambridge, generously arranged my access to the Darwin Papers; and Sydney Smith of St. Catherine's College provided expert guidance through the initially bewildering volume of Darwin material. On both visits, P. J. Gautrey, Under-Librarian, provided gracious and knowledgeable help with the Darwin materials in the Anderson Room.

In 1967, archivists in the Netherlands were most helpful in providing information and access to materials relating to the mail system and schedules between the Dutch East Indies and Europe in 1858. Harry Benda, then with the Southeast Asia Studies Program at Yale, provided initial guidance to these sources, for which I am in his debt. In the Hague, A. E. M. Ribberink, Chief Archivist, Second Section, of Algemeen Rijksarchief (General State Archives) and Dr. R. E. J. Weber, Director of the Netherlands Postal Museum, provided critical information and were most generous with their assistance. To them I am most grateful.

The only long segment of uninterrupted time devoted to this otherwise "after-hours" study was provided by a six-month sabbatical leave from the National Science Foundation, September 1980 through February 1981. I am pleased to acknowledge my gratitude to the Foundation, especially to Dr. Eloise E. Clark, Assistant Director for Biological, Behavioral, and Social Sciences, for approving my request; to Dr. Robert Rabin, Deputy Assistant Director of that Directorate, who encouraged me to apply for the sabbatical; and to Dr. Frank B. Golley, then Division Director, Environmental Biology, who endorsed my application.

My effective use of that time was in large part due to the facilities generously provided by the National Museum of Natural History, Smithsonian Institution. The Museum offered two essentials, quiet space and an excellent natural-history library. Special thanks go to Richard S. Fiske, Director of the National Museum of Natural History, for his enthusiastic endorsement of my request; Martin A. Buzas, Chairman of the Department of Paleobiology, for generously providing a room; and Robert M. Maloy, Director of the Smithsonian Institution Libraries, and Jack P. Marquardt, Senior Reference Librarian, for special kindnesses and unfailing help.

The sabbatical leave from the Foundation generously provided travel funds for consultation of archival sources and for the typing of the manuscript. P. Ackery, Assistant Curator of Entomology, British Museum (Natural History) kindly assisted in the location of some of Wallace's specimens of *Ornithoptera*. Discovery of records of the 1858 P & O mailing schedules came about through information on the possible existence of that material provided by Steven Rabson, Librarian, P & O Steamship Navigation Co., Beaufort House, London, who also provided the relevant dates; I am profoundly grateful.

R. W. Jones, in charge of the CHQ/Record Room, Postal Headquarters, London, and his assistant, Mrs. Constantinides, were patient and resourceful in helping me find what to all of us seemed a needle in a haystack.

Readers' comments were helpful, especially those of my former colleague, S. Dillon Ripley, Secretary of the Smithsonian Institution, a long-time expert on the fauna of Southeast Asia.

I am most grateful for permission to quote unpublished material from the American Philosophical Society, the Syndics of the Cambridge University Library, the Council of the Linnean Society, and the Trustees of the British Museum (Natural History).

Grateful thanks are due the typists who struggled to convert my handwriting to flawless typescript: Gloria McCabe, Sheila Matthews, and Janet Nevin Shepherd. It is a pleasure to acknowledge the helpful commitment of Susan Koscielniak, Associate Executive Editor of the Columbia University Press, and the meticulous concern of the Manuscript Editor, Amy Fass.

Finally, my greatest debt of gratitude is to my wife, Yvette, a debt the extent of which only she and I know.

Just Before the Origin

CHAPTER ONE

Beginnings

The odyssey began, if beginnings after birth can ever be identified, in 1844, just after Alfred Wallace attained his majority. He had arrived in Leicester, a small industrial city north of London, to teach at the Collegiate School. His duties were to assist the younger students in English reading and composition and in arithmetic, and to provide instruction in beginning drawing and surveying to students evincing an interest.

He had felt some trepidation about teaching, because he had been an apprentice land surveyor with his eldest brother, William, for the seven years since completing the curriculum at Hertford Grammar School. Long hours of rough field work left little time for reading, and the more remote parts of western England and southern Wales had offered little reading material. On his occasional idle days he had learned all he could from his brother's technical books—trigonometry, the rudiments of celestial navigation, and elementary astronomy. His curiosity had been increasingly drawn to the plants that were the environment for much of his daily toil. In 1841 he had spent one shilling from his meager supply for a paperbound book, published by the Society for the Diffusion of Useful Information, which dealt concisely with the elements of plant structure and provided descriptions of the common orders of British plants. This book had become Wallace's delight, because it enabled him to determine the major taxonomic assignment (Order) of most of the plants he collected. In order to make precise, specific identifications, he bought a botany textbook (Lindley's *Elements of Botany*), which proved on inspection to be of little utility in this regard. He then borrowed a large, expensive book that would provide this information. On the margins of Lindley, and on interleaved sheets, he made notes that encapsulated the desired descriptions. But he knew that knowledge of the natural world would have no more place in the curriculum at the Collegiate School than it had had at Hertford.

Alfred had enjoyed the way of life that surveying required—the rough, outdoor work with the opportunity to indulge his interest in the plants around him—but circumstance forced him to leave it. The spate of survey work that had enabled William to keep Alfred, and on occasion a second apprentice, had been required by the Commutation of Tithes Act of 1836. By late 1843, however, the surveys were largely completed, and the pace of William's business slackened. In December William was obliged to inform his brother that he could no longer provide employment, and Alfred soon left for London to seek some other job. Fortunately, he was able to share the lodging of his brother John. Teaching seemed one of the few possibilities, and the position open at the Collegiate School was one of two for which Alfred had felt qualified. Hertford Grammar School had provided classes in English, history, geography, arithmetic, algebra, and Latin—a standard curriculum but one that he had found quite uninspiring. He, like William, had some talent for drawing, and he had had adequate experience in surveying. For his interview with the headmaster Alfred had brought pencil sketches and a colored map he had drafted for an area near Neath, South Wales. Reverend Abraham Hill, the headmaster, proved kindly and was suitably impressed.

His fears about meeting the demands of his new job were unfounded. After a few misunderstandings about school protocol, Alfred found his duties easily performed. The school provided room and board, and in addition he received about thirty or forty pounds a year, compensation that seemed quite adequate. His brother had been able to provide only room and board. Money for clothes, and meager pocket money, had come from a small legacy left Alfred by his grandfather and carefully meted out by William.

More precious compensation was the free time every day for reading. When classes were over at four or five, his time was his own. A small subscription provided access to the Leicester library. Alfred's father had been librarian in Hertford, and as a boy Alfred had spent after-school hours in the town library. In his last year there, after John, who had been his closest companion, had left for London, the library had provided a welcome refuge. In his autobiography (*My Life*) Wallace recalled some of the books in the Leicester library that he believed were signal in shaping his future. Among others, he noted Humboldt's *Personal Narrative,* which first had awakened a desire to see the tropics. But he singled out Malthus' *Principles of Population,* "which I greatly admired for its masterly summary of facts and logical induction to conclusions. It was the first work I had yet read treating any of the problems of philosophical biology, and its main principles remained with me as a permanent possession, and twenty years later gave me the long-sought clue to the effective agent in the evolution of organic species" (Wallace 1905 1:232). Wallace read the sixth edition (1826), the last that Malthus himself prepared. A brief digression will indicate why knowledge of the edition is noteworthy.

The first edition of *An Essay on the Principle of Population* was a tract written in relative haste to call attention to what seemed to Malthus the inevitable and imminently disastrous outcome for society of unrestrained population growth. He appears to have been impelled by then-current expressions of optimism on this subject. The immediate occasion was the proposal of legislation to change the management of the Poor Law in Great Britain so that welfare payments would be in proportion to family size. In the opinion of Reverend Malthus such an act would be sheer folly; instead of solving the basic problem, he believed, the change would exacerbate it. As might be expected, publication of his tract in 1798 drew some approbation but a storm of criticism. The view presented in the first edition is the one that the name "Malthus" now usually conjures. The second and subsequent editions bore the same title as the first but were quite different in content and emphasis. The latter can be judged by the new subtitle, *A View on the Past and Present Effects on Human Happiness; with an Inquiry into Our Prospect Respecting the Future Removal or Mitigation of the Evils Which it Occasions.*

The extensive criticisms of the first edition had stirred Malthus to undertake a careful examination of all available literature on the population problem. He traveled to mainland Europe for further enlightenment—statistics, facts, theories. The resultant second edition, published in 1803, was, as noted, a quite different book. (The text was essentially unchanged by Malthus in subsequent editions; the supporting evidence was periodically updated.) It has been said that the first form of the *Essay on Population* was conclusive as an argument but was based on scant and questionable information. Its second form, on the other hand, while based on extensive information, was inconclusive as an argument. As Wallace later noted, this information was as important to him as the logic of the argument; indeed, it was this, not the argument, that provided Wallace with the "long-sought clue" two decades thence.

In reviewing the books that Wallace recalled having read at Leicester, one feels no surprise that Humboldt's should be among them. Malthus seems a less obvious choice for a self-taught naturalist. But Wallace, unlike many naturalists, was interested in the human condition, an interest that had been aroused at an impressionable age. At thirteen he had gone to London to lodge with his brother John, who was at that time apprenticed to a small builder. This arrangement was necessary because Alfred's parents had moved to a small house without room for him before William's surveying business was sufficiently established. As Alfred was only marking time until he could join William, he passed the days in the builder's milling and carpentry shop, watching, listening to the workmen, and helping out when possible. But at the finish of the ten-hour workday, John, being a good worker and of the required sixteen years of age, was completely free from seven until ten in the evening. The two then often roamed the streets examining the shops and other sights. "But our evenings were most frequently spent at what was termed a 'Hall of Science.' . . . It was really a kind of club or mechanics institute, for advanced thinkers among workmen, and especially for the followers of Robert Owen, the founder of the Socialist movement in England. Here we sometimes heard lectures of Owen's doctrines, or on the principle of secularism or agnosticism, as it is now called . . ." (Wallace 1905 1:87).

"Although later in my life my very scant knowledge of his work was not sufficient to prevent my adopting the individualist views of Herbert Spencer and of the political economists, I have always looked upon Owen as my first teacher in the philosophy of human nature and my first guide through the labyrinth of social science. He influenced my character more than I then knew . . ." (Wallace 1905 1:104).

Some years after that London experience, during a slack period the previous fall (1843), Alfred had written an account of the life and manners of the Welsh farmers as he had observed them during the several years he worked and lived among them. This article had been prepared for publication, but it was rejected by a London magazine as being more suited to an agricultural than to a popular magazine. Although this 10,000-word essay concentrated on the agricultural practices of "The South Wales Farmer," it commented as well on his domestic arrangements, customs, language, and character. Knowing all this, we can better comprehend the attraction of Malthus for young Wallace, browsing in the Leicester library the following year.

A fateful event of his year at Leicester was his making the acquaintance of a young man who was another natural-history enthusiast, Henry Walter Bates. Bates, whose name is familiar to biologists in the phrase "Batesian mimicry," was born two years later than Wallace into a family that had been associated with the hosiery manufacturing enterprises of Leicester for several generations. As it was intended that Henry continue in a business that had provided financial security for his parents, he had left boarding school at thirteen to be apprenticed to a hosiery manufacturer. Henry's avidity as a collector of insects during his schoolboy days was not diminished during his subsequent apprenticeships. Any leisure time was passed in the fields hunting insects, or attending classes at the Mechanic's Institute in Leicester (Clodd, in Bates 1892). By 1843 beetles entirely absorbed his collecting interest. He had contributed an article entitled "Notes on Coleopterous insects frequenting damp places" to the first volume of a periodical called the *Zoologist,* over a year before he and Alfred Wallace could have met. Although his name is most commonly associated with mimicry among Amazonian butterflies, beetles were a lifelong preoccupation.

By the time Alfred wrote his memoirs, his recollection of the circumstances of his first meeting with Bates was vague.

How I was introduced to Henry Walter Bates I do not exactly remember, but I rather think I heard him mentioned as an enthusiastic entomologist, and met him at the library. I found that his specialty was beetle collecting, though he also had a good set of British butterflies. Of the former I had scarcely heard, but as I already knew the fascinations of plant life I was quite prepared to take an interest in any other department of nature. He asked me to see his collection, and I was amazed to find the great number and variety of beetles, their many strange forms and often beautiful markings or colouring, and was even more surprised when I found that almost all I saw had been collected around Leicester, and that there were still many more to be discovered. If I had been asked before how many different kinds of beetles were to be found in any small district near a town, I should probably have guessed fifty or at the outside a hundred, and thought that a very liberal allowance. But I now learnt that many hundreds could easily be collected, and that there were probably a thousand different kinds within ten miles of the town. He also showed me a thick volume containing descriptions of more than three thousand species inhabiting the British Isles. I also learnt from him in what an infinite variety of places beetles may be found, while some may be collected all the year round, so I at once determined to begin collecting, as I did not find a great many new plants about Leicester. I therefore obtained a collecting bottle, pins, and a store-box; and in order to learn their names and classification I obtained, at wholesale price through Mr. Hill's bookseller, Stephen's ''Manual of British Coleoptera,'' which henceforth for some years gave me almost as much pleasure as Lindley's Botany, with my MS. descriptions, had already done. (Wallace 1905 1:236–237)

His friendship with Bates revealed to Wallace an entirely different ''department of nature.'' It also gave him someone with whom to share an enthusiasm for natural history. The earlier interest in flowering plants had developed and been sustained in essential solitude; having a companion for insect collecting was a novel experience. Alfred's early departure from Leicester did not interrupt this friendship. It was continued over the next years by occasional visits and through a regular correspondence, some letters of which have been preserved.

After William's unexpected death in February 1845, Alfred was permitted to leave the school at Easter. Soon after his return to Neath to continue the small building business that William had left, Alfred found that the great railroad mania which was to reach its peak that year would provide work for a surveyor. A supplement to the *Times* of London for November 17, 1845, carried a listing of "Railroad Interests of the United Kingdom." The summary stated that there were 47 completed railroads, 116 under construction, and 1,236 projected. Each projected line required extensive surveying. He worked in the field during the summer and into the autumn on a line to run through South Wales and then was required to go to London to rush the report to completion.

On November 9, 1845, while in London, Wallace concluded a letter to Bates by asking, "Have you read 'Vestiges of the Natural History of Creation' or is it out of your line?" "I well remember," wrote Wallace half a century later, "the excitement caused by the publication of the 'Vestiges,' and the eagerness and delight with which I read it. . . . The vague ideas of those who favoured evolution were first set forth in systematic form, with much literary skill and scientific knowledge . . ." (Wallace 1898:136, 137). *Vestiges of the Natural History of Creation* had first been published in October 1844. It aroused great interest and went through twelve editions, four in the first seven months. Only in the last, in 1884, was it revealed that the author had been Robert Chambers, then deceased. Robert Chambers was a well-known publisher and author, a Fellow of the Royal Society of Edinburgh, who had taken an amateur's interest in geology but did not claim to be a natural historian. In a "Note Conclusory" in the first edition the author had stated, "My sincere desire in the composition of the book was to give the true view of the history of nature, with as little disturbance as possible to existing beliefs, whether philosophical or religious." (Chambers 1844:389)

The book is a masterly development of an argument, supported by such information as the writer could find in the literature. Some of this supporting evidence was reasonably correct, some was naively incorrect. The author's hypothesis of development, toward which the first half of the book leads, is stated thus:

> The idea, then, which I form of the progress of organic life upon the globe—and the hypothesis is applicable to all similar theatres of vital being—is, *that the simplest and most primitive type, under a law to which that of like-production is subordinate, gave birth to the type next above it,*

that this again produced the next higher, and so on to the very highest, the
stages of advance being in all cases very small—namely, from one species
only to another so that the phenomenon has always been of a simple and
modest character. (p. 222)

The book slowly builds toward the concept that a natural law may
be effective in the formation of the organic world from a brief examination of the cosmos. The solar system is described with its laws
of planetary motion. This is followed by a consideration of the newly
discovered nebulae, or "nebulous stars." Noting their variety, the
author continues: "It may be presumed that all these are but stages
in a progress, just as if, seeing a child, a boy, a youth, a middle-
aged and an old man together, we might presume that the whole were
only variations of one being" (p. 8). Thus, the author early states an
analogy between progress in the cosmos and that in the organic world.
By then presenting the physical laws controlling progress in the cosmos, he prepares the reader for acceptance of the statement to be
made later that similarly pervasive laws operate in "organic life on
the globe . . . [and in] all similar theatres of vital being . . . ," as
the author stated in his hypothesis.

In the hundred pages that follow, the geological record is reviewed
and a strong case presented for progression from simple to complex
among the plants and animals in succeeding strata. "That there is a
progress of some kind, the most superficial glance at the geological
history is sufficient to convince us" (p. 149). This emphasis on progress in the life forms represented in successive geological strata is in
deliberate opposition to the concept of "nonprogressionism" on which
Charles Lyell and the orthodox still insisted, despite mounting evidence from the fossil hunters.

How, then, does this fact of the geological record come to be obvious?

A candid consideration of all these circumstances can scarely fail to
introduce into our minds a somewhat different idea of organic creation
from what has hitherto been generally entertained. That God created animated beings, as well as the terraqueous theatre of their being, is a fact so
powerfully evidenced, and so universally received, that I at once take it for
granted. But in the particulars of this so highly supported idea, we surely

here see cause for some re-consideration. It may now be inquired,—In what way was the creation of animated being effected? The ordinary notion may, I think, be not unjustly described as this,—that the Almighty author produced the progenitors of all existing species by some sort of personal or immediate exertion. But how does this notion comport with what we have seen of the gradual advance of species, from the humblest to the highest? How can we suppose an immediate exertion of this creative power at one time to produce zoophytes, another time to add a few marine mollusks, another to bring in one or two conchifers, again to produce crustaceous fishes, again perfect fishes, and so on to the end? This would surely be to take a very mean view of the Creative Power—to, in short, anthropomorphize it, or reduce it to some such character as that borne by the ordinary proceedings of mankind. And yet this would be unavoidable; for that the organic creation was thus progressive through a long space of time, rests on evidence which nothing can overturn or gainsay. Some other idea must then be come to with regard to *the mode* in which the Divine Author proceeded in the organic creation. . . . What is to hinder our supposing that the organic creation is also [as in the cosmos] a result of natural laws, which are in like manner an expression of his will? (p. 152–54)

The "law" which the author proposes is the developmental hypothesis initially quoted. A further word about the hypothesis as stated by Chambers is in order. It concerns the meaning of the clause: "a law to which that of like-production is subordinate. . . ." The author states that although ordinary observation suggests the truth of the dictum "like begets like," he considers it conceivable that like can beget unlike on rare occasions. Although such events may be so rare as to be yet unobserved, that does not prove them impossible.

The remainder of *Vestiges* views the classification of organisms, the early history of mankind, and the "mental constitutions of animals," including man, in the light of this developmental hypothesis.

Much contemporary opinion of this book was condemnatory, and Bates appears to have shared this opinion to some extent. In the following letter, written December 28, 1845, from London, Wallace responded to Bates's (unrecorded) reply with the words:

I have rather a more favourable opinion of the 'Vestiges' than you appear to have. I do not consider it a hasty generalization, but rather as an ingenious hypothesis strongly supported by some striking facts and analogies, but which remains to be proved by more facts and the additional light which more research may throw upon the problem. It [at all events] furnishes a subject for every observer of nature [to turn his attention to]; every fact he observes [must] make either for or against it, and it thus [furnishes] both an incitement to the collection of facts, and an object to which [to apply them] when collected. [I would observe that] many eminent writers [give great] support [to] the theory of the progressive development of species in animals and plants. There is a very philosophical work bearing directly on the question—Lawrence's 'Lectures on Man'—delivered before the Royal College of Surgeons, now published in a cheap form. The great object of these 'Lectures' is to illustrate the different races of mankind, and the manner in which they probably originated, and he arrives at the conclusion (as also does Pritchard in his work on the 'Physical History of Man') that the varieties of the human race have not been produced by any external causes, but are due to the development of certain distinctive peculiarities in some individuals which have thereafter become propagated through an entire race. Now, I should say that a permanent peculiarity not produced by external causes is a characteristic of 'species' and not of mere 'variety,' and thus, if the theory of the 'Vestiges' is accepted, the Negro, the Red Indian, and the European are distinct species of the genus Homo.

An animal which differs from another by some decided and permanent character, however slight, which difference is undiminished by propagation and unchanged by climate and external circumstances, is universally held to be a distinct *species;* while one which is not regularly transmitted so as to form a distinct race, but is occasionally reproduced from the parent stock (like Albinoes), is generally, if the difference is not very considerable, classed as a *variety*. But I would class both these as distinct *species,* and would only consider those to be *varieties* whose differences are produced by external causes, and which, therefore, are not propagated as distinct races. . . . As a further support to the 'Vestiges,' I have heard that in his 'Cosmos' the venerable Humboldt supports its views in almost every particular, not excepting those relating to animal and vegetable life. This work I have a great desire to read, but fear I shall not have an opportunity at present. Read Lawrence's work; it is well worth it. (Wallace 1905 1:254–55; McKinney 1972:11 is source for original text—in brackets—replacing slightly edited phrases published by Wallace.)

The "Lawrence" cited as author of "Lectures of Man" was William Lawrence, born in 1783, a gifted surgeon long active at St.

Bartholomew's Hospital in London. The "Lectures on Man" to which Wallace referred in the letter to Bates were originally published in 1819 under the title *Lectures on Physiology, Zoology, and the Natural History of Man, Delivered at the Royal College of Surgeons*. The book includes three lectures on physiology and the content of twelve lectures on "The Natural History of Man," given during the summer of 1818. The part about man has two sections: the first reviews the distinctions between man and animals; the second, nearly half of the book, is titled "On the Varieties of the Human Species." The general conclusions on the causes of variation in man are stated thus:

> The causes which operate on the bodies of living animals either modify the individual, or alter the offspring. The former are of great importance in the history of animals, and produce considerable alteration in individuals; but the latter are the most powerful, as they affect the species, and cause the diversity of races. Great influence has at all times been ascribed climate, which indeed has been commonly, but very loosely and indefinitely, represented as the cause of most important modifications in the human subject and other animals. . . . While, however, we have no precise information on the kind or degree of influence attributable to such [climatic] causes, we have abundance of proof that they are entirely inadequate to account for the differences between the various races of men. . . . (Lawrence 1819:324–25)
>
> It is obvious that the external influences . . . , even though we should allow to them a much greater influence on individuals than experience warrants us in admitting, would be still entirely inadequate to account for those signal diversities, which constitute differences of race in animals. These can be explained only by two principles already mentioned; namely, the occasional production of an offspring with different characters from those of the parents, as a native or congenital variety; and the propagation of such varieties by generation. It is impossible, in the present state of physiological knowledge, to show how this is effected. . . . (p. 329)

In taking this position Lawrence had come down against the prevailing opinion, which followed Buffon and the pioneer anthropologist Blumenbach, who had been persuaded that the differences between human races were environmental, i.e., "climatically" induced. Lawrence, on the other hand, was taking the position of James Cowles Prichard, author of *Researches into the Physical History of Man* (1813). Lawrence, acknowledging sources in his *Lectures,* started with Buffon and Blumenbach, ending with "and Dr. Prichard in this country, whose clear statements, convincing reasoning, and very extensive information, stamp the highest value on his interesting work, and distinguish it very advantageously from most other productions on the same subject'' (Lawrence 1819:82).

Looking back to this well-respected source, we find that in 1808, while in attendance at the Medical Faculty of the University of Edinburgh, Prichard prepared his medical dissertation on human races. He appears to have chosen the topic because he was unable to accept the view of Buffon, Blumenbach, and others, that racial differences were a result of a direct influence of environmental factors. He argued instead that any changes caused by external factors are limited to the individual affected, that they are not transmitted to the next generation and could therefore have no role in the establishment of racial differences. Instead he proposed that human races, as well as varieties of plants and animals, were to be attributed to accumulation of variations in the parental germinative cells that were invariably transmitted to the offspring, which he called "connate" variations.

A slightly expanded version of the original Latin dissertation was published in 1813, with the title "Researches into the Physical History of Man." Lawrence used the 1808 and 1813 editions as sources for his 1818 lectures. Interestingly, Dr. Prichard in later editions of this work yielded to strong criticism and backed away from his strong stance against the role of external factors. Fortunately Prichard's unusual views reached a wide readership through the medium of Lawrence's *Lectures,* which had many printings, including the "cheap form" alluded to by Wallace.

The publishing history of the *Lectures* is sufficiently unusual to merit comment. Published in 1819, they aroused severe criticism from colleagues at the Royal College of Surgeons because of Lawrence's attack on a colleague who, in the course of the previous year's lecture, had espoused John Hunter's vitalism. Lawrence himself strongly believed that a "vital spirit" had no place in physiology. Rather, he believed that all physiological phenomena, although extremely complex, are subject to the laws of physics and chemistry. Under threat of losing his hospital post as surgeon, he consented to withdraw his publication within a month of its release. Nonetheless, his book went through ten editions, one of which was pirated in 1822. Lawrence was unable to prevent this pirating because the Chancery Court denied him copyright on the grounds that parts of his book were "directed against the truth of the Scripture." One basis for this judgment was undoubtedly Lawrence's statement that mental activity was solely a function of the brain.

> If the intellectual phenomena of man require an immaterial principle superadded to the brain, we must equally concede it to those more rational animals, which exhibit manifestations differing from some of those of the human only in degree. If we grant it to these, we cannot refuse it to the next in order; and so on in succession to the whole series; to the oyster, the sea anemone, the polype, the microscopic animalcules. Is any one prepared to admit the existence of immaterial principles in all these cases? if not, he must equally reject it in man. (p. 22)

Whatever attitude Lawrence held about these unauthorized editions is unclear, but various printings continued to appear, thus ensuring a wide dissemination of Lawrence's words, despite two interdictions.

There is no indication that Wallace ever read Prichard's great work itself. His misspelling of Prichard's name in the Bates letter suggests a lack of direct acquaintance. It was only through the "cheap form" of Lawrence's *Lectures* that Wallace apparently learned of Prichard's perceptive views of the nature of variation and its significance for the establishment of human races and of the varieties of animals and plants.

This Bates-Wallace correspondence must have been fairly regular, although we have but fragments, because in a letter from Neath—dated April 11, 1846, less than four months later—Wallace remarked: "I was much pleased to find you so well appreciated Lyell. I first read Darwin's 'Journal' three or four years ago, and have lately re-read it. As the Journal of a scientific traveller, it is second only to Humboldt's 'Personal Narrative'—a work of general interest perhaps superior to it. He is an ardent admirer and most able supporter of Mr. Lyell's view" (Wallace 1905 1:255). A sentence later on in this letter reveals Wallace's sense of isolation: "I quite envy you, who have friends near you attached to the same pursuits. I do not know a single person in this little town who studies any one branch of natural history, so that I am quite alone in this respect" (Wallace 1905 1:256).

"Lyell" refers to Sir Charles Lyell's *Principles of Geology: Being an Attempt to Explain the Former Changes of the Earth's Surface by Reference to Causes Now in Operation.* In subsequent editions, the subtitle became *or, the Modern Changes of the Earth and its Inhabitants, Considered as Illustrative of Geology* (1847). When Lyell published the first volume of his *Principles,* in 1830, the majority of geologists adhered to one or another variant of catastrophism. Catastrophists believed that the surface of the earth and its inhabitants had been subject to violent alteration one or more times in the past by forces and events the like of which man has never witnessed. Those who believed in universal floods covering the land, for example, saw the vast valleys of today's rivers as the results of fierce erosive scouring when those floodwaters receded from the land. These catastrophes were seen as having been responsible for mass extinctions. God then created new suites of animals and plants to repopulate the face of the earth when once again it became habitable. The fact that the youngest strata contained fossils of more species living today was taken as an indication of God's wish that successive sets of his Creations should increasingly resemble that extant array of which man himself is a member. By such formulations natural philosophers of the early nineteenth century sought to explain two troublesome revelations of geology in ways compatible with Scripture. One was the former existence of life forms now extinct. The other was the evident progression up through the geological record from sometimes simpler, but usually unfamiliar, forms of life toward the assembly of complex forms that now share the earth with man.

Lyell had a different world view, one now generally accepted. He argued most ably in his first volume that geological events and forces were uniform through all time and were therefore observable today. By careful observation of forces now at work, he argued, the geologist would be able to comprehend the phenomena of the past as recorded in the rocks. Mighty valleys had been eroded, he said, not by some catastrophic flood but by erosion of the magnitudes now observable in the valley's river; slow, fitful erosion, but effective over immense stretches of time.

The second volume, published in 1832, offered his uniformitarian approach to changes in the living world through time. The challenge of demonstrating that such changes—the creation and extinction of species—were now observable was a formidable one. He chose to demonstrate that extinction could be the result of natural forces, even though the extinction of the dodo was the only unequivocal example during recent times. Lyell conceived of physiographic changes as being the cause of extinctions in two ways: by inducing climatic modification and by enabling alterations in the balance of species within biological communities. Lyell saw biological communities as quite stable, with each component species having a particular role. Too great a change in the composition of a biological community, such as the introduction of an aggressively growing plant or of a more efficient grazer or predator, might threaten the existence of a once-thriving member of the community, possibly leading to its extinction. The creation of species was more bothersome, and he invoked a supernatural force, a First Cause, the only such invocation in his entire formulation. He conceived of this "Creative Power" as spread more or less evenly over the habitable parts of the earth. Each new species was created with attributes to fit it precisely into a particular role in its biological community. But every creation was modeled, according to Lyell, "on types analogous to those of existing plants and animals, as to indicate, throughout, a perfect harmony of design and unity of purpose." But in this formulation Lyell essentially denied that there was an organic progression through the geological record toward the present constitution of the living world. Man was the exception.

This stance denying progression became more and more questionable in the decade following the appearance of the *Principles* and, as we have noted, was probably a strong factor in prompting Chambers to prepare *Vestiges*.

"Darwin's 'Journal' " refers, of course, to Charles Darwin's *Journal of Researches into the Geology and Natural History of the Various Countries Visited by H.M.S. Beagle Under the Command of Capt. Fitzroy, R.N. from 1832–36* (1839). This book, commonly referred to as *Voyage of the Beagle,* records observations during the five-year voyage, which had been largely occupied with a survey of the coast of South America. At the start of the voyage Captain Fitzroy presented Darwin with a copy of the recently published first volume of

Lyell's *Principles*. In his eyes Darwin's primary responsibility seems to have been geological reconnaissance in South America, to assess the possibilities for future mineral exploitation. At their first landfall Darwin, whose previous meager geological training had been with a confirmed catastrophist, found Lyell's approach immediately useful in field interpretations. Present conditions were, indeed, a key to understanding the past. He was a convert to uniformitarianism; his copy of the first volume of the *Principles* is heavily annotated. Devoted attention to geological phenomena in South America and, briefly, in the Pacific area produced significant contributions to the understanding of continental uplift and subsidence, and coral-reef formation. Lyell was delighted with these findings.

The science of the first edition of the *Journal* was largely geological. Subsequent editions had an increasing amount of biological detail as the various experts to whom the collections had been sent reported the identifications of the specimens Darwin had collected. This shift in emphasis is reflected in the changed wording of the subtitle; beginning with the second edition (Darwin 1845), *"natural history"* comes before *"geology."* But even in the last edition Darwin said nothing of evolution. There is no persuasive evidence that Darwin even considered the possibility of species transmutation until several months after his return to England (Kohn 1980). This fact requires emphasis only because some recent treatments of Darwin's life have suggested otherwise.

While the Wallace-Bates correspondence chiefly concerned insect collecting, it also provided an avenue for the exchange of ideas on philosophical biology and revealed a philosophical inclination more strongly developed in Wallace than in Bates. The letters of Wallace are especially valuable to us, as they furnish contemporary documentation of his quickening interest in evolutionary problems and of the literature that both satisfied and whetted this interest.

The spate of surveying work ceased abruptly when the massive railroad speculation ended in a panic, and Alfred and John, whom Alfred had persuaded to leave his London job and return to Neath, could make only a modest living with their general building business. Furthermore, this business provided none of the satisfactions that Alfred had derived from outdoor surveying work. Insect collecting was now his chief enjoyment. One minor satisfaction must have come from his capture of a rare beetle species in South Wales. A letter published in the *Zoologist* in 1846 marked the first appearance of the name Alfred R. Wallace in biological literature. It stated as introduction that the correspondent knew of no record of *Trichius fasciatus* having been recorded from the British Isles within the preceding two decades. "Capture of *Trichius fasciatus* near Neath—I took a single specimen of this beautiful insect on a blossom of *Carduus heterophyllus* near the falls at the top of the Neath Vale. Alfred R. Wallace—Neath." (Wallace 1847:1676)

It is not surprising, therefore, that when Alfred was again casting about for a means of livelihood, he should consider the vocational possibilities of natural-history collecting. Such collecting could, of course, be profitable only in a tropical region with a rich and relatively unknown fauna. Precisely when Alfred began to consider this possibility seriously is not clear. With reference to a visit to Neath made by Bates, Wallace said, "I think, in the summer of 1847 he came on a week's visit . . . and it must have been at this time that we talked over a proposed collecting trip to the tropics, but had not then decided where to go" (Wallace 1905 1:254). Alfred visited Paris in late September or early October, at the invitation of his sister Frances (Fanny), who had just returned home after teaching French for several years in the United States. After his return he wrote a long letter to Bates:

> After referring to a day spent in the insect room of the British Museum on my way home, and the overwhelming numbers of the beetles and butterflies I was able to look over, I add: "I begin to feel rather dissatisfied with a mere local collection; little is to be learnt by it. I sh[ould] like to take some one family to study thoroughly, principally with a view to the theory of the origin of species. By that means I am strongly of opinion that some definite results might be arrived at. Can you assist me in choosing one that it will be not difficult to obtain the greater number of the known species." (Wallace 1905 1:256; last sentence, omitted from published version, is from original text in McKinney 1969:12)

Definite plans must soon have been formulated to put these thoughts into action. Bates (1863) stated in the opening lines of the preface to *The Naturalist on The River Amazons:*

In the autumn of 1847 Mr. A. R. Wallace, who has since acquired wide
fame in connection with the Darwinian theory of Natural Selection, proposed to me a joint expedition to the river Amazon, for the purpose of
exploring the Natural History of its banks; the plan being to make for
ourselves a collection of objects, dispose of the duplicates in London to
pay expenses, and gather facts, as Mr. Wallace expressed it in one of his
letters, "toward solving the problem of the origin of species," a subject
on which we had conversed and corresponded much together.

Bates thus indicated that it was Wallace who made the proposal
that they go to Pará. The decision in favor of this particular area of
the tropics appears to have followed a perusal of *A Voyage up the
Amazon,* published that year (1847) by an American, Witt Edwards
(Wallace 1853g:iii). Edwards had written so glowingly of the beauty
and luxuriance of the tropical vegetation, the hospitality of the people, and the moderate cost of living that the two decided that this was
the ideal place for their work, provided that they could meet their
expenses by the sale of their duplicates. Mr. Doubleday of the British
Museum assured them that the fauna of northern Brazil was little
known and that by collecting all orders of insects, birds, mammals,
and land snails they should be able to cover their expenses. Encouraged, they began to make preparations, one of the first of which was
to find an agent to handle their affairs in London.

We were fortunate in finding an excellent and trustworthy agent in
Mr. Samuel Stevens. . . . He continued to act as my agent during my
whole residence abroad, sparing no pains to dispose of my duplicates
to the best advantage, taking charge of my private collections, insuring
each collection as its dispatch was advised, keeping me supplied with
cash, and with such stores as I required, and, above all, writing me
fully as to the progress of the sale of each collection, what striking
novelties it contained, and giving me general information on the progress of other collectors and on matters of general scientific interest.
During the whole period of our business relations, extending over more
than fifteen years, I cannot remember that we ever had the least disagreement about any matter whatever (Wallace 1905 1:266).

They planned to sail for Pará in early spring to take advantage of
the dry season. Leaving the faltering business in John's hands, and

gambling all on what he called his "wild scheme," Alfred took the £100 he had been able to save during the time of the railway surveying in 1845, met Bates in London in March 1848, and booked passage for Brazil. On April 20 they embarked from Liverpool on a small, fast sailing vessel. The two naturalists, the only passengers, had been assured that the *Mischief* was rated A-1 at Lloyd's.

CHAPTER TWO
Amazonian Venture

TO NATURALISTS, &c.

SAMUEL STEVENS, NATURAL HISTORY AGENT, No. 24 BLOOMSBURY STREET, BEDFORD SQUARE, begs to announce that he has recently received from South America *Two* beautiful Consignments of INSECTS of all orders in very fine Condition, collected in the province of Pará, containing numbers of very rare and some new species, also a few LAND and FRESHWATER SHELLS, and some BIRD SKINS and several small parcels of Insects, &c., from New Zealand, New Holland, India, and the Cape, all of which are for Sale by Private Contract.

Figure 2.1. Advertisement placed by S. Stevens, Agent, announcing arrival of first shipment of natural-history collections made by Wallace and Bates near Pará. (Inside cover, *Ann. Mag. Nat. Hist.* (1850), 2d ser. 5)

Despite the delight and excitement of the first months in the tropics after their arrival at Pará on May 26, 1848, Wallace and Bates must have been unable to suppress a feeling of concern as to whether they could make collecting pay their expenses. Fortunately, living was inexpensive and the district around Pará supports a remarkably diverse biota, especially rich in insect species. After two months of work they packed up their first shipment for Samuel Stevens. It contained specimens of more than 1,300 species of insects, 553 of which were Lepidoptera (some 400 species being butterflies likely to bring a good price) and about 450 beetles.

One means by which Stevens sought to interest prospective customers in these collections was the publication of excerpts from Wallace's letters, in the miscellany department of a journal widely read by naturalists, *Annals and Magazine of Natural History.* The letters provided many interesting facts relating to the collections themselves, as well as an impression of the problems that a professional collector faced. These excerpts from Wallace's early letters are the only contemporary documents known from this period of Wallace's travels. They appear to have been later overlooked by Wallace and by others.

I find no reference to them. Wallace refers to them neither in his account of his travels in Amazonia nor in his autobiography. Marchant (1916) does not include them in his list of Wallace letters.

Journey to Explore the Province of Parà [1]

Messrs. Wallace and Bates, two enterprising and deserving young men, left this country last April on an expedition to South America to explore some of the vast and unexamined regions of the province of Para, said to be so rich and varied in its productions of natural history. They have already forwarded two beautiful parcels of insects of all orders, containing about 7000 specimens in very fine condition, and a vast number of novelties, besides other rare species, some of which were known only to the entomological world by the beautiful figures in Cramer and Stoll, and a few shells and bird-skins. The last parcel is the result of their journey up the river Tocantins. The following passage is an extract from their letter to Mr. S. Stevens, dated Parà, Oct. 23, to whom the consignments have been forwarded, and who has the disposal of them (see Advertisement on cover). [Fig. 2.1]

If anyone is curious about our trip up the Tocantins, you may inform them that we ascended to about the 4th parallel of S. Lat. near the Rio Tabocas, having reached Arroya, the last abode of civilized people, and passed a little beyond to view the rapids called Guaribas. We hired one of the heavy iron boats with two sails for the voyage, with a crew of four Indians and a black cook. We had the usual difficulties of travellers in this country in the desertion of our crew, which delayed us six or seven days in going up; the voyage took us three weeks to Guaribas and two weeks returning. We reached a point about twenty miles below Arroya, beyond which a large canoe cannot pass in the dry season, from the rapids, falls and whirlpools which here commence and obstruct the navigation of this magnificent river more or less to its source; here we were obliged to leave our vessel and continue in an open boat, in which we were exposed for two days, amply repaid however by the beauty of the scenery, the river (here a mile wide) being studded with rocky and sandy islets of all sizes, and richly clad with vegetation; the shores high and undulating, covered with a dense but picturesque forest; the waters dark and clear as crystal; and the excitement in shooting fearful rapids, &c. acted as a necessary stimulant under the heat of an

1. In these letters the spelling of geographical names, including diacritical marks, is presented here as it was printed in the Annals, even though that spelling may be at variance with currently accepted usage.

equatorial sun, and thermometer 95° in the shade. Our collections were
chiefly made lower down the river. During the five weeks of our journey we had no rain till the last two days. The weather here is as de-
lightful as ever; the mornings invariably fine, and a shower in the after-
noon every third or fourth day, which cools and refreshes everything
delightfully. The heat is never oppressive; the nights always cool; there
can certainly be no climate in the world superior to this, and few equal.
Since sending our last collection, we have had further experience of the
rarity of insects in this country. The Lepidoptera are numerous in species, but not in individuals; the Coleoptera are exceedingly scarce, and
other orders are generally, like the Lepidoptera, sparing in individuals;
we attribute it to the uninterrupted extent of monotonous forest over
which animal life is sparingly but widely scattered. However this makes
a difference in the commercial value of the subjects. The present collection is the fruits of two months' devoted and almost exclusive attention to insects. Shells and Orchids continue to be exceedingly
scarce.   (Wallace 1849:74–75)

This trip up the Tocantins was the last joint Wallace-Bates collecting effort. On returning they decided that working separately would
be more profitable. Furthermore (and probably not unrelated to this
decision), Herbert, Alfred's younger brother, having had no success
in earlier jobs, arrived from England in July to try his hand at collecting as a livelihood. The botanist Richard Spruce arrived in Pará
on the boat with Herbert, although Alfred did not meet him until
October, in Santarém.
On January 19, 1850, Stevens forwarded a second letter, just received from Wallace:

Santarem, Sept. 12, 1849
I have got thus far up the river, and take the opportunity of sending
you a few lines. To come here, though such a short distance, took me
a month. I am now waiting here to get to Montalegre, but the difficulties of getting men even for a few days are very great. Here the country
is very sandy and dry, with a scrubby, shrubby vegetation; there are
however some patches of forest, and in these, Lepidoptera are rather
abundant; there are several lovely *Erycinidae* new to me, and many
common insects, such as *Heliconia Melpomene* and *Agraulis Dido,*

abundant, which we hardly ever saw at Parà: Coleoptera I am sorry to find as scarce as ever. I hope however to do better at Montalegre, as the hills there are near a thousand feet high, and must I should think produce some. I wish to know what is thought of Cuyaba in the province of Matto Grosso as a locality; it is at the head of the Tapajoz and Paraguay River; there is a communication from here, salt being taken up. I could also from Rio Nigro get up the Madeira to Matto Grosso city, or up some branches into Bolivia. Is Bolivia at all known? I see in the Museum Catalogue only five or six *Erycinidae* from it, from Mr. Brydges' collections. I see there is a branch of the Andes in it the highest in America, and its capital cities appear higher ground than even Bogota or Quito. Either of the localities can be I think quite as easily reached as the Andes up the Amazon; at all events, I should like to know if the ground is open and likely to be good, for some future time, if not just at present. I shall I think get up the Rio Nigro towards the sources of the Orinooko, but I am rather fearful that all N. Brazil is rather poor in Coleoptera.

September 14th.—I believe I shall now start for Montalegre tomorrow, having a canoe lent me; I have however found so many new species of Lepidoptera, that I shall probably stay here a month on my return before going to Rio Nigro, unless indeed I find Montalegre so very good as to induce me to spend till December there. I do not think that you need send me anything till I write again. Pray write whenever you can, and give me all the information you may be able to obtain, both as to what things are wanted in any class or order and as to localities.

The Tapajoz here is clear water with a sandy beach, and the bathing is luxurious; we bathe here in the middle of the day, when dripping with perspiration, and you can have no idea of the excessive luxury of it; the water is so warm that then is the healthiest time. Oranges are about a fourpence a bushel here, and are far the best fruit; large pineapples twopence to fourpence, but we seldom eat them. The more I see of the country, *the more I want to,* and I can see *no end* of, the species of butterflies when the whole country is well explored. Remember me to all friends,   (Wallace 1850a:156–57)

On November 20, 1850, Stevens submitted for publication extracts from two subsequent letters. The identifications that Stevens provided in footnotes to the original letters have here been inserted in brackets.

Santarem, Nov. 15, 1849 (500 miles above Parà)

I spent about three weeks at Montealegre and have now been back here nearly a month, so before I leave for the Rio Negro I send you a small lot of insects; they consist almost entirely of Lepidoptera, the *Beetles* not yet having made their appearance; in the wet season I hear there are plenty both at Montealegre and here, so I shall probably return here, unless I meet with something much better to keep me up above. Of the boxes sent, Nos. 1 and 2 only are for you to dispose of. Your lot, though a small one, I trust will be found a good one; there are a very considerable number of fresh species, one of which (No. 605) [Footnote: This beautiful species I find to be the rare *Callithea Sapphira*, Hub., of which hitherto only one example appears to have existed in the collections in this country. S. S.] is, I think, the *most beautiful thing* I have yet taken; it is very difficult to capture, settling almost invariably high up in trees; two specimens I climbed up after and waited for; I then adopted a long pole which I left at a tree they frequented, and by means of persevering with it every day for near a month have got a good series: the sexes I have no doubt whatever about, though I have not taken them *in copula;* the female flies lower and is easier to take than the male. The allied species (606) [Footnote: This is *Callithea Leprieurii* Feisthamel, also very rare.—S. S.] was rather abundant at Montealegre; the orange Heliconia-like insect occurred there plentifully. Of all *new species* and others which I know to be good, I have sent plenty; of old things I have sent a few only.

In the *Erycinidae* there are a great many species fresh to me, and I hope *some new* to Europe: I have now made descriptions of all the species sent, so that should I be obliged again to send home my duplicates or lose any of them, I can still recognize the species. The handsome species I hope will sell well. In box No. 3. I have put a lot of miscellaneous insects, which please take out and dispose of. There is also a small stuffed alligator, a species I think they have not in the Museum; it is the Jacare tinga, of which the tail is *eaten* and is very good; they are an immense deal of trouble in skinning. I have sent also a larger one, which I think is the common species; also a tortoise-shell and a few vertebrae of the large alligators of the Amazon I have put in to fill up; perhaps they may be interesting to geologists to compare with those of fossil Sauria. Shells there are none here. There are two painted calabashes in paper with your name outside; please accept them as a specimen of the Indian girls' work at Montealegre; the varnish, colours, &c., are all made by themselves from the leaves and bark of different trees and herbs; they paint them with bits of stick and feathers, and the patterns are all their own design; they are the usual drinking-vessels there, but less ornamented for common use. I am much in want of some work on the species of butterflies; I think the "Encyclopédie Méthodique," vol. ix. by Godard, is the only thing that will do. The leaf in the box is a segment of the *Victoria regia;* if any one wants it, you may sell it.

Barra de Rio Negro (1000 miles above Parà) [Manaus], March 20, 1850.

After sending off the box from Santarem (which I trust you have received safe), I was delayed a fortnight waiting for men to go up the river. After great difficulty I obtained them, but to Obidos only, a distance of about eighty miles (three days); there I was delayed four days, and then got others another stage of four days on to Villa Nova. There I was delayed a week, and was there indebted to the kindness of a trader, who lent me some of his men to get on to Barra. Now however the rains and head winds had set in, so that after rather an unpleasant journey owing to wet and mosquitoes, we arrived at Barra on the 30th of Dec. in thirty-four days from Santarem. I was so anxious to reach here before the wet season had regularly set in, that I never wasted an hour to go on shore but once a day to cook, so that I literally collected nothing on the road except at Villa Nova, where we had tolerably fine weather. After the muddy, monotonous, mosquito-swarming Amazon, it was with great pleasure we found ourselves in the black waters— *black as ink* they are, and well deserve their name; the shores are rugged and picturesque—and greatest luxury of all, mosquitoes are unknown except in the islands. Our voyage, however, was not near so bad as it might have been, for Mr. Spruce, who left Santarem for Obidos exactly a week before us, arrived there only the evening before, having taken *nine* days owing to the want of wind, without which it is impossible to stem the current. We are here staying with Sir Henrique Anthony, in the same house Edwards occupied; he is a most hospitable fellow, and his house is the general receptacle of strangers. I soon found that insects were exceedingly scarce here at this season, it being almost impossible to get half a dozen in a day worth bringing home. Birds too are equally scarce, so I resolved on a short trip up the Rio Negro to where the *Umbrella chatterers* are found. I spent a month there, and being fortunate in finding a good hunter, have got a small but pretty good collection of birds, considering the season.

With regard to living animals, &c., it is quite impossible to send them from here. At Parà they can only be bought at such high prices as not to make it worth the risk. The captains too require half the price for the passage. I had intended, if I could have been now on my voyage up the Rio Negro, to have returned about next Christmas, getting all the live animals I could on the way and coming home myself with them, calculating that I could get sufficient to pay all expenses to England and back; but I do not think now I shall do so, as I shall probably not be able to start for the frontiers till June or July, and it is nearly a two months' voyage. If therefore sufficient funds arrive by that time, I shall probably stay up in the neighbourhood of the Cassiquiare a year, and then on returning to Barra see about a journey up towards the Andes. I am anxiously waiting also to know about the fish and reptiles, as I do not want to get more if they do not pay.

Besides the umbrella birds, the little bristle-tailed manakin will, I think, be good; also the trumpeter, which is a species different from that at Parà; the muscovy ducks also. Both among the birds and insects there are, I know, many common as well as rare species. There are also two bad specimens of the celebrated "bell bird," which I believe is rare; they frequent the highest trees out of ordinary gunshot; my hunter fired five or six times at each of them, and after several ineffectual shots at another gave it up in despair. Of the curl-crested arçari, I have only at present got a single specimen. The arçaris I send are two species new to me, and are both much prettier than the curl-crested. I must now not forget to thank you for the prints you sent me, which I only discovered a short time ago, never having opened the box containing them. Any newspapers or scientific periodicals you can send me will be particularly acceptable.   (Wallace 1850b:494–96)

During the two rainy months, February and March, when Wallace and Bates were in Barra (Bates arrived three weeks after the Wallace brothers) they had much to discuss, including plans for future collecting. Bates later remembered, "Mr. Wallace chose the Rio Negro for his next trip and I agreed to take the Solimõens [upper Amazon]" (Bates 1892:177). Bates left for Ega, a town on the upper Amazon, at the end of March, and stayed there a year on this first trip. After a time he became discouraged and depressed by the lack of communication with the outside world. In a letter to Stevens written on December 31 of that year he stated his intention of returning to England soon, adding, "Mr. Wallace, I suppose, will follow up the profession, and probably will adopt the track I have planned out to Peru; he is now in a glorious country, and you must expect great things from him. In perseverance and real knowledge of the subject, he goes ahead of me, and is worthy of all success" (Bates 1851:3144). But Bates did not return then. Instead, he stayed on the Amazon until 1859. He and Wallace were not to meet again for twelve years, after Wallace had returned to England from the Malay Archipelago.

When Alfred started up the Rio Negro in August, Herbert stayed in Barra. A year's experience had demonstrated to both brothers that Herbert lacked the interest and perseverance to make collecting profitable. It was planned that he would collect around Barra for six months, then leave for Pará and home.

Alfred soon found that the Rio Negro district, while of great interest, did not yield bountifully for the professional collector. As the only Wallace letter from that period suggests, it was not the "glorious country" that Bates was at that moment imagining:

[Guia, Rio Negro, January 1851]

I have been spending a month with some Indians three days' journey up a narrow stream (called the Cobati River). From there we went half a day's journey through the forest to a rocky mountain where the celebrated "Gallos de Serra" (Cocks of the Rock) breed. But we were very unfortunate, for though I had with me ten hunters and we remained nine days at the Serra, suffering many inconveniences (having only taken farinha and salt with us), I only got a dozen gallos, whereas I had expected in less time to have secured fifty. Insects, there were none at all; and other good birds excessively rare.

My canoe is now getting ready for a further journey up to near the sources of the Rio Negro in Venezuela, where I have reason to believe I shall find insects more plentiful, and at least as many birds as here. On my return from there I shall take a voyage up the great river Uaupés, and another up the Isanna, not so much for my collections, which I do not expect to be very profitable there, but because I am so much interested in the country and the people that I am determined to see and know more of it and them than any other European traveller. If I do not get profit, I hope at least to get some credit as an industrious and persevering traveller.

Wallace added that the remainder of this letter "described the materials I was collecting for books on the palms and the fishes of these regions, and also for a book on the physical history of the Amazon valley" (Wallace 1905 1:285).

The biological collections from the Venezuela trip and his first ascent of the Rio Uaupés were weightily supplemented by artifacts acquired from the Uaupés Indians. Alfred's canoe was heavily laden as he returned to Barra in September 1851 to pack these materials for shipment to England. As Spruce was at that moment occupying a commodious house, Alfred stayed with him while he made the crates and packed his collections. Alfred was in an agitated state, because on arrival he had found a letter, months old, from Mr. Miller, the vice-consul in Pará, informing him that Herbert had suffered an attack of yellow fever so severe that there seemed little hope of recovery. Despite all efforts, Alfred could learn nothing further of his brother's condition.

A fortnight's work saw his packing finished. Worn by work and anxiety, he once again set out up the Rio Negro for his second attempt to penetrate the headwaters of the Rio Uaupés.

Yellow fever, spreading rapidly up the river, overtook him just as he reached the mouth of the Rio Uaupés.

> Sitio de Uanauacá
> Below the Falls of Saõ Gabriel
> Rio Negro, Dec. 28, 1851
>
> Mr. John Smith
> Royal Gardens, Kew
> I had sad news two days ago from my friend Wallace. He is at Saõ Joaquim, at the mouth of the Uaupés, a little above Saõ Gabriel, and he writes me by another hand that he is almost at the point of death from a malignant fever, which has reduced him to such a state of weakness that he cannot rise from his hammock or even feed himself. The person who brought me the letter told me that he had taken no nourishment for some days except the juice of oranges and cashews. Since I came to Pará the fevers of the Rio Negro have proved fatal to two of the persons mentioned in Edward's *Voyage*—Bradley and Berchenbrinck, very fine young men both. Wallace's younger brother, who came out from Liverpool along with me, died last May. He had gone there [Pará] to embark for England, took the yellow fever, and died in a few days.

The Rio Negro might be called the Dead River—I never saw such a deserted region. . . .

Mr. Wallace came up from the Barra more than a month before me, escaped the fever on his way, but the day he set foot in Saõ Joaquim was attacked. . . .

Richard Spruce
(Spruce 1908 1:267–68)

By the middle of February, having recovered to the point of being able to climb into and out of a canoe, Alfred set out finally for a second ascent of the Uaupés River. The best collecting season had passed while he lay prostrate. Not surprisingly, his collections were scant. He was able to buy more artifacts and a remarkable menagerie of tame animals from the Uaupés Indians. As his small canoe left the Rio Uaupés for the last time, it carried fifty-two live animals, mostly parrots and monkeys. Two days later he visited Spruce briefly, as he started down the Rio Negro.

His misfortunes between his arrival at Barra and his arrival in England are succinctly told in the following letter addressed to readers of the *Zoologist:*

Proceedings of Natural-History Collectors in Foreign Countries
Mr. A. R. Wallace. [Footnote: communicated by himself.]—As some account of the unfortunate accident that took place on my voyage home from South America may not be unacceptable to your readers, I beg to send you the following brief statement of the facts.

On the 2nd of July of the present year, I arrived in Pará from the river Uaupés, an unexplored branch of the upper Rio Negro. I had with me a considerable collection of birds, insects, reptiles and fishes, and a large quantity of miscellaneous articles, consisting of about twenty cases and packages. Nearly half of these had been left by me at Barra a year before to be sent home; but a new government, arriving there shortly after I left, took it into their heads that I was engaged in a contraband trade, and so I found them still there on my way down, in the present year, and had to bring them all with me.

On the 12th of July I embarked in the "Helen," 235 tons, for London, still suffering from fever and ague, which had nearly killed me ten months before on the upper Rio Negro, and from which I had never since been free.

The cargo of the vessel consisted of India-rubber, cocoa, arnatto, balsam of copaiba, and Piassaba. Almost all my cases were stowed in the hold. On the 6th of August, when in lat. 30°30′N., long. 52°W., at 9, a.m., smoke was discovered issuing from the hatchways, on opening which, and attempting to ascertain the seat of the fire, the smoke became more dense and suffocating, and soon filled the cabin, so as to render it very difficult to get any necessaries out of it. By great exertions the boats were got out, and bread, water, and other necessaries put into them. By noon the flames had burst into the cabin and on deck, and we were driven to take refuge in the boats, which, being much shrunk by exposure to the sun, required all our exertions to keep them from filling with water. The flames spread most rapidly, and by night the masts had fallen, and the deck and cargo was one fierce mass of flame. We staid near the vessel all night: the next morning we left the ship still burning down at the water's edge, and steered for Bermuda, the nearest point of land, but still 700 miles distant from us. For two days we had a fair easterly wind, but this afterwards changed to N. and N.W., and we could make but little way. We suffered much from the heat by day; and being constantly wet with the spray, and having no place to lie down comfortably, it may be supposed that we did not sleep very soundly at night. For food we did very well, having plenty of biscuit and salt pork,—raw, of course,—which we found very palatable, with a little water to wash it down. After a week, having seen no vessel, we put ourselves on short allowance of water, and then suffered much from thirst; and as we now were in a part celebrated for squalls and hurricanes, every shift in the wind and change of the sky was most anxiously watched by us. At length, after ten days and nights we heard the joyful cry of "Sail ho!" and by a few hours' hard rowing got on board the "Jordeson" from Cuba, bound for London, in lat. 32°48′N., long. 60°27′W., being still about 200 miles from Bermuda.

We now had a very tedious voyage, and soon got to be very short of provisions, the crew being doubled by our arrival: in fact, had not two vessels assisted us with provisions at different times, we should actually have starved; and as it was, for a considerable time we had nothing but biscuit and water. We encountered three very heavy gales, which split and carried away some of the strongest sails in the ship, and made her leak so much that the pumps could with difficulty keep her free. On the 1st of October, however, we safely landed at Deal, eighty days after we left Pará.

The only things which I saved were my watch, my drawings of fishes, and a portion of my notes and journals. Most of my journals, notes on the habits of animals, and drawings of the transformations of insects, were lost.

My collections were mostly from the country about the sources of the Rio Negro and Orinooko, one of the wildest and least known parts of South America, and their loss is therefore the more to be regretted. I had a fine collection of the river tortoises (Chelydidae) consisting of ten species, many of which I believe were new. Also upwards of a hundred species of the little known fishes of the Rio Negro: of these last, however, and of many additional species, I have saved my drawings and descriptions. My private collection of Lepidoptera contained illustrations of all the species and varieties I had collected at Santarem, Montalegré, Barra, the Upper Amazons, and the Rio Negro: there must have been at least a hundred new and unique species. I had also a number of curious Coleoptera, several species of ants in all their different states, and complete skeletons and skins of an anteater and cowfish, (*Manatus*); the whole of which, together with a small collection of living monkeys, parrots, macaws, and other birds, are irrecoverably lost.

I may also mention that I had taken some trouble to procure and pack an entire leaf of the magnificent Jupaté palm (*Oredoxia regia*), fifty feet in length, which I had hoped would form a fine object in the botanical room at the British Museum.

Alfred R. Wallace

P.S.—I left Mr. Spruce at S. Gabriel, on the falls of the Rio Negro, hard at work in good health, on the 29th of April last. On the 15th of June I called at Santarem, which place Mr. Bates had left a week previously on an excursion up the Tapajoz. A. W.

43 Upper Albany St., Regent's Park,
October 19, 1852.

(Wallace 1852a:3641–43)

CHAPTER THREE
Upland Species, Lowland Species

To appreciate the extent of Wallace's loss one must remember the basic objective of the two naturalists in undertaking the Amazonian venture. That was to seek indications of how species arise by examining the relationship between patterns of affinity and distribution among closely related species. While the disposal of duplicates and items judged readily salable paid their expenses, any specimens of scientific interest were retained in their private collections. A letter to Spruce, on the Rio Negro, written while Wallace was still on the brig *Jordeson* (''one of the slowest old ships going''), details the extent of his loss more explicitly than does his letter for publication. ''All my private collection of insects and birds since I left Para was with me, and comprised hundreds of new and beautiful species, which would have rendered (I had fondly hoped) my cabinet, as far as regards American species, one of the finest in Europe'' (Wallace 1905 1:306). Wallace had kept his intact private collection with him on his first trip up the Rio Negro, so that these specimens would be available for comparison with new finds.

Although Wallace does not state so explicitly, I think that another major objective was to record his experiences and observations with publication in mind. An account of his travels might have provided some much needed income. He had diligently kept a journal, parts of which were saved. These and reassembled letters home were the basis for the first and last parts of *A Narrative of Travels on the Amazon and Rio Negro* (1853g), as he noted in the preface. But he had to rely on his memory for the rest, because, as he stressed in the letter to Spruce, ''the three most interesting years of my journal'' were lost.

His observations and collections had, by the end of 1850, led him also to contemplate books on the physical history of the Amazon valley, on the fishes of the Rio Negro, and on the palm trees of the Amazon (letter from Guia). Only the plans for the last came to fruition. Wallace had been able to rescue his drawings of fishes and palms from his cabin on the burning *Helen*. These careful sketches were sufficient to identify the palms. Plates made from these, together with comments on distribution and the uses of each by various Amazonian Indians, comprised a small volume. *Palm Trees of the Amazon and Their Uses* (1853f) was published at the author's expense, but sales ultimately covered the cost. For fish, however, drawings alone do not suffice as adequate descriptions of new species; the specimens lost were irreplaceable. Wallace published only one brief paper (1853a) on these once-extensive collections. The substance of a planned book on the physical history of the Amazon was reduced to comprise one of the four chapters added to *A Narrative of Travels on the Amazon and Rio Negro*. Having salvaged from the burning *Helen* his compass mapping of the rivers and the latitude determinations made (by sextant) during his two trips up the Rio Negro and Uaupés, Wallace was able to prepare a large map of the region. On it he indicated major geographic and geological features and gave localities for several species of monkeys, as well as for the aboriginal Indian tribes. He presented the map to the Royal Geographical Society of London and read a paper, "On the Rio Negro" before the Society at its meeting in June 1853. The paper, with a reduction of the map, was published in the Society's journal. This map was completed too late for inclusion in the original edition of the *Narrative,* although it has been appended to a later edition.

The final four chapters of the *Narrative* provide overviews of the physical geography and geology, the vegetation, the zoology, and the aboriginal peoples, respectively, of the Amazon region. The first and third chapters of this final section of the *Narrative* will be noted here, because they offer a succinct view of Wallace's interpretation of the general features of the geologic history of the Amazon basin and of the consequent distribution patterns in certain animal groups. This, in turn, is background for interpreting our only clues to Wallace's thinking about the primary objective of his extensive collecting:

The general impression produced by the examination of the country is, that here we see the last stage of a process that has been going on, during the whole period of the elevation of the Andes and the mountains of Brazil and Guiana, from the ocean. At the commencement of this period, the greater portion of the valleys of the Amazon, Orinooko, and La Plata must have formed a part of the ocean, separating the groups of islands (which those elevated lands formed on their first appearance) from each other. The sediment carried down into this sea by the rapid streams, running down the sides of these mountains, would tend to fill up and level the deeper and more irregular depressions, forming those large tracts of alluvial deposits we now find in the midst of the granite districts. At the same time volcanic forces were in operation, as shown by the isolated granite peaks which in many places rise out of the flat forest district, like islands from a sea of verdure, because their lower slopes and valleys between them, have been covered and filled up by the sedimentary deposits. . . .

At the point where the mountains of Guiana approach nearest to the chain of the Andes, the volcanic action appears to have been continued in the interval between them, throwing up the serra of Curicuriarí, Tunuhy and the numerous smaller granite mountains of the Uaupés; and it is here probably that dry land first appears, connecting Guiana and New Granada [Ecuador], and forming that slightly elevated ridge which is now the watershed between the basins of the Amazon and Orinooko. The same thing occurs in the southern part of the continent, for it is where the mountains of Brazil, and the eastern range of the Bolivian Andes, stretch out to meet each other, that the sedimentary deposits in that part appear to have been first raised above the water, and thus to have determined the limits of the basin of the Amazon on the south. The Amazon valley would then have formed a great inland gulf or sea, about two thousand miles long and seven or eight hundred wide.

The rivers and mountain-torrents pouring into it on every side, would gradually fill up this great basin. . . . This process, continuing for ages, would at length narrow this inland sea, almost within the limits of what is now gapo, or flooded land.
(Wallace 1853g:425–27; 1889 ed.:294–96)

The Amazon basin, then, in Wallace's view, comprised extensive central alluvial lowlands derived from the erosion of the four surrounding uplands. These marginal uplands, which once were con-

sidered islands, are the Guiana highlands to the northeast, the Ecua-
dorian Andes to the northwest, the Peruvian (Bolivian) Andes to the
southwest, and the Brazilian highlands to the southeast.

A summary of the geographical distribution of animals is a major
section of the chapter on zoology, following an introductory survey
of the characteristic denizens of the region. It begins by noting that
animals tend to exist in small, local groups often occupying territories
with distinct boundaries. In the Amazon, Wallace had observed that
the Amazon River itself and its major tributaries form boundaries for
several animal groups. In particular, he notes the distribution of monkey species. He reviews briefly information that he also presented in
a paper to the Zoological Society of London. A closing paragraph in
that paper states the situation, and Wallace's interpretation, quite succinctly:

> During my residence in the Amazon district I took every opportunity
> of determining the limits of species, and I soon found that the Amazon,
> the Rio Negro and the Madeira formed the limits beyond which certain
> species never passed. The native hunters are perfectly acquainted with
> this fact, and always cross over the river when they want to procure
> particular animals, which are found even on the river's bank on one
> side, but never by any chance on the other. On approaching the sources
> of the rivers they cease to be a boundary, and most of the species are
> found on both sides of them. Thus several Guiana species come up to
> the Rio Negro and Amazon, but do not pass them; Brazilian species on
> the contrary reach but do not pass the Amazon to the north. Several
> Ecuador species from the east of the Andes reach down into the tongue
> of land between the Rio Negro and Upper Amazon, but pass neither of
> those rivers, and others from Peru are bounded on the north by the
> Upper Amazon, and on the east by the Madeira. Thus there are four
> districts, the Guiana, the Ecuador, the Peru and the Brazil districts,
> whose boundaries on one side are determined by the rivers I have men-
> tioned.   (Wallace 1852b: 109–10)

It must be noted here that although this paper gives the impression
that Wallace had become aware of the significance of rivers as faunal
boundaries early in his travels, he actually did not appreciate it until
he had begun exploring the Rio Negro. An anecdote related in a letter
to Bates several years later makes this point clear:

In a paper I read on "The Monkeys of the Lower Amazon and Rio Negro" I showed that the species were often different on the opposite sides of the river. Guayana species came up to the east bank, Columbian species to the west bank, and I stated that it was therefore important that travellers collecting on the banks of large rivers should note from which side every specimen came. Upon this Dr. Gray came down upon me with a regular floorer. "Why," said he, "we have specimens collected by Mr. Wallace himself marked "Rio Negro" only." I do not think I answered him properly at the time, that those specimens were sent from Barra before I had the slightest idea myself that the species were different on the two banks. . . .   (Wallace 1905 1:377)

Nowhere in the *Narrative* is any mention made of what had been Wallace's major preoccupation, his hypothesis of species formation. This fact is not surprising, in view of the loss of any supporting evidence that his collections might have provided. In the paper on the distribution of monkey species he dropped hints of the significance of knowing the precise distribution of species: "On this accurate determination of an animal's range many interesting questions depend. Are very closely related species ever separated by a wide interval of country? What physical features determine the boundaries of species and genera? Do the isothermal lines ever accurately bound the range of species, or are they altogether independent of them? . . ." (Wallace 1852b:110). But in the several publications reporting his Amazonian findings, only one carried a brief mention of what these "interesting questions" might be.

One brief, and usually overlooked, paragraph in a paper on butterflies provides the only clue to the direction of Wallace's thinking on the subject that we can be certain was never far from the center of his attention. Wallace read "On the Habits of the Butterflies of the Amazon Valley" to the Entomological Society of London in two installments, at its November and December meetings of 1853. The statement is brief and relates to only one family of butterflies:

In the beautiful family of *Heliconidae,* the glory of South American Entomology, the Amazon valley is particularly rich, at least sixty or seventy species being found there, of which a considerable number seem peculiar. And here the same thing takes place which we observed with regard to the Papilios,—that the more rare and restricted species are those which inhabit the forest, while the species found in the open grounds are generally widely distributed, and often seem mere stragglers from other parts of the continent. Among these latter are *Lycorea Halia, Tithorea Megara* and *Mechanitis Lysidice,* while most of the species of *Heliconia, Thyridia,* and *Ithomia,* which prefer the forest shades, are confined to a comparatively limited district. The most characteristic of the Amazon valley are those species of *Heliconia* with white or yellow spots on a shining blue or black ground, such as the *Antiocha, Thamar,* and several others; those with radiating red lines on the lower wing, such as *Erythaea, Egeria, Doris,* and several undescribed species; and, lastly, the delicate little clear wings of the genera *Thyridia, Ithomia* and *Sais.* All these groups are exceedingly productive in closely related species and varieties of the most interesting description, and often having a very limited range; and as there is every reason to believe that the banks of the lower Amazon are among the most recently formed parts of South America, we may fairly regard those insects, which are peculiar to that district, as among the youngest species, the latest in the long series of modifications which the forms of animal life have undergone. (Wallace 1853e: 257–58)

As a first step toward assessing the last sentence of that quotation as a clue to Wallace's thoughts, the space-time context of the cited observations must be established. The phrase "banks of the lower Amazon" excludes both the Pará district, for that is not on the Amazon proper, and the Rio Negro. We have learned from Wallace's letters that the only place on the lower Amazon where he spent much time was in the Santarém–Monte Alegre region. During his more than two months in these two localities he collected many new (to him) species, as his letters attest. Later, after the material had been identified, he found that he had collected about a hundred species of Lepidoptera in the Santarém district. Further evidence that Wallace was writing of the Santarém district is his naming of *"Heliconia Erythaea"* as one of the characteristic species. Bates, who several years later collected extensively around Santarém and studied the Heliconidae with particular care, stated that he considered the butterfly sometimes named *Heliconia erythaea* but a variety of the widespread species *Heliconius melpomene.* Further, this variety is found only in the vicinity of Santarém (Bates 1862). Wallace's cited observation must, therefore, have been made between the middle of September and the end of November 1849, when he was in the Santarém area.[1]

The Santarém region differs from all other parts of the lower (and much of the upper) Amazon valley in that hills approach close to the banks of the river itself. Everywhere else lowlands stretch inland for many miles from the banks of the river. As Wallace ascended the river, the obviously different character of the land near Monte Alegre as seen from the boat made him want to examine it, and its biota, more closely:

> On the north banks of the Amazon, for about two hundred miles, are ranges of low hills, which, as well as the country between them, are partly bare and partly covered with brush and thickets. They vary from three hundred to one thousand feet high, and extend inland, being probably connected with the mountains of Cayenne and Guiana. After passing them there are no more hills visible from the river for more than two thousand miles, until we reach the lowest ranges of the Andes: they are called the Serras de Paru, and terminate in the Serras de Montealegre, near the little village of Montealegre, about one hundred miles below Santarém.   (Wallace 1853g:226; 1889 ed.:95)

The slightly raised banks on the south side of the river at Santarém are a northern extension of the highlands of central Brazil, just as those near Monte Alegre on the north bank are the southern extension of the Guiana uplands to the north of the Amazon. The peculiar character of this portion of the Amazon's south bank was noted in Wallace's letter of September 12, 1849: "Here the country is very sandy and dry, with a scrubby, shrubby vegetation; there are however some patches of forest, and in these Lepidoptera are rather abundant. . . ."

1. The heliconian butterflies that led Wallace to believe that he had discovered new lowland forest species derived from those on adjacent highlands are a group now known to display a baffling complexity of distinctly different color patterns in each of many species. The morphs of different species in the same locality usually are closely similar. The color patterns are all visually distinctive so-called warning coloration: the butterflies are "advertising" their distastefulness to potential predators. A single warning pattern, shown by many species, is believed to have evolved because a predator learns more quickly if there is only one warning pattern to be learned. This shared pattern differs in its details from locality to locality, and it is believed that conditions in upland pleistocene refugia (see footnote 2) must be taken into account in attempting to understand lowland forms.

Two months of collections were to reveal distinct but similar species in the dry, shrubby "campos" as opposed to those in the forests growing on low-lying alluvium. The application of uniformitarian geological theories would have suggested to Wallace that the deposition of this alluvium had been a recent event in geological time, that the uplands near Santarém and Monte Alegre had been there long before these alluvial lowlands acquired their forest cover.

This situation, with two juxtaposed habitats, one old, the other quite new, and with somewhat similar species of animals in the two, may well have suggested to Wallace an opportunity to test what Lyell in his *Principles of Geology* had considered the definitive disproof of the Lamarckian hypothesis of species transmutation. Lyell had first established that each species of plant and animal occupied a limited "station," or, in other words, that each was adapted to a limited set of environmental conditions. Should there be an environmental change, the species composition of the area would alter if the limits of adaptation of the species present were exceeded. Other species, ones better adapted to the new conditions, would then replace the previously well-adapted forms. Changes affecting broad areas might even lead to the extinction of a species. Thus, Lyell's stance was that changes in the physical world might result in the extinction of a species, but never in its transmutation into another species better adapted to the altered environment:

> Lamarck, when speculating on the transmutation of species, supposed every modification in organization and instinct to be brought about slowly and insensibly in an indefinite lapse of ages. But he does not appear to have sufficiently considered how much every alteration in the physical condition of the habitable surface changes the relations of a great number of co-existing species, and that some of these would be ready instantly to avail themselves of the slightest change in their favour, and to multiply to the injury of others. . . . However slowly a lake may be converted into a marsh, or a marsh into meadow, it is evident that before the lacustrine plants can acquire the power of living in marshes, or the marsh-plants of living in a less humid soil, other species already existing in the region, and fitted for those several stations, will intrude and keep possession of the ground. . . .
>
> It is idle, therefore, to dispute about the abstract possibility of the conversion of one species into another, when there are known causes much

more active in their nature, which must always intervene and prevent the
actual accomplishment of such conversions. . . .
(Lyell 1842 3:227–28)

Lyell is not mentioned in Wallace's butterfly paper. But possibly
relevant here is a notation in the "Species Notebook" that Wallace
began six years later, in 1855, while collecting in Borneo, on the
other side of the earth. He then had jotted comments on Lyell that he
intended to use in a book on the formation of varieties and species.
"?Introduce this and disprove all Lyell's arguments first at the commencement of my first chapter" had been added over the following
statement: "Lyell argues that one species could not change into another by a change of external circumstances because while the change
was taking place other species already accustomed to those circumstances would displace them. But this must always be on the supposition of a rapid not a gradual change. . . ." (SN, p. 51).

To what extent Wallace appreciated the significance of his collections while still in Santarém will probably never be known for certain. But several bits of evidence hint that he might have done so
soon thereafter. On January 23, 1850, Bates arrived in Barra (Bates
1850:2940), just as two months of incessant rain were beginning. The
impossibility of collecting in such weather left ample time for Wallace and Bates to examine the collections that each had made on his
separate ascent of the Amazon. Such a comparison of collections might
be assumed, but we also have documentation in a letter Bates wrote
to Stevens from Santarém two years later: "I think Wallace cannot
have worked the locality, although he took, as I remember, the whole
series of species which he showed me at the Barra, and many butterflies that I had not yet seen. I think he was here at a better season.
. . ." (Bates 1852:3449). It seems likely that they discussed the relevance of their material to the evaluation of the hypothesis of species
transmutation, for this was the basic objective of their explorations.
What better time than the idle days enforced by weeks of torrential
rain?

More direct evidence is wanting. Our only hint is provided in the
narrative of Bates's travels. His narrative, prepared several years after
the Darwin-Wallace papers (1858) and Darwin's *Origin of Species*

(1859), contains but a single reference to the "origin of new species," and this concerns the forms of *Heliconius* in the dry and moist habitats of Santarém and Obidos, a town just across the Amazon (Bates 1892:133). This sole reference suggests that if the forms of *Heliconius* from Santarém were discussed there at Barra (Manaus) in relation to the dynamics of species formation, the discussion left a lasting impression on Bates, as it did on Wallace.

Evaluation of the Santarém heliconids in the manner noted in the paper (Wallace 1853e) on Amazonian butterflies seems to have suggested to Wallace that he seek similar patterns of distribution in other groups of plants and animals. As the Rio Negro flows through both lowlands and granitic uplands, he soon would have had ample opportunity to trace the distribution of upland and lowland species in any groups suitable for this purpose. He apparently sought evidence in the distribution patterns of both umbrella birds and palm trees. A theme common to both investigations, but one not emphasized in his publications for reasons that will become obvious, is the relation of the distribution of lowland species to that of closely related species in the ancient uplands.

When the Wallace brothers arrived at the Barra de Rio Negro (Manaus) in the final days of 1849, the rainy season had already started and collecting was poor. Alfred was told that these months were the time of year when the umbrella birds, briefly transcending their usual resemblance to short-legged crows, assumed their spectacular breeding plumage. He set out with an Indian hunter for the breeding grounds, islands in the middle of the miles-wide Rio Negro, where they collected for a month with fair success. When he returned to Barra, Bates had already arrived (and the discussion about butterflies followed). During the following weeks Wallace wrote a short paper on these birds (dated March 10, 1850, at Barra) and sent it to Stevens, who communicated it to the Zoological Society of London. On July 23, 1850, the Secretary of the Society read Wallace's first paper, "On the Umbrella-Bird (*Cephalopterus ornatus*), 'Ueramimbé' L.G. [Lingua Geral; the common name]." (This was reprinted in the "Miscellaneous" section of the November 1851 issue of the *Annals and Magazine of Natural History*.)

It can scarcely be doubted that the main purpose of the paper was to provide pertinent information that might awaken the acquisitive instinct of private collectors for the twenty-five skins he had just shipped. But the concluding paragraph suggests Wallace's scientific interest. Following a concise account of the "character and habits" of this crowlike bird, he wrote of its distribution:

> The Umbrella Bird inhabits the islands of the rivers, never having been seen on the mainland. . . .
> In ascending the Amazon, it first occurs opposite the mouth of the Madeira, in some islands. In the Sohuives [Upper Amazon], as far as the boundaries of Brazil, it also occurs, and probably further. The Rio Negro, however, is its headquarters; and there, in the numerous islands which fill that river, it is very abundant. It extends at least four hundred miles up the river, and very probably much farther. I have not heard of its occurring in the Rio Branco, Madeira, or any of the other great tributaries of the Amazon. I have been informed by a hunter, that towards the sources of the Rio Negro another species is found, and this I hope soon to have the means of verifying.   (Wallace 1850c:207)

The paragraph quoted suggests that Wallace may have looked upon these birds as a possible example of an upland-lowland pair of closely related species. The black *Cephalopterus ornatus* was an exemplary lowland species, common on islands near the mouth of the Rio Negro and on flooded banks of the Amazon itself but said to be unknown along the upper reaches of the Rio Negro. The sources of the Rio Negro are in remote highlands. The second, putative, species of umbrella bird, confined to this upland region, might well be ancestral to the lowland species.

Wallace's narrative provides evidence that, indeed, the discovery of that other species of umbrella bird may have been a primary goal in his explorations of the upper Rio Uaupés. On his first trip up the Rio Uaupés, at a season when the river was still sufficiently high to make the cataract-strewn ascent most arduous, he stopped halfway, deciding,

> after mature deliberation, to give up for the present my intended journey to the Andes, and to substitute another voyage up the river Uaupés, at least to the Juruparí (Devil) cataract, the *"ultima Thule"* of most of

the traders and about a month's voyage up from its mouth. Several
traders . . . as well as the more intelligent Indians, assured me that in
the upper districts there are many birds and animals not met with below. *But what above all attracted me, was the information that a white
species of the celebrated umbrella-chatterer was to be found there.*
[Italics added.] The information on this point from several parties was
so positive, that, though much inclined to doubt the existence of such
a bird at all, I could not rest satisfied without one more trial, as, even
if I did not find it, I had little doubt of obtaining many new species to
reward me.   (Wallace 1853g:341–42; 1889 ed.: 210–11)

He resolved to make the 1,500-mile round trip to Barra to pack his
collections and send them to England. He planned then to resume the
search during the months of low water, November to February, when
the ascent of the further reaches of the Rio Uaupés would be less
difficult. This plan would permit him to return to England during the
following summer, the best time to transport the collection of live
animals he hoped to take back. While he was on the return trip up
the Rio Negro, his near-fatal attack of yellow fever delayed ascent of
the Rio Uaupés until the middle of February 1852, the time when he
had planned to be quitting the region. Despite his enfeebled condition
he did reach Mucura, just east of the 72° meridian, an area to which
no European had before penetrated. "I was now," he said, "in the
country of the painted turtle and the white umbrella-bird and I determined to make a stay of at least a fortnight, to try and obtain these
much desired rarities" (Wallace 1853g:377; 1889 ed.:246). But after
a fortnight of searching he reported: "My expectations of finding rare
and handsome birds were quite disappointed. My hunter and Senhor
Nicoláu killed a few umbrella-birds of the Rio Negro species; but of
the white bird such contradictory statements were given,—many
knowing nothing whatever about it, others saying that it was sometimes, but very rarely seen,—that I am inclined to think it is a mere
white variety, such as occurs at times with our blackbirds and starlings at home, and as are sometimes found among the curassow-birds
and agoutis" (Wallace 1853g:380; 1889 ed.:249). He had been following a will-o'-the-wisp! The uplands member of what was to have
been an exemplary pair of closely related species did not exist. Fur-

thermore, he discovered that the species common in the flooded forests and islands of the alluvial lowlands ("the Rio Negro species") also occurred in the granitic uplands, in patches of flooded forest. *Cephalopterus ornatus* had obviously been able to establish itself in the flooded areas of the lowlands because it had become adapted to this "station" during its long existence in the granitic uplands. The new alluvial lands presented this environmental situation even more extensively than had the ancestral upland terrain.

The disappointment occasioned by finding that there was but a single species of *Cephalopterus* and that it lived in both the alluvial lowlands and the granitic uplands of the Rio Negro district must have been keenly felt, coming as it did on the eve of his departure from this *ultima Thule*. This had been his sole remaining hope for finding an upland-lowland pair of species.

The distribution of related species of palm trees had initially offered the greatest hope. The large size and immobility of the individuals make such species far more favorable for distributional studies than most animal groups. The study of palms had occupied much of Wallace's time and interest throughout these months, as his letter from Guia at the beginning of his Rio Negro adventure indicated. Yet his discussions of palms with Spruce after his first descent from the Rio Uaupés would have established the specific assignments of his materials and would have made it clear beyond doubt that the palm data failed to produce evidence of upland-lowland pairs such as he had found in the Santarém butterflies.

The palm-tree study is worth our attention because of the distributional patterns that it does reveal. Generally speaking, publication of data that fail to support a hypothesis is often difficult to justify and more difficult to accomplish. It is fortunate that Wallace's initial interest in palms was largely centered in his fascination with the myriad uses to which the Amazonian Indians put the many species provided in their verdant environment; fortunate also that he rescued from the burning ship the metal box with his pencil sketches of each species encountered. From these, and his notes on the distribution and the human uses of each, he put together the small book noted earlier, *Palm Trees of the Amazon and Their Uses* (Wallace 1853f). This is a systematic treatment of the forty-three palm species (assigned to seventeen genera) discovered in the Rio Negro district and the lower Amazon. Wallace's determination of the distribution of each is noted in detail, even though the book is addressed to the reading public as an essay in ethnobotany. Reflection on the general nature of this study is in order before beginning an analysis of the distributional data as they relate to the question of organic change.

The palm project was well suited to Wallace's talents and interests, quite aside from its relevance to his evolutionary formulations. Systematic botany had been his earliest scientific passion. His interest in subsistence activities is documented by the essay on the agricultural practices of Welsh hill farmers, written when he was twenty. Pencil sketching, for which Wallace had a talent, made the ideal way of recording and characterizing palm species. It had hitherto been difficult for botanists working in the tropics to convey a conception of a palm species to European colleagues and amateurs. Paintings were seldom accurate in detail; dried herbarium specimens of leaves often forty feet long are bulky to prepare, ship, store, and handle. His sympathy with the Indians helped him elicit the wealth of information that various tribes had accumulated about the palms in their respective areas. Furthermore, in studying palms in the Rio Negro district, he was walking literally and figuratively in the footsteps of the famous Alexander von Humboldt: literally, because they in part traced (in opposite directions) the same route from the Orinoco drainage through the upper section of the Rio Negro; figuratively, because Humboldt, with his botanical associates Bonpland and Kunth, described many palm species collected during his explorations of Spanish America.

Humboldt and Bonpland had named 20 new species of palms from their observations and collections in tropical America. When, in 1841, their colleague Kunth enumerated the palms of the world, the list reached 356. At present a similar listing would name about 2,800 species (Moore 1973). Some 387 of these are known from Brazil (Dahlgren 1936). When Wallace added his 11 new species over a century ago, the number known from that part of South America was scarcely half that. Wallace can, therefore, stand beside Humboldt as a student of palms. It must have given Wallace the greatest satisfaction when on the Estrada de Javita he discovered specimens of a hitherto undescribed species of palm, of which Humboldt knew nothing but the Indian name. Wallace, on the very footpath that Humboldt had trod, discovered and described specimens to go with the name—trees that had very likely been growing fifty years before. He had found what the great Humboldt had missed! This new species Wallace named *Leopoldina piassaba*. The genus *Leopoldina* had been created by von Martius, some thirty years before, to characterize a group of new species found in the region of the Upper Amazon and Rio Negro. The word that Wallace chose as the species name, "piassaba," is the Indian name for that particular kind of palm; it is also applied to the fiber derived from it, which at that time was extensively exported to Europe for the manufacture of coarse brooms and brushes.

There can be little doubt that Wallace's appreciation of palm systematics was greatly aided by his discussions with Spruce. Although systematic botany had been a passion during Wallace's adolescence, it had been displaced by an interest in animal systematics some years before he sailed to the tropics. As his preparatory studies had concentrated on the animal groups he was most likely to collect, his knowledge of the plants was sketchy. His association with Spruce helped acquaint him with current knowledge of the extremely rich and diverse Amazonian flora. Spruce, having studied this flora as thoroughly as the libraries and collections in London allowed, was a walking encyclopedia which Wallace was remarkably fortunate to have available for consultation. When Wallace returned to Barra to ship his collections after his first exploration of the Rio Uaupés, he spent two weeks at the house where Spruce was staying. As this was the first opportunity that Wallace and Spruce had had to talk since the days in Santarém over two years before, one can well imagine that they discussed palms. All of the palms that Wallace had seen in the Rio Negro region were new to his eyes, and he had no way of knowing for sure which ones had been described before and which ones were actually new to science. But Spruce would know, if anyone on that continent did. Spruce was in the midst of identifying the palms he had collected for himself. On September 24, 1851, during Wallace's stay, Spruce wrote a letter to the curator of Kew Gardens which began: "I trouble you with a letter to ask you to compare the specimens of Palms I have sent to your museum with the Plates, etc. in Martius's great work and give me your opinion on them.'' After continuing with comments on his own growing interest in palms despite the difficulty of collecting and preserving specimens, he adds: "Higher up the Rio Negro I am certain to find abundance of new palms. Mr. Wallace has just come down from the frontier and brought with him sketches of several palms, of which I have no doubt many are quite new. There are at least *two large Mauritias* quite distinct from any described by Martius. . . .'' (Spruce 1908 1:225–26). In *Palm Trees of the Amazon* there is frequent inclusion of bits of information attributed to Spruce that Wallace could have gleaned only during this visit.

Wallace's observations of five species of the genus *Mauritia* provided the most complete data available for testing his hypothesis concerning the derivation of lowland species from those of adjacent uplands. It is of interest for us to learn in what ways the data failed to support the hypothesis. He had found all five species living in the Guiana uplands, while in the lowlands only one had achieved a wide distribution. Although there were some slight differences in the size of the palms of what otherwise seemed like one widely spread species, he concluded that both upland and lowland representatives did in fact belong to the same species (Wallace 1853f:50). Thus, these data can only be interpreted to signify that the uplands are the ancestral home of the genus and that the lowland representative cannot be considered a different (and presumably newer) species derived from one of the five upland species.

Three *Mauritia* species were described and named by Wallace in his palm book: *Mauritia carana, Mauritia gracilis,* and *Mauritia pumila.* Not surprisingly, these three species, hitherto unknown to western science, are almost exclusively restricted to the little-explored Guiana uplands. The one species named by Humboldt, *M. aculeata,* is also thus restricted. The fifth species, the one noted above as enjoying a wide distribution in both uplands and lowlands, extends to the Atlantic coast. The early European explorers of these shores had brought parts of this palm back to Europe. Linnaeus, the great taxonomist, assigned these parts to a new genus, *Mauritia,* and named the species *Mauritia flexuosa.* Wallace considered this species to be "one of the most noble and majestic of American palms.''

The explanation for the striking difference between the distribution of *Mauritia flexuosa* and that of its four congeners is to be sought in the ecological requirements of each species, or as Lyell would have put it, in the "station" of each. It will suffice to consider the two upland species whose distribution was best known to Wallace. In the uplands adjacent to the upper reaches of the Rio Negro, he found that *Mauritia carana* Wallace is restricted to dry scrubby forest (catinga) or to "the sandy margins of streams well out of the reach of the highest flood." The occasional *M. carana* found beyond the limits of the Guiana uplands occurs on isolated bits of dry, elevated land that rise above the extensive alluvial plains through which the lower reaches of the Rio Negro flow. (Spruce later, in 1871, reported similar small, outlying populations of *M. carana*.) This species has been able to extend its geographical range only to those small, infrequent elevations of the lowlands which present a dry soil, to which *M. carana* had long been adapted in the Guiana uplands. These isolated elevations in the lowlands are less readily colonized by the palms of genera that thrive in the surrounding moist lowlands than they are by *M. carana*.

The ecological factors limiting the geographical distribution of the second upland species, *M. gracilis* Wallace, are less obvious. Like *M. carana*, *M. gracilis* is common; it grows in clumps at the margins of rivers and streams throughout the uplands in both the Rio Negro and Orinoco drainages. The geographical distribution of *M. gracilis* beyond the granitic uplands is very different from that of *M. carana*, because the ecological requirements of the two are so different. *M. gracilis* always grows close to the water's edge, and Wallace was able to chart its invasion of the banks of the lower reaches of the Rio Negro as he passed up and down the river. On his map of the Rio Negro (Wallace 1853b:212) he indicated the farthest point downstream where *M. gracilis* occurred—about 300 miles upstream from the mouth of the Rio Negro and 100 miles downstream from the edge of the granitic uplands. Its southward extension may be thwarted by competition from other palm species that are better adapted to the same ecological station.

The third species, *M. flexuosa* Linnaeus, was noted by Wallace often growing within yards of *M. carana* and *M. gracilis* in the granitic uplands, but is restricted to periodically flooded soil. Physiological adaptation to survival on periodically flooded soil has apparently enabled *M. flexuosa* to spread throughout the lowlands of the Amazon basin, in surprising contrast to its two upland neighbors and relatives. Wallace knew that *M. flexuosa* extended down the Rio Negro and Amazon to the Atlantic and was common on the tidal flooded lands at Pará. Spruce, who was later to ascend the upper Amazon, subsequently said that this species is "the most commonly distributed palm throughout the basins of the Amazon and Orinoco, or, say, from the Andes of Peru and New Granada [Ecuador] to the shores of the Atlantic. . . ." (Spruce 1871:77). This species has been preeminently successful on the tidally flooded banks of the lower Amazon. Wallace suggested that the larger size attained by trees of *M. flexuosa* on this diurnally flooded tidal land, as compared with the size attained in the uplands, may be related to the merely annual flooding in the ancestral environment.

Reflection on the patterns of distribution of the species of *Mauritia* and other palms would have revealed to Wallace, as it now reveals to us, the pertinence of Lyell's observations on the colonization of new situations. Newly transformed portions of the earth's crust are usually not inhabited by species newly modified from old ones to meet the special requirements of the new situation. Rather, they are invaded by preexisting species already adapted to the "stations" that the new situation offers. Only one *Mauritia* species of the Guiana uplands occupied an ecological station that the lowlands were to offer in abundance. *M. flexuosa,* alone and unmodified, invaded the newly formed lowlands and staked out *Mauritia*'s claim.

Twenty years later, when Spruce summarized his extensive studies of palms throughout the entire Amazon basin, he concluded that, abundant as palm species are in the lowlands of the Amazon basin, few if any are peculiar to them. Most of its species, he seemed satisfied, were derived from one of the adjacent highlands: the Guiana highlands to the north, the Central Brazilian highlands to the south, or the Andean foothills to the west (Spruce 1871:76).[2]

2. A century after Spruce found that the palms of the entire Amazon valley conformed to the pattern that Wallace discovered in the Rio Negro region, biologists again became interested in the distribution of lowland species in many plant and animal groups in relation to the populations in the surrounding uplands. The view that has developed over the past decade is that the extensions of the range of upland species into the adjacent lowlands is a much more recent

Let us pause to review our reconstruction of the trend of Wallace's efforts to test his provisional hypothesis of species change. Observations on the distribution patterns of heliconid butterflies at one area studied during his ascent of the lower Amazon in 1849 had suggested that species in the forest on newly formed alluvial plains had arisen from closely related species in adjacent, older uplands. As he began his exploration of the Rio Negro he observed an umbrella bird and some palm species which suggested ways to test his idea. His question must have been, Do the umbrella bird and the palm species common in the alluvial lowlands near the mouth of the Rio Negro have closely related upland counterpart species from which they arose? But strenuous efforts and careful study did not provide a positive answer.

In view of the complete lack of supporting evidence in his careful study of palm distribution, it is a little surprising that Wallace ventured to proclaim his allegiance to the heretical concept of species transmutation on the basis solely of the evidence of the Santarém–Monte Alegre butterflies. Possibly he was emboldened by the publication in 1852 of a brilliant analysis of the innate probabilities of the alternative theories—natural and supernatural—of the origin of species. This essay of some 2,000 words appeared in a London weekly newspaper, *The Leader,* as the second contribution in a regular anonymous column, "The Haythorne Papers." At a later date it became known that Herbert Spencer was the writer. Entitled "The Developmental Hypothesis" (an influence of the *Vestiges*?), the essay was an early manifestation of Spencer's philosophical interest in evolution:

> Those who cavalierly reject the theory of Lamarck and his followers, as not adequately supported by facts, seem quite to forget that their own theory is supported by no facts at all. Like the majority of men who are born to a given belief, they demand the most rigorous proof of any adverse doctrine, but assume that their own doctrine needs none. Here we find scattered over the globe vegetable and animal organisms numbering, of the one kind (according to Humboldt), some 320,000 species, and the other,

---

event, geologically speaking, than the one the known geology of the time led Wallace to postulate. It has now been postulated that during one (or more) periods of the glacial age, the Pleistocene, the lowland became so arid that the moisture-requiring species could survive only in the uplands surrounding the basin. When a climate like the present one was reestablished, the species reinvaded the lowlands. An excellent view of this subject is given in a publication (Prance 1982) which became available only after the manuscript for this book was completed.

if we include insects, some *two millions* of species (see Carpenter); and if to these we add the numbers of animal and vegetable species that have become extinct (bearing in mind how geological records prove that, from the earliest appearance of life down to the present time, different species have been successively replacing each other, so that the world's Flora and Fauna have completely changed many times over), we may safely estimate the number of species that have existed, and are existing on the earth, at not less than ten millions. Well, which is the most rational theory about these ten millions of species? Is it most likely that there have been ten millions of special creations? or is it most likely that by continual modifications, due to change of circumstances, ten millions of varieties may have been produced, as varieties are being produced still? One of the two theories must be adopted. Which is most countenanced by facts? . . .

And here we may perceive how much more defensible the new doctrine is than the old one. Even could the supporters of the development hypothesis merely show that the production of species by the process of modification is conceivable, they would be in a better position than their opponents. But they can do much more than this. They can show that the process of modification has effected and is effecting great changes in all organisms subject to modifying influence. Though, from the impossibility of getting at a sufficiency of facts, they are unable to trace the many phases through which any existing species has passed in arriving at its present form, or to identify the influences which caused the successive modifications, yet they can show that any existing species—animal or vegetable—when placed under conditions different from its previous ones, *immediately begins to undergo certain changes of structure fitting it for the new conditions*. They can show that in successive generations these changes continue until ultimately the new conditions become the natural ones. They can show that in cultivated plants, in domesticated animals, and in the several races of men, these changes have uniformly taken place. They can show that the degrees of difference so produced are often, as in dogs, greater than those on which distinctions of species are in other cases founded. They can show that it is a matter of dispute whether some of these modified forms *are* varieties or separate species. They can show, too, that the changes daily taking place in ourselves—the facility that attends long practice, and the loss of aptitude that begins when practice ceases—the strengthening of passions habitually gratified, and the weakening of those habitually curbed—the development of every faculty, bodily, moral, or intellectual, according to the use made of it—are all explicable on this same principle. And thus they can show that throughout all organic nature there *is* at work a modifying influence of the kind they assign as the cause of these specific differences—an influence which, though slow in its action, does, in time, if the circumstances demand it, produce marked changes—an influence which, to all appearance, would produce in the millions of years, and under the great varieties of conditions which geological records imply, any amount of change.

> Which, then, is the most rational hypothesis; that of special creations which has neither a fact to support it nor is even definitely conceivable; or that of modification, which is not only definitely conceivable; but is countenanced by the habitudes of every existing organism: . . .
> (Spencer 1852:280)

Spencer's strongest argument for the developmental hypothesis of changes over geological time was their similarity to the change that occurs in the development of every complex individual from a much less complex egg or seed.

> But the blindness of those who think it absurd to suppose that complex organic forms may have arisen by successive modifications out of simple ones, becomes astonishing when we remember that complex organic forms are daily thus produced. . . . Surely, if a single structureless cell may, when subjected to certain influences, become a man in the space of twenty years, there is nothing absurd in the hypothesis that under certain other influences, a cell may in the course of millions of years give origin to the human race. The two processes are generically the same, and differ only in length and complexity. (Spencer 1852:281)

Wallace could not have read this essay when the newspaper appeared, on March 20, 1852, because he had then just arrived at the Barra on his final homeward journey. But a statement made by Wallace as an old man suggests that he probably read it soon after its publication: "In 1852 Herbert Spencer published his essay contrasting the theories of Creation and Development with such skill and logical power as to carry conviction to the minds of all unprejudiced readers. . . ." (Wallace 1898:139).

The inclusion in his paper on the habits of Amazonian butterflies of even a brief statement of support for the hypothesis of gradual organic transformation must have taken courage. The audience may have been shocked or outraged, but there was apparently no immediate outcry; no comments on Wallace's evolutionary stance are recorded in the minutes of the Entomological Society of London. That there may have been behind-the-scenes comments of some adverse sort is suggested by some of the remarks made by the retiring president at the anniversary meeting in the following month, January 1854. Edward Newman, also editor of the *Zoologist,* extolled the activities of collectors in furthering the cause of science. But to appreciate his remarks we must review Wallace's relations with the membership of the Society.

Wallace's activities as a collector had been known to members of the Entomological Society since his agent, Samuel Stevens, who was usually treasurer of the Society, began exhibiting Wallace's specimens for sale at the monthly meetings. Three days after Wallace landed in England following his ordeal at sea he attended a meeting of the Entomological Society. The Society's minutes for the meeting of October 4, 1852, note as the second item: "Mr. Wallace was present as a visitor. He has lost the whole of the valuable collection of Natural History, made by him during several years' residence in South America, by the burning at sea of the ship in which he was bringing them to this country, and he narrowly escaped death in an open boat. . . ."

Attendance at these meetings meant much to Wallace. He must have hobbled to this first one, since in a postscript to a letter to Spruce written the next day, he lamented: "Here I am laid up with swelled ankles, my legs not being able to stand work after such a long rest in the ship" (Wallace 1905 1:309). To be granted permission to attend these meetings and those of the Zoological Society, societies at both of which his collections had made his name known, was important as betokening a measure of professional recognition and acceptance. He recalled that he attended their meetings with regularity, and "thus made the acquaintance of most of the London zoologists and entomologists" (Wallace 1905 1:321). But although Wallace might be something of a celebrity through his misadventures, he was only a collector, and a visitor at the Societies. He had read his "monkey" paper to the Zoological Society in December 1852; on June 6, 1853, he had read to the Entomological Society a small paper, "On the Insects Used for Food by the Indians of the Amazon" (1853d).

The paper "On the Habits of Butterflies of the Amazon Valley" (Wallace 1853e) is a well-conceived summary treatment of the ecology and distribution of these tropical butterflies, and it reveals acute observation and considerable deliberation on many topics. There might have been tolerance for his first, relatively unimportant paper on insects as food, but the competent nature of the ''butterfly'' paper may have seemed pretentious to some members of the Society. Possibly it was in response to such rumblings that Edward Newman made his remarks:

> On one subject I venture to express an opinion at variance with what appears a prescriptive practice. I repeatedly find in entomological works the indication of a desire to depreciate that particular branch of science which some one else has taken, or is supposed to be taking up. Such terms as ''species-man,'' ''mere collector,'' ''theorist,'' and many others, need but be quoted in explanation of my meaning. Now the sentiment implied by such expressions is unphilosophical; it is not in accordance with the catholicity of science; it implies that we are drawing a comparison between ourselves and others disadvantageous to the others, and it therefore has a direct tendency to foster, if not to create, feelings that ought not to exist. . . . We have long since been told that members of the human body must work together in concert: that the head must not say to the hand ''I have no need of thee,'' or the hand to the feet ''I have no need of you'': so with our science; the monographer cannot say to the collector, I have no need of you: the very admission of such a thought is a stumbling-block in our own way, a bar to our own progress. I wish to be understood as applying this last observation especially and emphatically to the case of the actual collector; to the man who, in *whatever station of life,* devotes his time, by night and by day; at all seasons in all weather; at home and abroad; to the positive capture and preservation of those specimens which serve as the objects for all our observations: he is the real labourer in the field, and if we would keep the lamp of our science constantly burning, it is to him alone that we can look for fuel to feed its flame.
>
>   . . . Another loss, truly, to be lamented . . . is that we have sustained . . . in the destruction of a zoological treasure; I allude, of course, to the collections made by our friend Mr. Wallace. That energetic traveller led by the thirst *I have already described* to behold with his own eyes, and not through the too often distorting medium of books, the exuberant luxuriance of animal and vegetable life as developed by the rays of a vertical sun, devoted himself to the acquisition of and actually acquired, a most intimate knowledge of the Natural History of the Valley of the Amazon . . . I cannot forbear to quote from his own pen the record of his feelings, when, no longer in jeopardy, he first realized the enormous loss he had sustained.
>
>   ''It was now, when the danger appeared past, that I began to feel fully the greatness of my loss! With what pleasure had I looked upon every rare and curious insect I had added to my collection! How many times, when almost overcome by the ague, had I crawled into the forest and been rewarded by some unknown and beautiful species! How many places, which

no European foot but my own had trodden, would have been recalled to my memory by the rare birds and insects they had furnished to my collection! How many weary days and weeks had I passed, upheld only by the fond hope of bringing home many new and beautiful forms from those wild regions; every one of which would be endeared to me by the recollections they would call up; which should prove that I had not wasted the advantages I had enjoyed, and would give me occupation and amusement for many years to come! And now everything was gone, and I had not one specimen to illustrate the unknown lands I had trod, or to call back the recollection of the wild scenes I had beheld! But such regrets were vain, and I tried to think as little as possible about what might have been, and to occupy myself with the state of things which actually existed."

Mr. Wallace is now on the eve of departure for the eastern instead of the western world. His face is familiar to us here; his writings are known to most of us, and some of them are on the point of publication in our "Transactions." I am sure that there is not one member of the Society but will wish him God speed!   (Newman 1854:144–147; italics added.)

Newman's choice of words makes it clear that this sermon was addressed principally to some members who had been making comparisons "disadvantageous" to Wallace, not only because Wallace was a "mere collector" but, as my italicizing of certain of Newman's phrases suggests, because he was a mere collector of inferior social station who had the temerity to present a challenge to the orthodox theory of creation.

CHAPTER FOUR
In the Malay Archipelago

Wallace left England for Singapore in the middle of March 1854, a year and a half after he had arrived there with the other survivors of the burning of the *Helen*. He had intended to start out much sooner. In a postscript to the letter to Spruce begun on the *Jordeson*, he stated:

> Fifty times since I left Pará have I vowed, if I once reached England, never to trust myself more on the ocean. But good resolutions soon fade, and I am already only doubtful whether the Andes or the Philippines are to be the scene of my wanderings. However, for six months I am a fixture here in London, as I am determined to make up for lost time by enjoying myself as much as possible for awhile. I am fortunate in having about £200 insured by Mr. Stevens' foresight, so I must be contented, though it is very hard to have nothing to show of what I took so much pains to procure.   (Wallace 1905 1:310)

He took a house near the offices of the Zoological Society and Stevens' office, and gathered what family was left in England—his mother and his sister Frances, now Mrs. Sims. John was in California, and as explained above, his other two brothers were dead. Mr. Sims practiced the new art of photography and was willing to shift his just-started business to London. Wallace attended the meetings of both the Zoological and the Entomological Societies with interest and regularity. While working on his books and scientific papers he was also assessing the potential of various unexplored parts of the tropics as future collecting sites. Discussions with naturalists at the meetings and examination of the collections at the old British Museum had satisfied him that the Malay Archipelago held the greatest promise for him. But passage to that area was expensive, and Wallace was nearly penniless.

The presentation of the paper on the physical geography of the Rio Negro area to the Royal Geographical Society of London, in the middle of June 1853, had served as the occasion for his making the acquaintance of Sir Roderick Murchison, the president of the Society. Within a few weeks Wallace had presented to the Society a request that the Council of the Society recommend to the Government that he be granted free passage to some convenient port in the Archipelago. In the application, preserved in the archives of the Society, Wallace said on his own behalf: "He proposes leaving England in the Autumn or Winter of the present year [1853], and, making Singapore his headquarters, to visit in succession Borneo, the Philippines, Celebes, Timor, the Moluccas and New Guinea, or such of them as may prove most accessible, remaining one or more years in each as circumstances may determine." He then noted that Sir James Brooke, the "White Rajah" of Sarawak and a Medallist of the Society, then in London, had promised his assistance in Borneo. He also requested the Society's endorsement of his applications to the governments of Spain and Holland for permission to visit the interiors of those islands "where they may have settlements." Sir Roderick and the Council looked with favor on this request; it bears the words "July 23. For the Earl of Clarendon." The matter dragged slowly through the summer, autumn, and winter, with various possibilities being offered, considered, rejected. Finally the question seemed settled in January 1854, with passage to Singapore arranged on the Navy brig *Frolic*. Wallace sent his heavy baggage ahead abroad a merchant ship, which would take months to arrive, since, of course, the ship went around the Cape of Good Hope. About the middle of February, Wallace recalled, he and his young assistant Charles Allen boarded the *Frolic* at Portsmouth. Time passed, and the *Frolic* was still at anchor. After some confusion new orders were issued: the *Frolic* was to carry stores to the Crimea. Back to London. Sir Roderick once again accommodated them, with a first-class ticket to Singapore overland by the next Peninsular and Oriental (P & O) steamship leaving England. The P & O was under contract to Her Majesty's Government to carry the

China and India mails. They left from Southampton on the *Euxine* and reached Alexandria via Gibraltar and Malta. The "overland" part of the passage began at Alexandria, whence canal boats carried the passengers to barges that ascended the Nile to Cairo. The following day horse-drawn carriages, with the horses changed every five miles, took them across the desert to Suez at the north end of the Red Sea. There they boarded the waiting P & O steamer *Bengal*, larger and more comfortable than the *Euxine*. A day at Aden, a stop at Galle, the old Dutch port city of south Ceylon, and then at Penang island in the straits of Malacca, and the *Bengal* arrived at Singapore on April 20, 1854. Wallace had been forty-five days en route.

This landfall signaled the beginning of eight years of wanderings among the islands of the vast Archipelago, which stretches over 4,000 miles from east to west and 1,300 from north to south. It covers an area of the earth's surface nearly equal to that of the continental United States. Wallace later estimated that about six of those eight years were actually occupied with collecting and "investigating the natural history of the area." The remainder of the time was passed in sixty-odd translocations between collecting sites—packing, arranging transportation, traveling, then unpacking and establishing another base. Illness and extremes of weather took time from collecting but also provided opportunity for reflection and writing; collecting days left little time or energy for such luxuries.

Malay Archipelago (Wallace 1869) provides a readable and scientifically informative account of these activities. It was not published until six years after Wallace's return to England, and much of its informativeness arises from this delay. The book is arranged geographically. Wallace felt, as he expressed in the preface, that a chronological arrangement of his wanderings would confuse the reader. He divided the Archipelago into the following five groups of islands:

    I   The Indo-Malay Islands:
       Malay Peninsula and Singapore, Borneo, Java, and Sumatra
   II   The Timor Group:
       Timor, Flores, Sumbawa, and Lombock (Lombok)
  III   Celebes (Sulawesi)
 IV   The Moluccan Group (Spice Islands):
       Bouru (Buru), Ceram (Seram), Batchian (Batjan), Gilolo (Hal-

mahera), Morty (Morotai), Ternate, Tidore, Amboyna (Ambon), and Banda

V   The Papuan Group:
New Guinea with outlying islands, Aru, Mysol (Misool), Salwatty (Salawati), and Waigiou (Waigeo)

Thirty-one narrative chapters are divided among these island groups. Following those covering each group Wallace added a chapter summarizing the natural history peculiar to that island group. It was the content of these chapters that profited from the six-year delay after his return to England, for this allowed time for detailed study and analysis of the collections. The narrative chapters themselves are taken essentially verbatim from the entries written in the field journal. Wallace also prepared an introductory chapter to the volume that describes the complex physical geography of the archipelago and the patterns of distribution manifest in its organic productions. Here he delineates the boundary between the biota of the western moiety, which is Asian in its affinities, and that of the eastern, with its Australian affinities. The line thus defined has been called "Wallace's line." He also noted that the western islands, initially occupied by peoples of the Malay race, can be separated from the eastern domain of the Papuans by a line that is not coincident with "Wallace's line" but lies further east. The final chapter, "The Races of Man in the Malay Archipelago," summarizes his years of careful attention to the nature and distinctions of the diverse representatives of the human species.

As admirably as *Malay Archipelago* achieves the goal the author set for himself, it reveals essentially nothing about what we know to have been his primary intellectual preoccupation, his hypothesis of organic change. Wallace had published important contributions to the theory of evolution over a decade before *Malay Archipelago* was published, yet it makes no mention of these papers. The two signal contributions, fortunately, are dated. "On the Law Which Has Regulated the Introduction of New Species" (1855c) concludes with the notation "Sarawak, Borneo, Feb. 1855." The second, "On the Tendency of Varieties to Depart Indefinitely from the Original Type" (1858e), ends with "Ternate Feb. 1858." Two other important contributions that follow the first of these are applications of the hypoth-

esis therein proposed. The first considers a problem in natural classification. The second compares Wallace's explanation of organic
affinities on a series of islands of known physiographic histories with
the explanation that Lyell's hypothesis of supernatural creation would
offer. But neither "Attempts at a Natural Arrangement of Birds
(1856d) nor "On the Natural History of the Aru Islands" (1857f)
bears any indication of time and place of composition.

One of the objectives of this book is to determine as fully as possible the nature of Wallace's observations that were antecedent, and
probably contributory, to the concepts expressed in these four papers.
An obvious first step is to examine *Malay Archipelago* for relevant
information, not just on the immediately antecedent events to be eval-
uated, but on the sequence of his observations—for each event was
but the latest in the continuum of events that shaped his thoughts and
concepts.

The geographical arrangement of *Malay Archipelago* makes the
chronology of Wallace's wanderings difficult to follow. The following tabulation of his itinerary is divided into four phases; for each,
the major collecting sites are noted in sequence, the relevant narrative
chapters in *Malay Archipelago* are shown in chronological order, and
titles of theoretical papers assignable to that phase are given.

Preliminary Exploration, April 1854 to April 1856
    Singapore, Malacca, Borneo
        Malay Archipelago chs. 2–6
        "On the Law Which Has Regulated the Introduction of New Species"
        (1855c)
        "Attempts at a Natural Arrangement of Birds" (1856d)

Bali, Lombock, Celebes, Aru Islands, June 1856 to March 1858
    Singapore, Bali, Celebes, Aru, Celebes, Ternate, Gilolo
        Malay Archipelago chs. 10–12, 15, 31–33, 16, part of 19, 20
        "On the Natural History of the Aru Islands" (1857f)
        "On the Tendency of Varieties to Depart Indefinitely from the Original
        Type" (1858e)

New Guinea, March to September 1858
    New Guinea (at Dorey), Ternate, Gilolo
        Malay Archipelago chs. 21, 22, 25

Moluccas, Timor, North Celebes, October 1858 to November 1860
  Ternate, Batchian, Timor, North Celebes, Ceram, Waigiou, Bouru
    Malay Archipelago chs. 23–24, 13, 17, 20, 25, 35–37, 26
    "On the Zoological Geography of the Malay Archipelago" (1860)

Departure: Java, Sumatra, June 1861 to January 1862
  Java, Sumatra
    Malay Archipelago chs. 7, 8

In future chapters the antecedents of each of the first four papers will be examined in detail. Our immediate purpose is to consider possible explanations for lack of information about these papers in *Malay Archipelago*.

The "law" paper was inscribed "Sarawak, Borneo, Feb. 1855." The first line of the first chapter on Borneo states that Wallace arrived there November 1, 1854. The second paragraph continues: "The first four months of my visit were spent in various parts of the Sarawak River, from Santubong at its mouth up to the picturesque limestone mountains and Chinese gold-fields of Bow and Bede. This part of the country has been so frequently described that I shall pass it over, especially as, owing to its being the height of the wet season, my collections were comparatively poor and insignificant." The next paragraph begins "In March, 1855. . . ." So much for the events of February!

The narrative pertaining to the time of composition of the 1858 paper, Wallace's contribution to the joint Darwin-Wallace statements read to the Linnean Society of London on July 1, is not a complete blank, but it is not particularly illuminating either.

Let us address the paper, dated "Ternate, Feb. 1858." Chapter 21 of *Malay Archipelago,* "Ternate," is short, a composite of narratives relating to several visits to this port, which was home base for Wallace's wanderings in the eastern part of the Archipelago. It begins with his first arrival on January 8, 1858, preparatory to a trip to New Guinea. After a description of this beautiful but earthquake-ridden volcanic island, known for centuries in Europe as a major port in the spice trade, Wallace continues: "Soon after my first arrival in Ternate I went to Gilolo. . . ." A close neighbor, Gilolo was reached by three hours of rowing and sailing. As collecting proved poor at

the landing site, Wallace made his way to a village named Dodinga—
and there the narrative stops. The following chapter, "Gilolo," is
dated "March and September 1858," and picks up the story: "My
first stay was at Dodinga. . . ." This statement is followed by less
than a page of description of the terrain and the people living there.
Then: "The village is occupied entirely by Ternate men. The true
indigenes of Gilolo, 'Alfuros' as they are here called, live on the
eastern coast, or in the interior of the northern peninsula." "I got
some very nice insects here, though, owing to illness most of the
time, my collection was a small one" (1890 ed.:240–41) concludes
that paragraph. The next paragraph describes his September 1858 visit.
To summarize, the Gilolo chapter (ch. 22), under the date "March,"
directly continues but soon ends the narrative of this first trip and
provides no other dates. But Chapter 35, on New Guinea, begins
"After my return from Gilolo to Ternate in March 1858. . . ." In
short, then, *Malay Archipelago* informs the determined reader only
that Wallace was on the neighbor islands Ternate and Gilolo from the
first of January to sometime in March. The one relevant bit of information is the mention of his illness on Gilolo during what must have
been February.

In comparison with this total lack of notice of the important evolutionary contribution, there is an account of a significant anthropo-
logical discovery two pages further on in the Gilolo narrative (September 1858). After a second examination of the indigenes of northern
Gilolo, whom Wallace had just referred to as "Alfuros," he concluded that they were distinct from all other Malay races, that they
were more "semi-Papuan." "Here then I had discovered the exact
boundary line between the Malay and Papuan races, and at a spot
where no other writer had expected it. I was very much pleased at
this determination, as it gave me a clue to one of the most difficult
problems in Ethnology. . . ." (p. 243). Obviously, Wallace's reti-
cence related only to his own evolutionary discoveries.

In regard to the two papers that are based on the hypothesis of the
1855 paper, we find that the first, on the classification of birds as
seen in the context of organic evolution, is nowhere mentioned in
Malay Archipelago. There is, however, a counterpart in the narrative
to the second paper, concerning the natural history of the Aru Is-

lands. This is chapter 33, "The Aru Islands—Physical Geography and Aspects of Nature." Wallace interpreted the unique geological characteristics of these islands as an indication of their relatively recent separation from the adjacent island of New Guinea, from which Aru is separated by some 100 miles of shallow sea. He then uses this as a situation to test the relative success of his "law" of organic change as opposed to the Lyellian version of supernatural creation in explaining the faunal similarities and differences among Aru, New Guinea, Borneo, and Australia. Evolution wins, hands down. Yet in *Malay Archipelago,* while the physical geography is described at great length, the comparison of the two hypotheses is totally omitted. Instead, the reader is referred for further information on the biota of islands to "Sir Charles Lyell's *Principles of Geology* and Mr. Darwin's *Origin of Species."* Recall that Wallace's paper was published in December 1857, two years before the publication of the *Origin of Species.*

One can only conclude that a decade after the publication of the *Origin,* when *Malay Archipelago* was written, the social climate in the scientific circles in which he moved was such that Wallace wished to suppress any indication of his own contributions to the theory of organic evolution. Analysis of the intellectual currents of 1868 is outside the scope of this book. Possibly the events recorded in coming chapters will provide some appreciation of why Wallace took this stance.

Wallace's deferral to Darwin is such that a casual reader, vague about the date of the *Origin of Species,* might think that all of Wallace's travels were undertaken after its publication. The dedication of the book is "To Charles Darwin—Author of 'The Origin of Species'—I dedicate this book—not only as a token of personal esteem and friendship but also to express my deep admiration for his genius and his works." Wallace, of course, had been studying the natural history of the Archipelago five years before the publication of the *Origin.*

It has been necessary to seek sources other than *Malay Archipelago* for the missing information. Fortunately, Wallace's autobiography is helpful in recalling the immediate circumstances of the composition of the papers of 1855 and 1858. The autobiography was published in

1905, however, nearly fifty years after the events in question. Contemporary documents supply other details that must be pieced together. There are, fortunately, several such documents, some unpublished, which together with published papers can offer clues to the stepwise development of Wallace's concepts.

Wallace kept five manuscript documents during these years:

Registry of Consignments to Mr. Stevens (RC)
Species Registry (two notebooks) (SR)
Daily Register of Insect Collections (IC)
Species Notebook (in terminology of McKinney 1972) (SN)
Field Journal (four notebooks) (FJ)

All but the "Species Registry" are in the library of the Linnean Society of London. The Species Registry is in the library of the British Museum (Natural History). The titles are not Wallace's; they are convenient descriptors.

Reference will be made periodically to these documents. A brief description of the content of each will provide the reader with the kinds of field information that an experienced naturalist and collector recorded, and also help the reader to distinguish between them.

The "Registry of Consignments to Mr. Stevens" is the smallest in size (page size 4″ x 6″), but not in importance to Wallace. It recorded the shipments the sale of which would provide his income. The first consignment was sent from Singapore on May 28, 1854, five weeks after his arrival. As beetle collecting in Singapore proved unexpectedly good, he was able to ship 1,087 specimens of 222 species. The last shipment recorded, a mixed and heavy one—Java birds and sculpture, hornbills, palm leaves, and assorted collections from the Moluccas—closed out the operation. The notation reads "Left at Batavia [Djakarta]—Nov. 1, 1861 addressed to S. Stevens." The forty intervening pages record the shipments of seven and a half years' worth of collections: pages with shipping dates, often the name of the ship, special instructions to Stevens, estimates of how much money each shipment should yield, and sometimes how much it actually did. Aside from miscellaneous notes filling the end papers, the only irrelevant information in this business record is a three-page listing of the thirteen mammalian species collected in Malacca. (This is the kind of information more properly belonging in a species registry—see below—but the sparse collecting of the well-known vertebrates of Malacca and Singapore did not merit a book.)

The "Species Registry" records the unique designation of each species collected. There are three elements in the designation: animal group, locality, and a number. The vertebrates are entered in sections by class, i.e., birds and mammals, while the insects are divided into orders, e.g., Coleoptera (beetles), Lepidoptera (butterflies and moths), and dragonflies. The localities are designated by the island. If a species is represented by more than one specimen, each bears the same unique species designation. Nonnaturalists are reminded that most animals are sufficiently distinct that it is usually possible to sort newly collected specimens into species even if one has no idea whether a name has been previously assigned to that species and, if so, what that name might be. The problem of learning whether a species has been described and a Latin binomial assigned is much greater. Wallace addressed this need with some feeling many years later in his autobiography:

Among the great wants of a collector who wishes to know what he is doing, and how many of his captures are new or rare, are books containing a compact summary with brief descriptions of all the more important known species; and, speaking broadly, such books did not then nor do now exist. Having found by my experience when beginning botany how useful are even the shortest characters in determining a great number of species, I endeavoured to do the same thing in this case. I purchased the "Conspectus Generum Avium" of Prince Lucien Bonaparte, a large octavo volume of 800 pages, containing a well-arranged catalogue of all the known species of birds up to 1850, with references to descriptions and figures, and the native country and distribution of each species. Besides this, in a very large number—I should think nearly half—a short but excellent Latin description was given by which the species could be easily determined. In many families (the cuckoos and woodpeckers, for example) every species was thus described, in others a large proportion. As the book had very wide margins, I consulted all the books referred to for the Malayan species, and copied out in abbreviated form such of the characters as I thought would enable me to determine each, the result being that during my whole eight years' collecting in the East, I could almost always identify every bird already described, and if I could not do so, was pretty sure that it was a new or undescribed species.

No one who is not a naturalist and collector can imagine the value of this book to me. It was my constant companion on all my journeys, and as I had also noted in it the species not in the British Museum, I was able every evening to satisfy myself whether among my day's captures there was anything either new or rare.   (Wallace 1905 1:328)

Each volume of the "Species Registry" is written from both ends; Birds and Mammals begin at one end, Insects at the other. The first bird description is: "1. Trichophorus gularis Horsf. (Bon, p. 262) Sarawak iris olive brown, feet pale buff, upper mandible bknd lower [illegible]." From page 262 of Bonaparte we learn that "Horsf." represents Horsfield, the describer of the species. The colors noted by Wallace are characters of the living bird either missing or unreliable in a prepared skin. The eye is obviously not preserved, and while feet and mandibles are part of the "bird skin," their color often changes after death. In general the structural color of the feathers is a much more reliable character, and its pattern often is paramount in species differentiation. For example, of the eight species of *Trichophorus* that Bonaparte lists from Asia, six had been named from the islands of the Archipelago, while *T. gularis* Horsf. was listed from Malacca and Java. Two others from Borneo are distinguished from *T. gularis* and from each other by size and by color of throat and abdomen. Given these three possibilities, Wallace decided that his specimen belonged to *T. gularis,* not only on the basis of the colors he noted, but because of its similarity to one he had collected in Malacca some months before (Wallace 1855a).

Aside from the usual miscellaneous notations in the end pages, the registry is a straightforward listing, except for Borneo. The earlier pages list ninety-eight bird and twenty-three mammal species for Borneo, but the eighteen following pages are filled with body measurements of orangutan specimens and several pages of text on this great ape. The only other exceptional page, numbered "6," bears pencil sketches of the bill of a hornbill species, with notations on its coloration.

The insect half of each registry is also straightforward, but where listings occupy only part of a page the blank portions have been largely filled with miscellaneous notations, seldom dated. To identify the insects he would collect, Wallace had forearmed himself as best he could. Following the comments in his autobiography quoted above, on the usefulness of Bonaparte's *Conspectus*, he added:

> The only other book of much use to me was the volume by Boisduval, describing all the known species of the two families of butterflies, the Papilionidae and Pieridae. The descriptions by this French author are so clear and precise that every species can be easily determined, and the volume, though dealing with so limited a group, was of immense interest to me. For other families of butterflies and for some of the beetles I made notes and sketches at the British Museum, which enabled me to recognize some of the larger and best known species; but I soon found that so many of the species I collected were new or very rare, that in the less known groups I could safely collect all as of equal importance   (Wallace 1905 1:330).

A notebook that I have designated "Daily Register of Insect Collections" contains daily notations of the numbers of species (and of "new" species) whenever insect collecting was extensive between March 14, 1855 (Borneo), and December 1859 (Ceram, in the Moluccas). On the first page, for example, Wallace entered "Sunday March 25th 100—55 sp. 23 new fine"; meaning that the weather was fine on that date and that the 100 specimens collected were assignable to 55 species, 23 of which he judged to be new (i.e., undescribed). Then, "March 26th 120—76 sp. 34 new . . . to me. Long. 18 sp 8 new—fine." "Long." refers to the family Longicornes, characterized by long antennae. Longicorns are commonly wood-eaters, and they were well represented in these Bornean collections because trees were being felled to provide access to newly discovered coal deposits. In later entries the number of specimens is not recorded; Wallace was more interested in indicating the family representation.

The only major hiatus in this register is from page 4 to page 39, after Borneo and before Celebes ("Makassar"). These pages are devoted to two subjects: a comparative study of Bornean beetles (wings glued on to the page and head appendages drawn) and another on the life stages of several Aru butterflies.

The beetle study is usually only on the left-hand pages. Of the miscellaneous entries on the right-hand pages, the most tantalizing occupies page 14. Under the heading "Sketch of Mr. Darwin's 'Natural Selection'" is a list of titles of fourteen chapters with some phrases noting the contents of each. This entry and a discussion of its possible dating and significance are shown in chapter 10.

The fourth notebook ("Species Notebook") is headed by Wallace "Entomological Notes Sadong River Borneo" and begins: "On March the 12th 1855 I arrived at the landing place in the Si Munjon River. There I found a thatch house erected by Mr. Coulson, the superintendent of the coal mines at the neighbouring mountain." For the next several pages the narrative is devoted to insects. But by the middle of March the eagerly anticipated orangutan becomes the center of attention. The daily notations for the next ten weeks all relate to "Mias," the name given to this ape by the Malays. Much of this narrative has been included, at various places, in the fourth chapter of *Malay Archipelago*. The narrative ends with the entry for June 27 (p. 30), never to be resumed, although there is a brief dated entry on page 55: "March 1856 Singapore Bee-Eater (Merops)." After a brief note of its behavior, the entry ends, "At Singapore and Malacca migratory—appears in November, leaves in March, April—."

The twenty-five pages between the entry of June 27, 1855, and that of the following March are filled with brief statements: "Proof of Design," "Skeleton of Birds," "Notes from Lyell's 'Principles,'" "Note for Organic law of change." Then follow seventeen pages of argument with various of Lyell's assertions. Following these pages, and just preceding the entry dated Singapore—March 1856, there is a page-long item on hornbills, beginning, "The Hornbills of Africa feed on reptiles, insects, such as grasshoppers, lizards etc. and even small mammals, whereas those of India eat *only* fruit. Yet both have exactly the same general structure and form of bill. . . ."

The hundred-odd pages following the Singapore entry are a miscellany of notes and observations in no particular chronological sequence or substantive relationship. When Wallace began his serious general narrative at Bali later in 1856, he used a new notebook, thus leaving blank pages in the Species Notebook for jottings throughout the remainder of his wanderings.

The nature of the contents of pages 31 to 55 is the obvious reason for McKinney's assignment (1967) of the designation "Species Notebook." His interpretation of these as notes for the projected book that Wallace mentioned in a letter to Bates several years later makes sense. His contention that the pages were written *before* the "law" paper, however, is contrary to the obvious dating of the first page of narrative as March 12, 1855. The "law" paper, as already noted, was inscribed "Feb. 1855." Although the date of actual composition is nowhere stated, the fact that these notes for a book follow a relatively complete and coherent chronology from March 12 to June 27 suggests a time after the end of June. In *Malay Archipelago,* the paragraph after Wallace's transcription of the Species Notebook entry for June 27 begins: "At this time I had the misfortune to slip among some fallen trees, and hurt my ankle, and, not being careful enough at first, it became a severe inflamed ulcer, which would not heal, and kept me a prisoner in the house the whole of July and a part of August" (1869:40). Periods of physical inactivity forced by extreme weather or illness gave Wallace time to speculate and often to write papers. Possibly this period, or his second rainy Bornean December (1855), or even a later time in Singapore awaiting a ship to Celebes, provided opportunity for extended speculation and writing.

As already mentioned, Wallace's field journal, in four notebooks, begins with his arrival in Bali on the long-awaited trip from Singapore to Macassar, Celebes. A remarkably complete sense of the content of this field journal is provided by the narrative chapters of *Malay Archipelago,* if taken in their proper chronology. A few departures from its essentially verbatim transcriptions will be discussed later.

It seems appropriate to close this chapter with the tally of his Eastern collections with which Wallace concluded his preface to *Malay Archipelago.* He found that he had collected 125,660 natural-history specimens—just over one-eighth of a million—in the six years actually devoted to collecting. The preparation of over 8,000 bird skins and the mounting and drying of over 100,000 insects represent many additional hours of painstaking work, often under the cramped and trying circumstances that his temporary housings offered. It also meant that Wallace had examined the distinguishing morphological characteristics and exact distribution of more individual animals, especially of birds and insects, than anyone before him, or indeed, after him. Fortunately he was able to use this remarkable experience in codifying the major features of animal geography in the two-volume treatise *The Geographical Distribution of Animals,* published in 1876, seven years after *Malay Archipelago.*

CHAPTER FIVE

Species, Gaps, and Groupings

Wallace's first contribution to the theory of organic evolution was written at Sarawak, Borneo, in February 1855, less than a year after his arrival in Singapore. Although his contemporary account, *Malay Archipelago,* is silent on the circumstances of the composition of "On the Law Which Has Regulated the Introduction of New Species" (1855c), he did recall them in his autobiography, *My Life,* published in 1905, fifty years after the event remembered:

> Before giving a general sketch of my life and work in less known parts of the Archipelago, I must refer to an article I wrote while in Sarawak, which formed my first contribution to the great question of the origin of species. It was written during the wet season, while I was staying in a little house at the mouth of the Sarawak river, at the foot of Santubong mountain. I was quite alone, with one Malay boy as cook, and during the evenings and wet days I had nothing to do but to look over my books and ponder over the problem which was rarely absent from my thoughts. Having always been interested in the geographical distribution of animals and plants, having studied Swainson and Humboldt, and having now myself a vivid impression of the fundamental differences between the Eastern and Western tropics; and having also read through such books as Bonaparte's "Conspectus," already referred to, and several catalogues of insects and reptiles in the British Museum (which I almost knew by heart), giving a mass of facts as to the distribution of animals over the whole world, it occurred to me that these facts had never been properly utilized as indications of the way in which species had come into existence. The great work of Lyell had furnished me with the main features of the succession of species in time, and by combining the two I thought that some valuable

conclusions might be reached. I accordingly put my facts and ideas on
paper, and the result seeming to me to be of some importance, I sent
it to the *Annals and Magazine of Natural History*, in which it appeared
in the following September (1855).   (Wallace 1905 1:354–55)

We are interested, as noted earlier, in learning the nature of Wallace's observations during the preceding ten months—"of the vivid
impression of the differences between the Eastern and Western tropics"—that stimulated him to make a quite novel interpretation of these
facts of organic distribution. Because the paper itself may furnish
clues, we begin with a summary of the argument.

Synopsis of the "Law" Paper

Wallace's essay begins with a summary of the geological history
of the earth: it stated that the surface of the earth has undergone
successive changes throughout its immense, but unknown, time course;
"mountain chains have been elevated; islands have been formed into
continents, and continents submerged till they have become islands.
. . ." While the physical aspects of the earth's surface have been
undergoing gradual but continuous alteration, the manifestations of
organic life have been altering. "This alteration has also been gradual, but complete; after a certain interval not a single species existing
which had lived at the commencement of the period." Wallace points
out "that the present condition of the organic world is clearly derived
by a natural process of gradual extinction and creation of species
from that of the latest geological periods. We may therefore safely
infer a like gradation and natural sequence from one geological epoch
to another."

Wallace continues, "The great increase of our knowledge within
the last twenty years, both of the present and past history of the
organic world, has accumulated a body of facts which should afford
a sufficient foundation for a comprehensive law embracing and explaining them all, and giving a direction to new researches. It is
about ten years since the idea of such a law suggested itself to the
writer of this paper, and he has since taken every opportunity of

testing it by all the newly ascertained facts with which he has become acquainted, or has been able to observe himself. These have all served to convince him of the correctness of his hypothesis."

He then presents a list of propositions codifying the patterns of distribution of organisms through space at the present time ("Geography") and through geological time ("Geology").

Geography.

1. Large groups, such as classes and orders, are generally spread over the whole earth, while smaller ones, such as families and genera, are frequently confined to one portion, often a very limited district.

2. In widely distributed families the genera are often limited in range; in widely distributed genera, well-marked groups of species are peculiar to each geographical district.

3. When a group is confined to one district, and is rich in species, it is almost invariably the case that the most closely allied species are found in the same locality or in closely adjoining localities, and that therefore the natural sequence of the species by affinity is also geographical.

4. In countries of a similar climate, but separated by a wide sea of lofty mountains, the families, genera, and species of the one are often represented by closely allied families, genera and species peculiar to the other.

Geology.

5. The distribution of the organic world in time is very similar to its present distribution in space.

6. Most of the larger and some small groups extend through several geological periods.

7. In each period, however, there are peculiar groups, found nowhere else, and extending through one or several formations.

8. Species of one genus, or genera of one family occurring in the same geological time are more closely allied than those separated in time.

9. As generally in geography no species or genus occurs in two very distant localities without being also found in intermediate places, so in geology the life of a species or genus has not been interrupted. In other words, no group or species has come into existence twice.

10. The following law may be deduced from these facts:—*Every spe-*

> *cies has come into existence coincident both in space and time with*
> *a pre-existing closely allied species.*   (pp. 142–43)

Wallace then examines the utility of his "law" in explaining four arrays of facts, namely, the system of natural affinities (classification), the distribution of animals and plants in space, their distribution through geologic time, and the existence of rudimentary organs.

He begins his explanation of the system of natural affinities with a statement of the kinds of affinity relationships that would develop if each species arose from a closely related one. He also introduces an important new insight: the realization that extinction within such lineages together with the gradual modification of species was both necessary and sufficient to explain all of the affinity relationships evident in the organic world. "If the law above enunciated be true," Wallace says, "it follows that the natural series of affinities will also represent the order in which the several species came into existence, each one having had for its immediate antitype [antecedent] a closely allied species existing at the time of its origin." He continues by indicating that the lines of affinity will be simple when only one species arises from each antecedent.

But if two or more species have been independently formed on the plan of a common antitype, then the series of affinities will be compound, and can only be represented by a forked or many-branched line. Now, all attempts at a Natural classification and arrangement of organic beings show, that both these plans have obtained in creation. Sometimes the series of affinities can be well represented for a space by a direct progression from species to species or from group to group, but it is generally found impossible so to continue. . . . We are also made aware of the difficulty of arriving at a true classification, even in a small and perfect group;—in the actual state of nature it is almost impossible, the species being so numerous and the modifications of form and structure so varied, arising probably from the immense number of species which have served as antitypes for the existing species, and thus produced a complicated branching of the lines of affinity, as intricate as the twigs of a gnarled oak or the vascular system of the human body. Again, if we consider that we have only fragments of this vast system, the stem and main branches being represented by extinct species of which we have no knowledge, while a vast mass of limbs and boughs and minute twigs and scattered leaves is what we have to place in order, and determine the true position each originally occupied with regard to the others, the whole difficulty of the true Natural System of classification becomes apparent to us. (pp. 186–87)

If we now consider the geographical distribution of animals and plants upon the earth, we shall find all the facts beautifully in accordance with, and readily explained by, the present hypothesis. A country having species, genera, and whole families peculiar to it, will be the necessary result of its having been isolated for a long period, sufficient for many series of species to have been created on the type of pre-existing ones, which, as well as many of the earlier-formed species, have become extinct, and thus made the group to appear isolated. If, in any case, the antitype had an extensive range, two or more groups of species might have been formed, each varying from it in a different manner, and thus producing several representative or analogous groups. . . . (p. 188)

The phaenomena of geological distribution are exactly analogous to those of geography. Closely related species are found associated in the same beds, and the change from species to species appears to have been as gradual in time as in space. Geology, however, furnishes us with positive proof of the extinction and production of species, though it does not inform us how either has taken place. (p. 190)

Wallace then states that "Sir C. Lyell" has suggested a *modus operandi* for extinction: "Geological changes, however gradual, must occasionally have modified external conditions to such an extent as to have rendered the existence of certain species impossible."

Wallace proceeds to apply his hypothesis to the questions of interpretation of two sets of geological phenomena. The first is the problem of whether the succession of organic forms through geological time represents a true progression from simpler to more complex; the second is Edward Forbes's recent conclusion that the number of genera had been highest early and late in geologic time with a minimum at an intermediate time.

"Much discussion has of late years taken place on the question, whether the succession of life upon the globe has been from a lower to a higher degree of organization? The admitted facts seem to show that there has been a general, but not a detailed progression.'' To be sure, Mollusca existed before vertebrates, and fish before mammals, but many of the Mollusca of an early period seem to have been more highly organized than many now living. "Now it is believed that the present hypothesis will harmonize with all these facts, and in great measure serve to explain them; for though it may appear to some readers essentially a theory of progression, it is in reality only one of gradual change.''

In examining this apparent nonprogressive replacement in Mollusca, he returns to the image of the branching tree. A species-rich class of highly organized mollusks that had flourished at an earlier geologic time could be imagined as a large branch of a tree. But, as a consequence of physiographic change, this class had become extinct. Subsequently a new group might arise from some less highly organized species, placed lower on the trunk, that had survived the period of stress. In time this new group might come to replace the former class, but "may never attain so high a degree of organization as those preceding it. . . . Thus every case of apparent retrogression may be in reality a progress, though an interrupted one: when some monarch of the forest loses a limb, it may be replaced by a feeble and sickly substitute. . . . In this manner alone, it is believed, can the representative groups at successive periods, and the risings and fallings in the scale of organization, be in every case explained.''

Forbes's statement of his polarity hypothesis had just recently set forth a novel interpretation of the distribution of the richness of organic diversity as revealed in the fossil record, as well as a hypothesis of supernatural design to account for it. Wallace takes exception to both the interpretation and the metaphysical explanation. Wallace first states Forbes's interpretation: there is an "abundance of generic forms at a very early period and at present, while in the intermediate epochs there is a gradual diminution and impoverishment, till the minimum occurred at the confines of the Palaeozoic and Secondary epochs. . . .''

Wallace then says that this interpretation of the known fossil record can readily be explained by differences in the relative rates of extinction and formation of representative groups of species in different geological epochs. He seeks an analogy in the present abundance of organic diversity in the tropics as contrasted with that of temperate and arctic regions: "Now it appears highly probable that a long period of quiescence or stability in the physical conditions of a district would be most favourable to the existence of organic life in the greatest abundance, both as regards individuals and also as to variety of species and generic groups, just as we now find . . . [in] the tropics in comparison with the temperate and arctic regions. On the other hand, it seems no less probable that a change in the physical conditions of a district, even small in amount if rapid, or even gradual if to a great amount, would be highly unfavourable to the existence of individuals, might cause the extinction of many species, and would probably be equally unfavourable to the creation of new ones," a situation possibly analogous to that in temperate and frigid zones. He adds that "it seems a fair assumption that during a period of geological repose . . . the creations . . . exceed in number the extinctions, and therefore the number of species would increase. In a period of geological activity, on the other hand, it seems probable that the extinctions might exceed the creations, and the number of species consequently diminish." And, he continues, the geological record appears, indeed, to show that periods of great crustal activity and "violent convulsions" preceded the time when the "poverty of forms of life is most apparent." For this perceived pattern of abundance, he concludes, there is a natural cause, and "a cause so simple may surely be preferred to one so obscure and hypothetical as polarity" (Wallace 1855c:192, 193).

Then Wallace questions the validity of the assumptions basic to Forbes's interpretation of the fossil record. "Now, the hypothesis of Professor Forbes is essentially one that assumes to a great extent the *completeness* of our knowledge of the *whole series* of organic beings which have existed on the earth. This appears to be a fatal objection to it, independently of all other considerations" (p. 195). "Our knowledge of the organic world during any geological epoch is necessarily very imperfect. Looking at the vast numbers of species and groups that have been discovered by geologists, this may be doubted; but we should compare their numbers not merely with those that now exist upon the earth, but with a far larger amount. We have no reason for believing that the number of species on the earth at any former

period was much less than at present. . . . Now we know that there
have been many complete changes of species; new sets of organisms
have many times been introduced in place of old ones which have
become extinct, so that the total amount which have existed on the
earth from the earliest geological period must have borne about the
same proportion to those now living, as the whole human race who
have lived and died upon earth, to the population at the present time.''
But how little we must know of all these manifestations of life in
ages past. ''In order then to understand our possible knowledge of
the early world and its inhabitants, we must compare, not the area of
the whole field of our geological researches with the earth's surface,
but the area of the examined portion of each formation separately
with the whole earth'' (p. 194).

After stressing the incompleteness of our knowledge of the numbers of extinct species, Wallace comments on the incompleteness of
knowledge of their nature. Here he applies to geology his new insight
into the significance of the extinction of intermediate species for patterns of geographical distribution and affinity:

> But yet more important is the probability, nay, almost the certainty,
> that whole formations containing the records of vast geological periods
> are entirely buried beneath the ocean, and for ever beyond our reach.
> Most of the gaps in the geological series may thus be filled up, and
> vast numbers of unknown and unimaginable animals, which might help
> to elucidate the affinities of the numerous isolated groups which are a
> perpetual puzzle to the zoologist, may there be buried, till future revo-
> lutions may raise them in their turn above the waters, to afford mate-
> rials for the study of whatever race of intelligent beings may then have
> succeeded us.   (p. 194–95)

Wallace finally addresses his law, as the only natural explanation
for the existence of what he called rudimentary organs. (The examples he cites would be called ''vestigial'' by present-day biologists,
because each represents the remnant of a part now known once to
have been functional.) Every part with a highly specialized function
must have developed, Wallace believed, from a simpler, rudimentary
condition. Incorporating this consideration with the preceding geolog-

ical one, the paper sweeps to its grand finale and conclusion in the last two paragraphs:

Another important series of facts, quite in accordance with, and even necessary deductions from the law now developed, are those of *rudimentary organs*. That these really do exist, and in most cases have no special function in the animal oeconomy, is admitted by the first authorities in comparative anatomy. The minute limbs hidden beneath the skin in many of the snake-like lizards, the anal hooks of the boa constrictor, the complete series of jointed finger-bones in the paddle of the Manatus and whale, are a few of the most familiar instances. In botany a similar class of facts has been long recognised. Abortive stamens, rudimentary floral envelopes and undeveloped carpels, are of the most frequent occurrence. To every thoughtful naturalist the question must arise, What are these for? What have they to do with the great laws of creation? Do they not teach us something of the system of Nature? If each species has been created independently, and without any necessary relations with pre-existing species, what do these rudiments, these apparent imperfections mean? There must be a cause for them; they must be the necessary results of some great natural law. Now, if, as it has been endeavoured to be shown, the great law which has regulated the peopling of the earth with animal and vegetable life, is that every change shall be gradual; that no new creature shall be formed widely differing from anything before existing; that in this, as in everything else in Nature, there shall be gradation and harmony,—then these rudimentary organs are necessary, and are an essential part of the system of Nature. Ere the higher Vertebrata were formed, for instance, many steps were required, and many organs had to undergo modifications from the rudimental condition in which only they had as yet existed. We still see remaining an antitypal sketch of a wing adapted for flight in the scaly flapper of the penguin, and limbs first concealed beneath the skin, and then weakly protruding from it, were the necessary gradations before others should be formed fully adapted for locomotion. Many more of these modifications should we behold, and more complete series of them, had we a view of all the forms which have ceased to live. The great gaps that exist between fishes, reptiles, birds, and mammals would then, no doubt, be softened down by intermediate groups and the whole organic world would be seen to be an unbroken and harmonious system.

It has now been shown, though most briefly and imperfectly, how the law that *"Every species has come into existence coincident both in time*

and space with a pre-existing closely allied species," connects together
and renders intelligible a vast number of independent and hitherto unexplained facts. The natural system of arrangement of organic beings,
their geographical distribution, their geological sequence, the phaenomena of representative and substituted groups in all their modifications,
and the most singular peculiarities of anatomical structure, are all explained and illustrated by it, in perfect accordance with the vast mass
of facts which the researches of modern naturalists have brought together, and, it is believed, not materially opposed to any of them. It
also claims a superiority over previous hypotheses, on the ground that
it not merely explains, but necessitates what exists. Granted the law,
and many of the most important facts in Nature could not have been
otherwise, but are almost as necessary deductions from it, as are the
elliptic orbits of the planets from the law of gravitation.   (195–96)

Formative Experiences

Even this brief synopsis makes it evident that the consequences of
extinction within affinity-arrays are crucial to each of Wallace's four
areas of application. In order to identify those of Wallace's experiences of the preceding year that could have contributed to the development of that insight, the text concerning each application must be
scrutinized.

There can be little doubt from the pages on geological (paleonto-
logical) phenomena that Edward Forbes's presentation of his polarity
hypothesis prompted Wallace's response. Any lingering doubt is removed by a letter dated January 4, 1858, to Henry Bates, who had
expressed surprise that Wallace had published his (and, in part,
Bates's) views so soon. "It was the promulgation of Forbes' theory
which led me to write and publish, for I was annoyed to see such an
ideal absurdity put forth when such a simple hypothesis will explain
all the facts" (Marchant 1916 1:65–67).

While the polarity hypothesis prompted Wallace to present his own
views, the four and a half pages of Forbes's supporting text do not
even include the word "extinction." One can conclude, then, that
Forbes's paper was not a source of new information for Wallace on

the role of extinction. It was, however, a source of information about life of the past; it offered a concise statement about distribution patterns of life through geological time.

The section on geographical distribution is a more likely source, since Wallace himself refers to the "vivid impression of the fundamental differences between the Eastern and Western tropics." At the conclusion of the introductory paragraph on the application of the law to the facts of geographical distribution listed as proposition 4 (see synopsis above), several sets of organisms are named as examples of the distribution patterns thus explained. "The *Sylviadae* of Europe and the *Sylvicolidae* of North America, the *Heliconidae* of South America and the *Euploeas* of the East, the group of *Trogons* inhabiting Asia, and that peculiar to South America. . . ." (1855c:188). All but the first pair of "warbler" groups could have been observed by Wallace.

His proposition 3 includes data on the existence of localized, species-rich groups that supported his (and Bates's) initial hypothesis: "The natural sequence of the species is also geographic." After noting several such groups that he had observed in Amazonia, he cites examples relevant to our inquiry: "Why are the genera of Palms and of Orchids in almost every case confined to one hemisphere? Why are the closely related species of brown-backed Trogons all found in the East, and the green-backed in the West? Why are the Macaws and the Cockatoos similarly restricted? Insects furnish a countless number of analogous examples; the Goliathi of Africa, the Ornithopterae of the Indian islands; the Heliconidae of South America, the Danaidae of the East, and in all, the most closely allied species found in geographical proximity" (pp. 189, 190). All but two groups— Goliathi (giant African beetles) and Australian cockatoos—live in lands that Wallace had visited either in South America or during the preceding months in the eastern tropics.

Wallace's letters and scientific papers written during his first nine months in the East (late April 1854 to January 1855) reveal a sequence of observations the interpretation of which seems to lead stepwise to the conceptions expressed in the "law" paper, written in February 1855.

1. Butterflies of the Eastern genus *Euploea* in comparison with the family Heliconidae of the Amazon (May 1854)
2. Trogons of the Malay forest as compared with the very similar birds of the Amazonian forest (July 1854)
3. Discovery and description of a new species of bird-wing butterfly, genus *Ornithoptera,* in Sarawak, Borneo (December 1854–January 1855)
4. Forbes's polarity hypothesis (it is not clear exactly when Wallace read Forbes's paper; it could probably not have reached Singapore or Sarawak much before autumn of 1854)

Euploea and Heliconidae

The first observations of *Euploea* were on Singapore soon after his arrival. The expansion of the city of Singapore had led to the deforestation of most of the island. At the time of Wallace's arrival only a few patches of virgin forest remained. The plantations of nutmeg and Oreca palm that had replaced most of the forest supported but a meager fauna, even of insects. During his first week, before he established quarters in the center of the island near the remnants of forest (where he collected innumerable species of beetles), his sweepings of the most likely places in the cultivated area had small yield: a few beetles, several genera of butterflies. The genus *Euploea* was one, and in a letter written three weeks after his first sight of Singapore he noted: "The Euploeas here quite take the place of the Heliconidae of the Amazons, and exactly resemble them in their habits" (Wallace 1854a:4396). In November, six months later, in summarizing the entomology of Singapore and Malacca, he compared various groups of butterflies in the East and in America. "The Euploeas, though very beautiful, cannot compete with the exquisite Heliconidae, to which they are so closely allied. . . ." (Wallace 1854b:4637).

Trogons

There were few birds to be collected in Singapore. His first chance to see a representative bird fauna came when, in July, he sailed a hundred miles north from Singapore to the old port of Malacca on the Malay peninsula proper. Losing not a day in town, he settled in an outlying village within easy walking distance of the vast forest. A letter to his mother described the situation:

> We have been here a week, living in a Chinese house or shed, which reminds me remarkably of my old Rio Negro habitation. I have now for the first time brought my rede [hammock that he had used in Brazil] into use, and find it very comfortable. . . .
>
> Malacca is an old Dutch city, but the Portuguese have left the strongest mark of their possession in the common language of the place being still theirs. I have now two Portuguese servants, a cook and a hunter, and find myself thus almost brought back again to Brazil by the similarity of language, the people, and the jungle life.
> (Marchant 1916 1:49–50)

This sense of déjà vu must have been strengthened by his finding birds that behaved just as had the trogons of Brazil—characteristic denizens of the deep Amazonian forest. Recounting the experiences of the first day in which he fired his gun in the Malayan forests, he noted trogons as part of the first day's bag: "The lovely Eastern trogons, with their rich brown backs, beautifully pencilled wings, and crimson breasts, were also soon obtained. . . ." (Wallace 1869). But the dorsal coloration must have brought him back from a remembered American forest: here the backs of the males were brown; the Amazonian species had green backs.

We must now ask the question, How could Wallace be so certain that all the American trogons were green-backed, all Eastern ones brown-backed? How could he be certain that all the American species resembled the green-backed species he had seen in Amazonia, or that all Eastern species were brown-backed, when he had just begun to explore the Eastern Archipelago they inhabited? He could be sure because he had with him, as he noted, a list with brief descriptions of all then-known species and genera of birds, Bonaparte's *Conspectus Generum Avium*. In the margins he had added further notations on all Malay species. Wallace probably did not actually have Bonaparte's *Conspectus* with him in Malacca, but he would be able to consult it two months later in Singapore. A letter to his mother from Singapore on September 30 (Marchant 1916 1:52) noted that his heavy baggage, his "books and instruments," had just arrived. The reader will recall that Wallace had shipped all such baggage ahead just before his quickly aborted embarkation the preceding January in the brig *Frolic* with its "scanty accommodations."

Ornithoptera: Bird-Wing Butterflies

The third challenge to Wallace's working hypothesis came in the form of a splendid bird-wing butterfly, a specimen that Wallace could not assign to any known species of the genus *Ornithoptera*. His analysis of the relationship of the new Bornean species, which he described on the basis of this single male specimen, to the other species of "green-marked" *Ornithoptera*, all known from the lands near New Guinea, provided a completely new insight into the relationship between affinity and geographical distribution. It provided a clue to the hitherto puzzling relationships that Wallace had observed between the biotas of the eastern and western tropical forests. It revealed the way in which the extinction of one or more intermediate species, within a group that had been produced by gradual modification, could generate all of the hitherto puzzling patterns of affinity and distribution. To appreciate the steps in this revelation, it will be necessary to look back at Wallace's experiences during his first months in Borneo and to examine the classification and distribution of the genus *Ornithoptera* as it was then construed.

When Wallace returned to Singapore from Malacca late in September 1854, chance had it that Sir James Brooke, the Rajah of Sarawak, was there. Wallace wrote to his mother, "I have called on him. He received me most cordially, and offered me every assistance at Sarawak." Sir James not only was most affable but also was actively interested in natural history, so that Wallace's prediction that "I shall have some pleasant society at Sarawak" proved correct. As Sir James was not proceeding to Borneo immediately, he gave Wallace a letter to his nephew Captain Brooke, requesting him "to make me at home till he arrives, which may be a month, perhaps," as Wallace wrote on October 15, the day before he was to sail (Marchant 1916 1:52). Wallace arrived in Borneo on the first day of November, and although he made some trips up and down the Sarawak River, his collections were "comparatively poor and insignificant" because the rainy season was at its height (Wallace 1869:27). Wallace used these times of enforced physical inactivity to write. The first paper he wrote during this period, "The Entomology of Malacca" (Wallace 1854b), dated "Sarawak, November 25, 1854," was published in the *Zoologist* early in 1855. It must also have been about this time that his host, Captain Brooke, presented him with a specimen of a magnificent bird-wing butterfly with a wingspread of six and a half inches, which Wallace immediately perceived to be unlike any of the species of *Ornithoptera* that had hitherto been described, a judgment made possible by his annotated copy of Boisduval.

He prepared a description of this new species on the basis of the specimen, a male, and sent it to Stevens to be read before the Entomological Society of London. Stevens presented it on April 2, 1855, exhibiting at the same time a drawing Wallace had enclosed. As the mail from Borneo to England, via the overland route, required at least two months, the description must have been dispatched some time late in January. The dating of this description is of importance because, as I shall discuss at length, it dates Wallace's recognition of a phenomenon the analysis of which provided insight into the biological significance of extinction. The "law" paper was completed less than a month after the description of *Ornithoptera brookiana* must have been mailed!

To appreciate properly Wallace's heuristic analysis of interspecific relationships within *Ornithoptera*, it is necessary to consider the genus as it was construed at that time. Although the name *"Ornithoptera"* was not proposed until 1832, several of the species which Boisduval placed in his new genus had been known to Linnaeus in 1758, when he produced the tenth edition of the *Systema Naturae*, the listing of the names of all then-known animals. The names assigned in the tenth edition are now accepted by zoologists as the earliest valid specific names. The early interest on the part of European maritime nations in the islands where spice and pepper grew had led to the introduction of these spectacular butterflies into the cabinets of European entomologists. Even the most desultory collector on these innumerable voyages was attracted to them. Linnaeus placed them in the genus *Papilio,* since he placed all of the 192 species of butterflies known to him in this genus, but he placed those from the East in the first of six series. It was clearly their large and spectacular nature that led Linnaeus to give first place to these *"Papilio Equites Trojani,"* among which are found the species that Boisduval later transferred to the genus *Ornithoptera.* Linnaeus' listing began with *Papilio priamus.* (As might be expected, this was followed by *P. hector, P. paris, P. helenus, P. troilus,* etc.) Of *P. priamus* Linnaeus remarked, as if giving the reason for putting it first, *"Papilionum omnium Princeps longe augustissimus . . . ut dubitem pulchrius quidquam a natura in insectis productum."* [Of all butterflies the most outstanding and respected . . . so that I doubt whether anything more beautiful among insects has been produced by nature.][1] The advantage of his system of designating each species by two names, those of its genus and species, over the earlier system of using a descriptive phrase can be seen in the history of the taxonomic treatment of this species. It had early been cataloged as *"Papilio amboinensis viridi & nigro-holosericeus insignis."* Linnaeus conveyed this information, and more, after assigning a binomial by saying *"Habitat* in Amboina" and adding a sixteen-line description in which black and green color patterns of upper and lower surfaces of both wings, among other characteristics, are indicated. He obviously considered the fact that it was all silky (*totus holosericeus*) a significant indication that it was one of the insect world's most splendid creations.

In the 1830s, while studying a new collection of butterflies from the Archipelago, Boisduval noted that the males of some species of what Linnaeus had called *Papilio* bore exceptionally large anal claspers, used in holding the female genitalia during copulation. He decided that the species so characterized formed a natural group apart from other *Papilio,* and for this group he proposed the name *Ornithoptera.* In Boisduval's 1836 treatment of the Lepidoptera, the book that Wallace took with him, there are listed nine species in the genus, mostly species that had hitherto been assigned to *Papilio.* Linnaeus' *Papilio priamus* and *Papilio helenus* were transferred, becoming *Or-*

1. Translation courtesy of Dr. Harold Cannon, Director, Division of Research Programs, National Endowment for the Humanities.

nithoptera priamus and *O. helena*, respectively, and quite naturally (and correctly) *O. priamus* was also placed first in this new genus. Boisduval himself had named only a single species, *O. haliphron*. Research at the British Museum had apprised Wallace of the five other species that biologists had assigned to *Ornithoptera* since 1836.

All of the species at that time assigned to *Ornithoptera*, deriving from a vast area from India through Malaya and New Guinea and into northern Australia, had either of two kinds of color pattern. The green and black colors noted for *O. priamus* were characteristic of one group, while the other (including *O. helena*) had various black and yellow patterns. Wallace had seen specimens of each type in the British Museum but since his arrival in the East had seen only *O. amphrisius*, which, like *O. helena*, was black and yellow. In fact, Wallace had prepared an account of this encounter in *"The Entomology of Malacca"* in November 1854, shortly before writing the description of his new species, *O. brookiana*.

> It was at my earliest station [Malacca] that I first fell in with the magnificent Ornithoptera Amphrisius, but for a long time I despaired of getting a specimen, as they sailed along at great height, often without moving the wings for a considerable distance, in a manner quite distinct from that of any other of the Papilionidae with which I am acquainted. To see these and the great Ideas on the wing is certainly one of the finest sights an entomologist can behold.
> (Wallace 1854b:4636)

Idea is the name given to a genus of handsome, large, black-and-white butterflies. In retrospect we might play on these words, saying that there were indeed "great ideas on the wing" while Wallace pondered the significance of his new species of *Ornithoptera*.

The role of coloration in the assessment of the affinities of the new species is evident from the description:

Description of a New Species of Ornithoptera
Ornithoptera Brookiana. *Wallace*

Expansion 6½ inches. Wings very much elongated; black, with horizontal band of brilliant silky green. On the upper side this band is formed of seven spots of a subtriangular form, the bases of the four outer being nearly confluent, and of the three inner quite so, forming a straight line across the centre of the wing; the attenuated apex of each spot very nearly reaches the other margin at each nervule. On the lower wings the green band occupies the centre half, and has its upper margin tinged with purple. The lower wings are finely white-edged. There are some azure atoms near the base of the upper wings. The collar is crimson, and the thorax and abdomen (?) black. Beneath black, upper wings with the green spots opposite the bases of those above, small and notched, the basal one with brilliant purple reflexions, also a purple streak on the anterior margin at the base. Lower wings with a submarginal row of diamond-shaped whitish spots divided by the nervures; base of wings with two elongated patches of brilliant purple. Body obliquely banded with crimson, abdomen black.

Hab. N.W. Coast of Borneo.

This magnificent insect is a most interesting addition to the genus Ornithoptera. The green-marked species have hitherto been found only in N. Australia, New Guinea and the Moluccas, and all those yet known so much resemble each other in their style of marking, that most of them have been considered as varieties of the original Papilio Priamus of Linnaeus. Our new species is therefore remarkable on two accounts; first, as offering a quite new style of colouring in the genus to which it belongs; and secondly, by extending the range of the green-marked Ornithopterae to the N.W. extremity of Borneo. As it has not been met with by the Dutch naturalists, who have explored much of the S. and S.W. of the island, it is probably confined to the N.W. coast. My specimen (kindly given me by Captain Brooke Brooke) came from the Rejang river; but I have myself once seen it on the wing near Sarawak. I have named it after Sir J. Brooke, whose benevolent government of the country in which it was discovered every true Englishman must admire.   (Wallace 1855b:104, 105)

Wallace made no comment at the time about the genesis of the 1855 paper except his allusion in a letter to Bates several years later to the need for controverting Edward Forbes's polarity theory. But the above reconstruction of the lines of Wallace's thought, as revealed in his writings during the four months prior to February 1855, suggests that Captain Brooke Brooke's specimen of the new Bornean bird-wing played a crucial role. Wallace's analysis of its distribution and color pattern in relation to the same attributes of the other green-marked *Ornithoptera* could have suggested an explanation for disjunct distributions, other examples of which, such as that of trogons, had been puzzling. The range of the green-marked *Ornithoptera*, as Wallace conceived it, extended from Borneo eastward to northern Australia, although the central part of the range was known to be devoid of these spectacular butterflies (see fig. 5.1). The green bird-wings had never been recorded from a region that not only had been explored but was, relatively speaking, quite well known to Europeans. The known territory of the *Ornithoptera priamus*-like forms lay far to the southeast of Borneo. They had been found in the islands surrounding New Guinea, islands that provided safe landfall for European voyagers, as New Guinea itself did not. Amboina, an island in the Moluccas (Spice Islands) lying to the west of the northern tip of New Guinea, was early settled by the Dutch, and it was there that specimens of *O. priamus* were first procured for Western science. Between the Moluccas and the northwest coast of Borneo, the principal land masses had long been home for Dutch colonials: these comprised much of the huge island of Borneo and all of the sizable island of Celebes. Boisduval recorded that a variety of *O. priamus* had been found in Celebes (Wallace later found this an error), along with several of the yellow-marked species of *Ornithoptera*, some of which were also recorded as being found in Amboina. But no green-marked *Ornithoptera* had ever been found by Dutch naturalists in southern and southwestern Borneo. If, as Gray had noted in an 1852 paper, two of the yellow-marked species were known from Borneo, it must have seemed to Wallace highly unlikely that the larger and even more spectacular males of green-marked bird-wings would have gone unnoticed. He could feel relatively confident, therefore, that *Ornithoptera brookiana* did not occur in the southern and southwestern parts of Borneo. There was, then, a large distribution gap between the Sarawak population of *O. brookiana* and the Celebesian and Moluccan populations of *O. priamus*-like forms.

To one as committed as Wallace to the concept that a species could have arisen only from a contiguously preexisting species, the then-current Lyellian solution that *Ornithoptera brookiana* was a separate creation without necessary relation to other existing bird-wings was unthinkable. The fact that *O. brookiana* now occupied a range sepa-

Figure 5.1. Bird-wing butterflies. Two green-marked forms discovered by A. R. Wallace. Area shown as white on wings is actually a "brilliant silky green." Males depicted are all at least 6 inches from wingtip to wingtip. Wallace's discovery of a male in Sarawak, north Borneo, with a color pattern totally distinct from the other known green-marked forms immediately preceded the preparation of his first essay on the law of organic change. He named this new species *Ornithoptera Brookiana.* The other forms then known were *Ornithoptera priamus,* from Amboina, a small island in the Moluccas, and *O. poseidon,* then recently described from the islands around New Guinea. The pattern of black and green coloration is similar

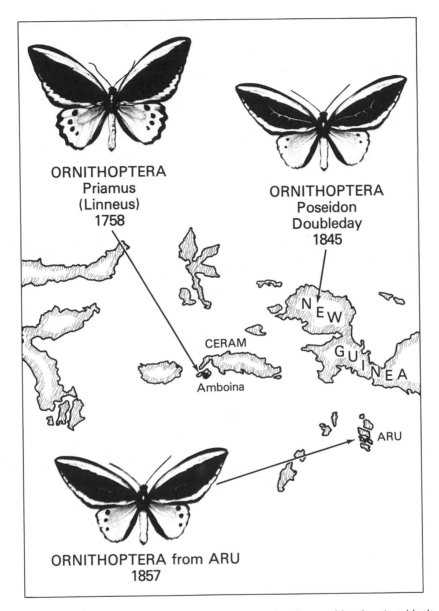

ORNITHOPTERA
Priamus
(Linneus)
1758

ORNITHOPTERA
Poseidon
Doubleday
1845

CERAM

Amboina

NEW

GUINEA

ARU

ORNITHOPTERA from ARU
1857

in those two species. Diagnostic differences are that *O. poseidon* has two black spots on the hind wing where *O. priamus* has four; also, a central nervule in the forewing of *O. poseidon* is green for about half the length of the wing. The nervule in *O. priamus* lacks green.

Wallace's second discovery, in the Aru Islands, was a form similar to both *O. priamus* and *O. poseidon*. In fact, its coloration is precisely intermediate between the two in amount of green or forewing nervule and in number of spots on hind wing. See text for discussion of theoretic significance of this discovery for Wallace.

rated from that of other *Ornithoptera* could be made compatible with
his hypothesis of species formation only if a form of green-marked
Ornithoptera had once also occupied the remainder of Borneo. Furthermore, this form, which must have become extinct after the formation of *O. brookiana,* must have been intermediate in characteristics between that species and the *O. priamus-*like forms on islands to
the southeast, if the law of gradual modification was valid. While
Wallace nowhere made this analysis explicit, he draws attention to
all of the salient points for such an interpretation in the paragraph on
distribution that concludes the above-quoted description of *O. brookiana,* written in January 1855.

Wallace appears to have generalized immediately the explanation
of the isolated position of *Ornithoptera brookiana.* He perceived that
extinction of ancestral, intermediate species or groups of species would
explain all cases of the disjunct distribution of isolated but closely
related groups. The biological distinctiveness of disjunct moieties is
the necessary result of the extinction of the intermediate links in what
must once have been a continuous chain of affinities. The continuing
gradual modification of the species at the ends of the now-disjunct
range would produce clusters of closely related species. This was the
explanation of green-backed trogons' being restricted to tropical
America and the brown-backed to the Oriental tropics. Here, too,
was the explanation of the restriction of the genus *Euploea* to the
Orient, while the related South American species were represented
by a greatly expanded cluster that had become so large as to constitute its own family, the Heliconidae.

As noted, Wallace himself never commented on the role of *O.
brookiana* in the formulation of his hypothesis. A possible reason
was that, as he collected and thus became better acquainted with the
forms close to *O. priamus,* he realized that *O. brookiana* could not
be a close relative. In 1865, three years after returning to England,
he published a monographic treatment of the Papilionidae of the Archipelago. In it he classified the species of bird-wings in three groups,
the first two of which corresponded to the "green-marked" and the
"yellow-marked" species, respectively, of the 1855 paper; *Ornithoptera brookiana* alone comprised the third group. Of it he remarked,
"I have been in much doubt about the position of this remarkable

species, and was for some time inclined to place it among the Papilios. It agrees, however, far better with *Ornithoptera* in the form and stoutness of the wings. . . . It is peculiar . . . in its altogether unique style of coloration, and must be considered as the type of a distinct group of the genus *Ornithoptera.*" (Wallace 1865b:41) Much later, but before Wallace wrote his autobiography, the Bornean bird-wing (now also known from Sumatra) had been transferred to its own genus, *Trogonoptera,* which is now placed not even close to its original genus within the classification of *Papilio*-like butterflies (Munroe 1961; Zeuner 1943; D'Abreda 1975; Haugum and Lowe 1978.) Even though subsequent knowledge has demonstrated the naïveté of Wallace's initial taxonomic judgment, the generalization he made from the 1855 analysis of relationships within *Ornithoptera* has been accepted as a general truth.

Forbes's Polarity Hypothesis

It is not clear exactly when Wallace read Forbes's statement of the polarity hypothesis, which comprised the conclusion of a long Anniversary Address he presented to the Geological Society of London at the end of his year as its president. The date was February 17, 1854. It seems most unlikely that the issue of the Society's *Quarterly Journal* carrying the address could have reached Singapore much before Wallace's return from the Malay Peninsula in September of that year. But whenever and wherever Wallace read it, he was likely impressed not only by the "absurdity" of the hypothesis but also by the relevance of Forbes's summary of the distribution of groups of similar organisms through geological time. This statement was the preamble to the presentation of the Forbes hypothesis:

> Doubtless a principal element of this difference [between palaeozoic and "neozoic" life] lies in *substitution* in the replacement of one group by another, serving the same purpose in the world's oeconomy. Paradoxical must be the mind of the man, a mind without eyes, who in the present state of research would deny the limitation of natural groups to greater or less, but in the main continuous, areas or sections of geological time. Now, that greater and lesser groups—genera, subgenera, families, and orders, as

the case may be—or, in truer words, genera of different grades of extent—
have replaced others of similar value and served the same purpose or played
the same part, is so evident to every naturalist acquainted with the geological distribution of animals and plants, that to quote instances would be a
waste of words. This replacement is *substitution of group for group*—a
phaenomenon strikingly conspicuous on a grand scale when we contrast
the palaeozoic with the after-faunas and floras. A single instance of these
greater substitutions may be cited to assist my argument, viz., the substitution of the Lamellibranchiata of later epochs by the Palliobranchiata during the earlier. In this, as in numerous other instances, it is not a total
replacement of one group by another that occurred; both groups were represented at all times, but as the one group approached a minimum in the
development of specific and generic types, the other approached a maxi-
mum, and *vice versa*. I think few geologists and naturalists who have studied both the palaeozoic and the after—I must coin a word—*neozoic* mollusca will doubt that a large portion of the earlier Brachiopoda—the
Productidae for example—performed the offices and occupied the places of
the shallower-water ordinary bivalves of succeeding epochs.

Now in this substitution the replacement is not necessarily that of a lower
group in the scale of organization by a higher. There is an appearance of
such a law in many stances that has led over and over again to erroneous
doctrines about progression and development. The contrary may be the
case. Now that we have learned the true affinities that exist between the
Bryozoa and the Brachiopoda, we can see in these instances the *zoological*
replacement of a higher by a lower group, whilst in the former view, equally
true, of the replacement of the Brachiopoda by the Lamellibranchiata, a
higher group is substituted for a lower one. Numerous cases might be cited
of both categories.

But can we not find something more in these replacements and inter-
changes than mere *substitution,* which is a phaenomenon manifested among
minor and major groups within every extended epoch? Is there no law to
be discovered in the grand general grouping of the substitutions that characterize the palaeozoic epoch when contrasted with all after-epochs considered as one, the Neozoic? It seems to me that there is, and that the
relation between them is one of contrast and opposition—in the natural
history language, is the relation of POLARITY.

The manifestation of this relation in organized nature is by contrasting
developments in opposite directions. The well-known and often-cited instance of the opposition progress of the vegetable and animal series, each
starting from the same point—the point at which the animal and vegetable
organisms are scarcely if at all distinguishable,—may serve to illustrate the
idea, and make it plain to those to whom the use of the term POLARITY
in geological science may not be familiar. In that case we speak of two
groups being in the relation of polarity to each other when the rudimentary

forms of each are proximate and their completer manifestations far apart.
This relation is not to be confounded with divergence, nor with antago-
nism. (Forbes 1854: lxxviii–lxxix)

While the hypothesis proposed by Forbes could appropriately be
dubbed an "ideal absurdity" by Wallace, the preceding text could
not. "Paradoxical must be the mind of the man, a mind without eyes,
who in the present state of research would deny the limitation of
natural groups to greater or less, but in the main continuous, areas or
sections of geological time" must have seemed familiar to Wallace.
Wallace himself might well have written that sentence—if one strikes
out the phrase, "of geological time." He might well have also written Forbes's following sentence, if the words made parenthetical here
were omitted: "Now, that greater and lesser groups—genera, sub-
genera, families, and orders, as the case may be—(or, in truer words,
genera of different grades of extent)—have replaced others of similar
value and served the same purpose or played the same part, is so
evident to every naturalist acquainted with the (geological) distribution of animals and plants, that to quote instances would be a waste
of words." The fact that these slight emendations of Forbes's statement apply to the facts of *geographical* distribution makes the analogy between the distribution of related organic entities in space and
in time evident. It is unlikely that this analogy escaped Wallace. In
fact, Forbes's statement could well have been the inspiration for the
geological propositions (see synopsis above) of the "law" paper, am-
plified by information from Lyell's *Principles*.

These, then, were the observations that challenged Wallace's hypothesis of gradual species modification during his first months in the
East. The final realization that the extinction of intermediate species
would explain these puzzling distribution patterns also gave his hypothesis a robustness that emboldened him not only to present it for
public scrutiny but even to assert, "It also claims a superiority over
previous hypotheses, on the ground that it not merely explains, but
necessitates what exists" (Wallace 1855c:196). Superior as it seemed
to be, its statement had to be brief, isolated as its author was in a
cottage near the mouth of the Sarawak River, waiting for an end to
rain that had been nearly incessant for four months. In the introduc-

tion he wrote: "Fully to enter into such a subject would occupy much space, and it is only in consequence of some views having been lately promulgated, he believes in a wrong direction, that he now ventures to present his ideas to the public, with only such obvious illustrations of the arguments and results as occur to him in a place far removed from all means of reference and exact information" (p. 185).

Only two of the "obvious illustrations" are not based primarily on his own observations, or on the statements on geological phenomena in Forbes's paper. The exceptions are the explanations of the origin of the "true Natural System of classification" and of the peculiar nature of the Galapagos biota in the section on geographical distribution.

Strickland on Natural Systems

The final paragraph in the short explanation of the natural system of classification is: "We shall thus find ourselves obliged to reject all those systems of classification which arrange species or groups in circles, as well as those which fix a definite number for the divisions of each group" (p. 187). As difficult as it is for today's reader to understand, the use of such symmetrical arrangements, particularly the circular, had been on the increase in the decade preceding 1855. It is necessary to appreciate that the proponents of these systems held to the belief that God had created each species according to a grand plan. What more God-like than a plan based on perfect circles? Swainson's text (1835) on geographical distribution and classification, well studied by Wallace, promulgated the circular system. But Wallace had found the approach unworkable. "We have, however, never been able to find a case in which the circle has been closed by a direct and close affinity. In most cases a palpable analogy has been substituted, in others the affinity is very obscure or altogether doubtful (p. 187). He concluded, "Their ['purely artificial arrangements'] death-blow was given by the admirable paper of the lamented Mr. Strickland, published in the 'Annals of Natural History,' in which he so clearly showed the true synthetical method of discovering the Natural System" (p. 188). (News of Strickland's tragic accidental death was included in the opening part of Forbes's presidential address.)

The paper by Hugh Edwin Strickland had appeared over a decade earlier, in the November 1840 issue of the *Annals and Magazine of Natural History,* under the title "On the true Method of discovering the Natural System in Zoology and Botany." Before indicating Strickland's views on natural systems, it is helpful to note his definitions of "affinity" and "analogy" in relation to Wallace's statement, just quoted:

> If we suppose that by a repetition of this process [assignment of degrees of resemblance] every species is placed in its true position, we obtain a definition of those much-disputed terms, *affinity* and *analogy,*—the former consists in those *essential* and *important* resemblances which determine the place of a species in the natural system, while the latter term (analogy) expresses those *unessential* and (so to speak) *accidental* resemblances which sometimes occur between distantly allied species without influencing their position in the system. (Strickland 1840:185)

The evident circularity in Strickland's definitions is at least theoretically resolved by Wallace, who states, "The natural series of affinities will also represent the order in which the several species came into existence . . ." (1855c:186), or, briefly stated, affinity betokens evolutionary descent. But the pragmatic difficulty of deciding whether, for example, similar bill shape in two bird groups indicates descent from a common ancestor (affinity) or parallel or convergent modification in relation to a similar style of feeding (analogy) is not removed by the theoretical clarification. Wallace acknowledges this: "We thus see how difficult it is to determine in every case whether a given relation is an analogy or an affinity, for it is evident that as we go back along the parallel or divergent series, toward the common antitype, the analogy which existed between the two groups becomes an affinity" (p. 187).

It is most unlikely that Wallace had a copy of Strickland's paper in hand; it is much more likely that he remembered what he had read a year or so before in London, while trying to resolve questions about bird classification raised by observations in the Amazon.

Strickland's essay is largely devoted to a general comparison of attributes of a true natural system of classification with those designed to satisfy some a priori symmetrical plan. In particular he dissects and devastates Swainson's use of circular designs in the classification of birds. Two quite fundamental statements about natural systems are noteworthy because they demonstrate ways in which Wallace's hypothesis provided dynamic, natural interpretations of what Strickland conceived as a static, permanent system of life forms.

Strickland begins: "The postulate with which I commence the inquiry is, to let it be granted that there are such things as *species,* distinct in their characters and permanent in their duration. This being admitted, we define the natural system to be *the arrangement of species according to the degree of resemblance in their essential characters"* (Strickland 1840:184). This is Wallace's introductory sentence: "If the law above enunciated be true, it follows that the natural series of affinities will also represent the order in which the several species came into existence, each one having had for its immediate antitype a closely allied species existing at the time of its origin" (1855c:186).

Although there is much to suggest that Strickland's ideas had been important in shaping Wallace's, the only one that need be mentioned here is his suggestion that a tree might offer a useful analogy to a system of classification: "The natural system may, perhaps, be most truly compared to an irregularly branching tree, or rather to an assemblage of detached trees and shrubs of various sizes and modes of growth. And as we show the form of a tree by sketching it on paper, or by drawing its individual branches and leaves, so may the natural system be drawn on a map. . . ." (Strickland 1840:190). Wallace used the tree simile (see the earlier quotation in the synopsis of the "law" paper) to express the intricate relationships that the continued gradual modification of many related species can produce, "a complicated branching of the lines of affinity, as intricate as the twigs of a gnarled oak. . . ," and to introduce the significance of extinction:

> Again, if we consider that we have only fragments of this vast system, the stem and main branches being represented by extinct species of which we have no knowledge, while a vast mass of limbs and boughs and minute twigs and scattered leaves is what we have to place in order, and determine the true position each originally occupied with

regard to the others, the whole difficulty of the true Natural System of classification becomes apparent to us. (Wallace 1855c:187)

Darwin on the Galapagos Biota

Wallace made reference in his section on geographical distribution to a phenomenon with which he was not directly conversant: the biota of the Galapagos Islands. Although no explicit mention is made of it, the source of information was, almost without doubt, the second edition of Charles Darwin's *Journal of Researches into the Natural History and Geology of the Countries Visited During the Voyage of H.M.S. Beagle Under the Command of Captain Fitz Roy, R.N.* (1845). The second edition contained a wealth of biological information lacking in the first, which had been prepared immediately after Darwin's return to England (1839). By 1845 various experts had provided identifications of the specimens Darwin had collected. Wallace had noted in a letter to Bates dated April 11, 1846, "I first read Darwin's 'Journal' three or four years ago, and have lately re-read it" (Wallace 1905 1:255–56). Although it is nowhere so stated, it seems not unreasonable to assume that the rereading was occasioned by the appearance of the second edition. The second edition provided more detail on both the plants and the animals to which Wallace makes reference. I quote here from Darwin only the text relating to birds, for only here did Darwin make any comments on the problems of their origin, other than some general remarks, also quoted here.

The paragraph in question begins, "Of land birds I obtained twenty-six kinds, all peculiar to the group and found nowhere else, with the exception of one lark-like finch from North America (Dolichonyx oryzivorus), which ranges on that continent as far north as 54°, and generally frequents marshes." After listing the other species, he treats the most unusual group of birds:

> The remaining land-birds form a most singular group of finches, related to each other in the structure of their beaks, short tails, form of body, and plumage: there are thirteen species, which Mr Gould has divided into four sub-groups. All these species are peculiar to this archipelago; and so is the whole group, with the exception of one species of the sub-group Cactornis,

lately brought from Bow Island, in the Low Archipelago. Of Cactornis, the two species may be often seen climbing about the flowers of the great cactus-trees; but all the other species of this group of finches, mingled together in flocks, feed on the dry and sterile ground of the lower districts. The males of all, or certainly of the greater number, are jet black; and the females (with perhaps one or two exceptions) are brown. The most curious fact is the perfect gradation in the size of the beaks in the different species of Geospiza, from one as large as that of a hawfinch to that of a chaffinch, and (if Mr Gould is right in including his sub-group, Certhidea, in the main group), even to that of a warbler. Seeing this gradation and diversity of structure in one small, intimately related group of birds, one might really fancy that from an original paucity of birds in this archipelago, one species had been taken and modified for different ends. (Darwin 1845:345–46)

Darwin's sentence ending "one might really fancy that from an original paucity of birds in this archipelago, one species had been taken and modified for different ends" surely provided nothing unacceptable to strict deists among the contemporary readership. At the same time, it was sufficiently ambiguous to provoke debate among future historians of biology. Was Darwin making a tentative, but cryptic, statement that species might be modified by *natural* causes?

While it is impossible to give a decisive answer to that question, it is possible to say without provoking argument that Darwin's attitude toward the general significance of the Galapagos biota had undergone a change since 1839. In his first edition he appears to have been principally impressed by the "American character" of the biota of this oceanic archipelago:

I will not here attempt to come to any definite conclusions, as the species have not been accurately examined; but we may infer, that, with the exception of a few wanderers, the organic beings found on the archipelago are peculiar to it; and yet that their general form strongly partakes of an American character. It would be impossible for any one accustomed to the birds of Chile and La Plata to be placed on these islands, and not feel convinced that he was, as far as the organic world was concerned, on American ground. This similarity in type, between distant islands and continents, while the species are distinct, has scarcely been sufficiently noticed. The circumstance would be explained, according to the views of some authors, by saying that the creative power had acted according to the same law over a wide area. (Darwin 1839:474)

Toward the end of the discussion of the Galapagos Islands in the second edition, Darwin indicated the aspect of this peculiar biota that he found most unexpected:

> The distribution of the tenants of this archipelago would not be nearly so wonderful, if, for instance, one island had a mocking-thrush, and a second island some other quite distinct genus;—if one island had its genus of lizard, and a second island another distinct genus, or none whatever;—or if the different islands were inhabited, not by representative species of the same genera of plants, but by totally different genera, as does to a certain extent hold good; for, to give one instance, a large berry-bearing tree at James Island had no representative species in Charles Island. But it is the circumstance, that several of the islands possess their own species of the tortoise, mocking-thrush finches, and numerous plants, these species having the same general habits, occupying analogous situations, and obviously filling the same place in the natural economy of this archipelago, that strikes me with wonder. It may be suspected that some of these representative species, at least in the case of the tortoise and of some of the birds, may hereafter prove to be only well-marked races; but this would be of equally great interest to the philosophical naturalist. (Darwin 1845:362)

Wallace believed that his law of gradual modification provided the answer:

> Such phaenomena as are exhibited by the Galapagos Islands, which contain little groups of plants and animals peculiar to themselves, but most nearly allied to those of South America, have not hitherto received any, even a conjectural explanation. The Galapagos are a volcanic group of high antiquity, and have probably never been more closely connected with the continent than they are at present. They must have been first peopled, like other newly-formed islands, by the action of winds and currents, and at a period sufficiently remote to have had the original species die out, and the modified prototypes only remain. In the same way we can account for the separate islands having each their peculiar species, either on the supposition that the same original emigration peopled the whole of the islands with the same species from which differently modified prototypes were created, or that the islands were successively peopled from each other, but that new species have been created in each on the plan of the pre-existing ones. (Wallace 1855c:188)

A footnote added to the text of the "law" paper shows that Wallace had hoped to attract the attention of Forbes to his own hypothesis. At the conclusion of the Presidential Address in which he had presented the polarity hypothesis, Forbes had called for reactions. By developing an alternative hypothesis that in part reacted explicitly to Forbes, Wallace apparently hoped to elicit some serious consideration of his ideas about organic change. He was probably mindful of the hostile, unthoughtful response that had followed his earlier brief, speculative remarks before the Entomological Society. But Wallace's hope was destined to be frustrated. Edward Forbes died suddenly at the age of forty, on November 18, 1854. His death probably came within a month of the time when Wallace read his address. Wallace, of course, could not have learned this sad news until several months after the event. The footnote read: "Since the above was written, the author has heard with sincere regret of the death of this eminent naturalist, from whom so much important work was expected. His remarks on the present paper—a subject on which no man was more competent to decide—were looked for with the greatest interest. Who shall supply his place?" (p. 192).

It must have seemed to Wallace that there was, indeed, no one to respond. Samuel Stevens, his agent, reported that the only reaction in the Entomological Society was grumblings that he should stop theorizing and get on with his collecting.

CHAPTER SIX

Borneo: Birds, Brutes, and a Book

The fifteen months Wallace spent in Borneo may be divided into four phases. For the first four months after his arrival in November 1854, heavy, nearly incessant rain made field work sporadic and unproductive. It was limited to trips on the Sarawak River. Wallace's energies were directed instead to the preparation of a series of papers, a series that culminated in the "law" paper, dated February 1855. The second, much longer phase began when the rains finally slackened and field work became possible. Wallace moved to a site at Simunjon (Simunjan) near the newly opened coal mines on the Sadong River, which lies some miles east of the Sarawak. In nine months here, over half his total time in Borneo, Wallace's diligence yielded an extraordinarily rich collection of beetles; most of his 2,000 Bornean species, represented by nearly 10,000 specimens, were taken here. These, and specimens of the orangutan, whose presence there had drawn him to Simunjon, provided the income needed to finance his projected travels to the eastern islands of the Archipelago. Of these nine months, some six weeks were lost because of a badly ulcerated ankle. Evidence suggests that during this period of enforced physical inactivity, Wallace's interest was directed toward expansion and application of the hypothesis of the "law" paper. An innovative application, to the understanding of the systematic affinities among families of perching birds, was at least begun then. So was the extraction from Lyell's *Principles* of a series of statements to which he took exception. Wallace considered these notations to constitute the beginning of a book-length elaboration of his views on organic change.

Collecting activities, when resumed, soon proved unproductive.

Toward the end of November, Wallace left Simunjon, to begin the third phase of his travels in Borneo. He wanted to explore the interior. Hitherto his activities had been restricted to riverbanks and adjoining swampy areas. His plan was to ascend the Sadong River to its headwaters, then to cross the divide to the headwaters of the Sarawak and return down the Sarawak River to Kuching. This journey provided an opportunity to become acquainted with the Hill Dyaks (Dayaks), for comparison with the other Bornean Malays. One aspect of life in various Dyak villages that fascinated Wallace was the use made of bamboo; it invited comparison with the uses that Wallace had observed Amazonian Indians to make of palms. The short final phase, except for Christmas week, was passed at a cottage owned by the Rajah of Sarawak on an isolated mountain twenty miles from Kuching. Here Wallace had the greatest success of his entire Eastern sojourn in collecting moths; a lamp on a whitewashed veranda facing a vista of the forested mountain attracted a steady influx on dark, wet nights. On a record night he collected 200 specimens, representing 130 species. In all, about ten times that number of species of moth were taken, most of them previously undescribed. Wallace left Borneo in late January 1865.

It should be emphasized that Wallace's travels in Borneo yielded rich collections but provided little challenge to his hypothesis. At that time he foresaw a lifetime devoted to the analysis of these collections and the amassing of evidence to support his hypothesis. It was two almost incidental specimens that appear to have provided immediate challenges. The first was the specimen of a beautiful new bird-wing butterfly presented to him by Captain Brooke Brooke. The scientific consequences of this one specimen, named *Ornithoptera brookiana* by Wallace, have been considered in a previous chapter. The second specimen was a large, almost grotesque bird, a hornbill. This bird was one of his small collection of Bornean birds, an assemblage Wallace characterized in his summary of the zoology of Borneo as "remarkably scarce and uninteresting . . ." Yet, as evidence to be presented below will suggest, it was speculation about the affinities of this aberrant bird that appears to have stimulated his first application of his hypothesis to analysis of the relationships among a large group of variously related families of animals.

I shall first briefly examine Wallace's experiences with the orang-utan, then analyze more extensively his thoughts on the affinities of perching birds. Finally, a few remarks will relate his "Species Notebook" jottings to the foregoing material.

One of the three papers reporting the results of his observations of the orangutan carried some comments of more general interest. This paper provided an opportunity for Wallace, now possessed of an unsurpassed knowledge of the habits of this great ape, to make a public statement of his belief that man and orangutan had a shared ancestry. This was a courageous, if not foolhardy, act at that time, but his firsthand observations had strengthened a belief in the common ancestry of apes and man that Wallace had brought with him to Borneo.

In his delineation of the characteristic features of the zoology of Southeast Asia, Swainson had written in 1835: "Commencing with the quadrupeds, we find a striking characteristic of this region, in the numerous but disgusting races of apes and baboons; of whose existence in Europe, even at the most remote period, there is not the slightest record. These satyr-like creatures seem to congregate as we advance to the equinoctial line; the long armed gibbons being principally found on the isthmus of Malacca, while the oran-utangs appear more especially to be natives of the great islands" (p. 48). Wallace was not disgusted but rather fascinated with what he had learned of the orangutan, and the possibility of observing this creature was a prime attraction of Borneo. Before departing for Singapore early in 1854, he had discussed Borneo as a collecting site with Sir James Brooke, Rajah of Sarawak, who was a naturalist with a particular interest in these great apes.

On the first of November Wallace arrived in Sarawak from Singapore. The heavy rains arrived at about the same time, and collecting was poor. The Rajah returned home in December, and Wallace celebrated that Christmas and the next as his guest, in the "pleasant society" he had anticipated in his letter home. Spencer St. John, Sir James Brooke's private secretary and later his biographer, recorded Wallace's arrival in late 1854 with these words:

> We had at this time in Sarawak the famous naturalist, traveller, and
> philosopher, Mr. Alfred Wallace, who was then elaborating in his mind

the theory which simultaneously was worked out by Darwin—the theory
of the origin of species; and if he could not convince us that our ugly
neighbours, the orang-outangs, were our ancestors, he pleased, delighted,
and instructed us by his clever and inexhaustible flow of talk—really good
talk. The Rajah was pleased to have so clever a man with him as it excited
his mind, and brought out his brilliant ideas. No man could judge the Rajah
by seeing him in society. It was necessary to get him at his cottage at
Paninjow, with his clever visitor Wallace, or with his nephew Charles, the
present Rajah . . . ; or with Mr. Chambers, the present Bishop. . . .
With these, either at our house in Kuching or in our mountain cottage, we
were ever in discussion and our discussions were always either philosophical or religious.   (St. John 1879:274–75)

The Rajah was one of the few of his countrymen to have seen this
great ape living in the wild, to have seen its similarities to man. Yet
he obviously held, as most others did, to the comforting belief that
God had created the human species in His own image. The orangutan
was but a highly organized species of animal to which it had pleased
God to give some passing similarities to man.

An alternative assessment of the significance of these similarities
of man to the great apes had been presented in the second volume of
Lyell's *Principles*. It was not an assessment which Lyell himself accepted; rather it was a signal part of Lyell's translation and summary
of the thoughts of Jean Baptiste Lamarck in his *Zoologie Philoso-
phique,* which had been published in Paris in 1809. Lyell used Lamarck's speculation about the transformation of orangutan to man as
an example of Lamarck's conception of species transformation. Lamarck made two basic postulations. The first was "the tendency to
progressive advancement" which, if it acted alone on organisms would
raise "the humblest to the most exalted degree of intelligence." The
second was that "the force of external circumstances perpetually in-
terferes with this progressive tendency, and through retardations and
accelerations maintains the spectrum of organic types that has long
characterized the living world."

One of the races of quadrumanous animals which had reached the highest state of perfection, lost, by constraint of circumstances (concerning the
exact nature of which tradition is unfortunately silent), the habit of climbing trees, and of hanging on by grasping the boughs with their feet as with

hands. The individuals of this race being obliged, for a long series of generations, to use their feet exclusively for walking, and ceasing to employ their hands as feet, were transformed into bimanous animals, and what before were thumbs became mere toes, no separation being required when their feet were used solely for walking. Having acquired a habit of holding themselves upright, their legs and feed assumed, insensibly, a conformation fitted to support them in an erect attitude, till at last these animals could no longer go on all-fours without much inconvenience.

The Angola-orang (*Simia troglodytes,* Linn.) is the most perfect of animals; much more so than the Indian orang (*Simia Satyrus*), which has been called the oran-outang, although *both* are *very inferior* to man in corporeal powers and intelligence. These animals frequently hold themselves upright; but their organization has *not yet* been sufficiently modified to sustain them habitually in this attitude, so that the standing posture is very uneasy to them. When the Indian orang is compelled to take flight from pressing danger, he immediately falls down upon all-fours, showing clearly that this was the original position of the animal. Even in man, whose organization, in the course of a longer series of generations, has advanced so much farther, the upright posture is fatiguing, and can be supported only for a limited time, and by aid of the contraction of many muscles.
(Lyell 1842, vol. 3, ch. 1, pp. 18, 19)

Lyell concluded this summary of the transformation of orangutan to man thus: "It may be proper to observe that the above sketch of the Lamarckian theory is no exaggerated picture, and those passages which have probably exerted the greatest surprise in the mind of the reader are literal translations from the original" (p. 22). Many indications suggest that one of Lyell's basic difficulties in accepting any theory of species transmutation or organic evolution was that it must, implicitly or explicitly, require that man had evolved from a brute. As he himself said, he couldn't go the whole orang!

Wallace, however, had accepted as a possibility the view espoused by the author of the *Vestiges*—that under certain circumstances, species might be transformed. To him it was quite thinkable that an apelike species was ancestral to man. It is no surprise, however, that he did not convince his audience at the Rajah's; for them it was still unthinkable.

The rains continued for two months after Christmas. Collecting was still not possible. Wallace prepared the description of *Ornithoptera brookiana* and the "law" paper, but not until early March could field work be resumed. On March 12, 1855, as recorded in the first item in the "Species Notebook," Wallace arrived at the landing place in the Simunjon River, close to the new coal mines. After a week of intensive beetle collecting, he noted, "Monday March 19th. This was a white date for me. I saw for the first time the Orang-utan or 'Mias' of the Dyak in its native forest. I was out after insects not more than a quarter of a mile from the house when I heard a rustling in a tree near and looking up saw a large red haired animal moving slowly along hanging from the branches by its arms. It passed in this manner from tree to tree till it disappeared in the jungle which was so swampy that I could not follow it." A letter written three weeks later for publication in the *Zoologist* describes the terrain:

> St. Munjon Coal Works, Borneo, 8th April, 1855. You will see by the heading of this letter that I have changed my locality. I am now up the river Sadong, about twenty miles N.E. of Sarawak. A small coal-field has been discovered here, and is now being worked. At present the jungle is being cleared, and a road made to carry the coals to the river side, and it is on account of the scarcity of roads in this country that I thought it advisable to come here. Another reason was, that this is the district of the "Mias" or Orang-utan, the natural history of which I am very anxious to investigate, so as to determine definitely whether or no three species exist here, and also to learn something of their habits in a state of Nature. An English mining engineer has the direction of the works here, and has about a hundred Chinese labourers engaged. I am residing with him, at the foot of the hill in which the coal is found. The country all round us is dead level and a perfect swamp, the soil being vegetable mud, quite soft, and two or three feet deep, or perhaps much more. In such a jungle it is impossible to walk; a temporary path has, however, been made from the river (about a mile and a half) by laying down trunks of tree longitudinally. Along this path is very good collecting-ground, but many fine insects are daily lost, and butterflies can hardly be captured at all, from the impossibility of stepping out of the path, and the necessity of caution in one's movement to preserve balance and prevent slipping, not at all compatible with the capture of active tropical insects. (Wallace 1856b:5113–14)

Most of Wallace's observations and collections of orangutans were made between March 19 and June 24, 1855 ("Species Notebook").

He published three papers about them. One addressed the question of how many species of orangutan exist in Borneo. He concluded that there were two species, not three, as the letter had noted as a possibility. In another, "On the Habits of the Orang-Utan of Borneo," he addressed two topics relevant to the question of the relationship of this great ape to the human species. The first was its behavior when attacked. Lyell had said "When the Indian orang is compelled to take flight from pressing danger, he immediately falls down on all-fours, showing clearly that this was the original position of this animal." The observed behavior was more complex:

> It is a singular and most interesting sight to watch a Mias making his way leisurely through the forest. He walks deliberately along the branches, in the semi-erect attitude which the great length of his arms and the shortness of his legs give him: choosing a place where the boughs of an adjacent tree intermingle, he seizes the smaller twigs, pulls them towards him, grasps them, together with those of the tree he is on, and thus, forming a kind of bridge, swings himself onward, and seizing hold of a thick branch with his long arms, is in an instant walking along to the opposite side of the tree. He never jumps or springs, or even appears to hurry himself, and yet moves as quickly as a man can run along the ground beneath. When pursued or attacked, his object is to get to the loftiest tree near; he then climbs rapidly to the higher branches, breaking off quantities of the smaller boughs, apparently for the purpose of frightening his pursuers. Temminck denies that the Orang breaks the branches to throw down when pursued; but I have myself several times observed it. It is true he does not throw them *at* a person, but casts them down vertically; for it is evident that a bough cannot be thrown to any distance from the top of a lofty tree. In one case, a female Mias, on a durian tree, kept up for at least ten minutes a continuous shower of branches and of the heavy spined fruits, as large as 32-pounders, which most effectually kept us clear of the tree she was on. She could be seen breaking them off and throwing them down with every appearance of rage, uttering at intervals a loud pumping grunt, and evidently meaning mischief.   (Wallace 1856a:27)

The second topic addressed was the possible descent of both man and orangutan from some now-extinct ancestors:

It is a remarkable circumstance, that an animal so large, so peculiar, and of such a high type of form as the Orang-Utan, should yet be confined to such a limited district,—to two islands, and those almost at the limits of the range of the higher mammalia; for, eastward of Borneo and Celebes, the Quadrumana and most of the higher mammalia almost disappear. One cannot help speculating on a former condition of this part of the world which should give a wider range to these strange creatures, which at once resemble and mock the "human form divine,"—which so closely approach us in structure, and yet differ so widely from us in many points of their external form. And when we consider that almost all other animals have in previous ages been represented by allied, yet distinct forms,—that the bears and tigers, the deer, the horses, and the cattle of the tertiary period were distinct from those which now exist, with what intense interest, with what anxious expectation must we look forward to the time when the progress of civilization in those hitherto wild countries may lay open the monuments of a former world, and enable us to ascertain approximately the period when the present species of Orangs first made their appearance, and perhaps prove the former existence of allied species still more gigantic in their dimensions, and more or less human in their form and structure! Some such discoveries we may not unreasonably anticipate, after the wonders that geology has already made known to us. Animals the most isolated in existing nature have been shown to be but the last of a series of allied species which have lived and died upon the earth. Every class and every order has furnished some examples, from which we may conclude, that all isolations in nature are apparent only, and that whether we discover their remains or no, every animal now existing has had its representatives in past geological epochs. (p. 32)

This was the first declaration (however oblique) of belief in the evolution of man from some antecedent, more apelike species (and possibly of an ape from a more manlike one) by a biologist who had actually observed one of the great apes in a state of nature. This was in late 1855 or early 1856.

It may be noted that forty-five years after Wallace wrote the above lines, a "monument of a former world" was discovered on the nearby island of Java that was intermediate in character between man and ape. Eugène Dubois, a Dutch anatomist and geologist, unearthed in central Java the fossilized femur and parts of the skull of what became widely known as the "Java ape-man." Dubois interpreted the shape of the femur as an indication that the primate of which it had once been a part had walked with an erect posture. But the low, flattened skull he took to indicate a brain more like that characteristic of apes. He named his find *Pithecanthropus erectus,* the erect ape-man. The generic name had been proposed by the speculative German biologist Ernst Haeckel after the publication in 1859 of Darwin's *Origin of Species,* for an intermediate between ape and man whose existence he postulated. Darwin himself had been remarkably unforthcoming in the *Origin of Species* about the question of man's ancestry, although it was a common myth, then as now, that he had said that man descended from ape. He had actually said only; "I may add that some little light can apparently be thrown on the origin of these differences [between the races of man], chiefly through sexual selection of a particular kind, but without here entering on copious details my reasoning would appear frivolous" (Darwin 1859:199).

Wallace's 1856 paper predicting that fossils intermediate between ape and man would surely be uncovered was entirely forgotten; nonetheless, he was proved correct. Dubois' find partook of such an intermediate character that the zoologists who examined it declared it was human, while the anthropologists declared it an ape. After decades of controversy about the validity of these and similar fossils in Asia and Africa, the consensus of experts is that they indicate the existence (more than half a million years ago) of a species intermediate between earlier ape-man and true man, *Homo sapiens.* As it is agreed that this creature was basically manlike, it has been placed in the genus *Homo* and named *Homo erectus.*

A more extensive paper, "Attempts at a Natural Arrangement of Birds" (1856d), appeared in the September 1856 issue of the *Annals and Magazine of Natural History.* The "law" paper (Wallace 1855c), published a year earlier, had addressed the apparent dilemma for a theory of gradual organic change posed by the discreteness of the major groups of vertebrates now living. Wallace had stated then that if we knew of all of the extinct species, "the great gaps that exist between fishes, reptiles, birds and mammals would then, no doubt, be softened down by intermediate groups, and the whole organic world would be seen to be an unbroken and harmonious system." With the "birds" paper he extended his analysis to one of these major groups. Since birds, especially land birds, constitute the largest systematically well-known, cohesive group of vertebrates, indeed probably of all animals, they are exemplary for this purpose.

Aside from the umbrella birds of the Rio Negro, I have not mentioned Wallace's scientific interest in birds. Now we need to explore the observations and experience that led to the formulation of the ideas expressed in the "birds" paper. The date and place of writing are not given, but the publication date provides a starting point. The "law" paper, published exactly a year before, had been sent from Sarawak, Borneo, in February 1855. The "birds" paper, then, was probably mailed in February or March of 1856. Wallace had returned to Singapore from Borneo in early February, so that the manuscript was probably mailed from Singapore. The circumstances of its composition are conjectural. The earliest likely time was the previous summer during a long period of imposed inactivity. An undated entry in the "Species Notebook" follows the entry for June 27 (1855): "At this time I had the misfortune to slip among some fallen trees, and hurt my ankle, and not being careful enough at first it became a severe inflamed ulcer, which would not heal, and kept me a prisoner in the house the whole of July and a part of August" (SN, p. 30). The "house" was near the coal mines on the Simunjon River. This entry concludes the narrative that fills the first part of the notebook. The pages following are occupied by a variety of undated notations, the nature of which will be described later.

The next step is to examine the major new elements of the paper for items that can be identified as part of Wallace's recent experience. The "birds" paper can be said to have two objectives. The first was to propose the inclusion of hummingbirds and hornbills—among the smallest and the largest of land birds, respectively—as highly divergent members of a tribe, Fissirostres, with which neither was customarily identified. The second objective was to demonstrate that the great gaps among bird families of the Fissirostres and those among the families of another tribe, Scansores, or climbing birds, are the result of the extinction of intermediate groups. The hornbills, then, present themselves as the stimulus for the thoughts presented in this paper. (It cannot be the hummers, because they are restricted to

America. The observations adduced in support of their new systematic alignment obviously derive from Wallace's Amazonian experience.)

Hornbills are not mentioned anywhere in the three chapters devoted to Borneo in *Malay Archipelago*. But in a letter dated May 1855 from the Simunjon Coal Works, Wallace stated: "The only striking features of the animal world are the hornbills which are very abundant and take the place of the toucans of Brazil, though I believe they have no real affinity with them; and the immense flights of fruit-eating bats" (Marchant 1916 1:54).

In the first volume of the "Species Registry" of Birds and Mammals, entry 25 records a specimen of *Hydrocissa*, a hornbill. The opposite page (numbered "6" although on the right) contains a pencil sketch of the bills of an adult and an immature hornbill, with notes on coloration. It should be noted that this is the only one of the some 100 species taken in Borneo accorded any attention other than the standard notations (see ch. 4). The rest of the page bears remarks on habits and behavior, information included in the paper:

> Hornbills have a very short tongue rather fleshy than horny and not at all serrated (?) or fibrous at end. They *never* hop from bough to bough but by short jumps sideways along the same branch as far as their weight will allow them to go, to gather the fruit.
> —The large sp.—The smaller ones do hop.
> —In a small trogon I found a grasshopper which was exactly the length of the *body* of the bird.   (SR, p. 6)

This entry (like most) is undated; in a list of mammals on the preceding page, the last entry is dated "Dec." [1854].

The pages in the "Species Registry" following page 6 are devoted to measurement of orangutans, the first specimen being recorded as "May 12th." Of the December to May interval thus bracketed, the weeks through February were largely lost to field work because of the heavy rains. Thus, the only hornbill listing for Borneo falls into the March to May period, a conclusion consistent with the May letter.

This is an appropriate place to describe what we may term Wallace's background experience with birds. He never indicated a particular interest in birds during his early years. He learned to shoot birds and to prepare their skins before his departure for Brazil, only because exotic bird skins, he had learned, found a ready market. But he quickly became an ornithologist by practice; as he noted early in the "birds" paper:

> The writer of this paper has enjoyed the great privilege of observing the habits of many tropical birds in a state of nature in S. America and is at present doing so in the Indian Islands. Every naturalist knows how important this is towards a proper appreciation of the affinities of Birds, to which their habits are generally a sure guide, or at all events of much value in conjunction with other structural characters. Without pretending to have any great knowledge of anatomy, he believes that no intelligent person can be in the constant habit of skinning birds without obtaining much information on very important parts of their internal structure. Even mere external characters, such as the texture and arrangement of the feathers, the form and structure of the torso, the form of the nostrils and of the tongue, can be examined far better in a recently killed bird than in a dried or mounted specimen. In the process of skinning we also ascertain the thickness and tenacity of the skin, the solidity of the bones, the form and strength of the skull, and the texture and contents of the stomach, which characters are perhaps, for the determination of affinities, of as much importance as any which can be pointed out.   (Wallace 1856d:194–95)

The earliest indication of his interest in the bearing of the habits of birds on the revelation of their affinities was given in his *Narrative of Travels on the Amazon and Rio Negro* (1853g). The following section, incidentally, was selected for reprinting in the miscellany section of the January 1854 issue of the *Annals and Magazine of Natural History,* which also carried reviews of this book and the one on palm trees:

Habits of Birds

In all works on Natural History, we constantly find details of the marvellous adaptation of animals to their food, their habits, and the localities in which they are found. But naturalists are now beginning to look beyond this, and to see that there must be some other principle regulating the infinitely varied forms of animal life. It must strike every one, that the numbers of birds and insects of different groups, having scarcely any resemblance to each other, which yet feed on the same food and inhabit the same localities, cannot have been so differently constructed and adorned for that purpose alone. Thus the goatsuckers, the swallows, the tyrant flycatchers, and the jacamars, all use the same kind of food, and procure it in the same manner: they all capture insects on the wing, yet how entirely different is the structure and the whole appearance of these birds! The swallows, with their powerful wings, are almost entirely inhabitants of the air; the goatsuckers, nearly allied to them, but of a much weaker structure, and with largely-developed eyes, are semi-nocturnal birds, sometimes flying in the evening in company with the swallows, but most frequently settling on the ground, seizing their prey by short flights from it, and then returning to the same spot. The flycatchers are strong-legged, but short-winged birds, which can perch, but cannot fly with the ease of the swallows: they generally seat themselves on a bare tree, and from it watch for any insects which may come within reach of a short swoop, and which their broad bills and wide gape enable them to seize. But with the jacamars this is not the case: their bills are long and pointed—in fact, a weak kingfisher's bill—yet they have similar habits to the preceding: they sit on branches in open parts of the forest, from thence flying after insects which they catch on the wing, and then return to their former station to devour them. Then there are the trogons, with a strong serrated bill, which have similar habits; and the little hummingbirds, though they generally procure insects from the flowers, often take them on the wing, like any other fissirostral bird.

What birds can have their bills more peculiarly formed than the ibis, the spoonbill, and the heron? Yet they may be seen side by side, picking up the same food from the shallow water on the beach; and on opening their stomachs, we find the same little crustacea and shell-fish in them all. Then among the fruit-eating birds, there are pigeons, parrots, toucans and chatterers,—families as distinct and widely separated as possible—which yet may be often seen feeding all together on the same tree; for in the forests of South America, certain fruits are favourites with almost every kind of fruit-eating bird. It has been assumed by some writers on natural history, that every wild fruit is the food of some bird or animal, and that the varied forms and structure of their mouths may be necessitated by the peculiar character of the fruits they are to feed on; but there is more of imagination than fact in this statement: the number of wild fruits furnishing food for birds is very limited, and birds of the most varied structure and of every size will be found visiting the same tree.—Wallace's Travels on the Amazon and Rio Negro. (Wallace 1853g:58–59)

The native bird population on the island of Singapore, Wallace's first station, had been virtually eliminated by the deforestation which was at that time being completed. His only bird collecting prior to Borneo had been during the summer of 1854 on the Malay Peninsula at Malacca, where he had collected some hornbills: "My stay was too short to obtain many of the larger birds. The Hornbills are very numerous in species, but I only procured three, *Buceros rhinoceros* L., *B. intermedius* Blyth (at Singapore), and *B. malayanus* Raffl. (*anthracinus* Temm.). This last species has the bill white in the male and black in the female, which latter is the *B. nigrorostris* of Blyth" (Wallace 1855a:98). While he had briefly speculated in that short paper on the affinities of another bird group, his chief interest in the hornbills seemed to lie in pointing out that the separate name that Blyth had given to a female with a black bill was an invalid synonym, the earlier name given to the male having priority. The hornbills collected in Borneo about May 1855, therefore, represented his second encounter with these strange heavy-billed birds.

At the beginning of the "birds" paper Wallace indicates that he is limiting his comments to the "Perching Birds"—the Passeres: Insessores, as they were then recognized. This was a not inconsiderable task, as more than 5,000 of the 7,000 bird species then known were perchers. The system proposed by Cuvier, still in general use at that time, separated birds into five groups (orders): "1. Raptores, or birds of prey; 2. Insessores, or perchers; 3. Rasores, or fowls; 4. Grallatores, or waders; 5. Natatores, or swimmers" (Swainson 1835:344). These orders were accepted by Wallace as valid divisions, but he observes that as one proceeded with an examination of the families within the Insessores, similar clear-cut divisions are seldom evident. "We must therefore give up altogether the principle of *division*, and employ that of *agglutination* or juxtaposition" (Wallace 1856d:195).

It might then be possible to establish an "arrangement" if not a "classification."

Wallace proceeds to demonstrate the inadequacies he found in the Cuvierian division of the Insessores into tribes, as then followed by most ornithologists. Those tribes, as given in Swainson, are: "1. *Conirostres*, with a conical bill, and pre-eminently perchers. 2. *Dentirostres*, or perchers of prey, with sharp claws, and living chiefly upon insects. 3. *Fissirostres*, with large heads, flat bills, and weak feet, as the swifts and swallows. 4. *Tenuirostres*, with small eyes and mouth, and long bills, like the hummingbirds. And lastly, 5. The *Scansores*, or climbers, which brings on the woodpeckers, parrots, and cuckoos" (p. 345). Wallace believed this generally accepted division into tribes to be artificial and unacceptable:

> These divisions being accepted, every bird is forced into one of them, and the result has been the most incongruous and unnatural combinations. For instance, in the Tenuirostres are combined the Humming Birds and the Sun Birds (*Nectarinia*), families which in a natural arrangement would have, in our opinion, the masses of the other Passeres intervening between them. In the case of these two families, a mere outward resemblance appears to have been universally mistaken for an affinity. A similarity in size, in the prevalance of metallic colours, and in the slenderness of a very variable bill, has been taken to over-balance the most important structural differences. The universal aspects of the Hummers are, excessively long wings and as excessively small feet, with more or less united toes. They take their food exclusively on the wing. Every motion is made upon the wing. The feet are solely used as means of support, never for locomotion. The Sun Birds and their allies, the *Coerebidae* of America, have on the other hand long legs and toes, the hinder toes especially being very long and powerful; they are therefore as capable of hopping and perching as any of the most highly developed Passeres. Their wings, too, are short and round, quite incapable of any powerful flight, and their tail almost invariably short and even. . . . . There is therefore no general agreement of structure to unite these groups, except the solitary and trivial one of an elongate and slender bill.
>
> On similar principles we believe the Conirostres and Dentirostres to be equally untenable and unnatural. . . . .

The remaining groups, the Scansores and the Fissirostres, we believe to be much more natural, and in fact to be the only ones which can be distinctly separated from the Passeres, of which they form an abnormal development. It is to the arrangement of these two groups that we more particularly address ourselves.

The Fissirostres are those passerine birds whose feet are adapted solely for a state of rest,—all motion being performed by the wings. With rare exceptions, they never move the shortest distance by means of their feet,—a character which distinguishes them at once from all other Passeres, which either hop, climb, or walk almost incessantly. Such a peculiar oeconomy must evidently depend upon corresponding peculiarities of organization; and it is a remarkable proof of how little importance is the form of the bill alone as an index of affinity, that in this highly natural group we find every form of bill,—conical, toothed, hooked, serrated, spear-shaped, curved, and flat. The external characters which distinguish these birds are, very short and weak legs, long, or at all events powerful wings, and a wide gape. Their characteristic habit is to sit motionless, watching for their prey, to dart after it and seize it on the wing, and to return to their original position to swallow it. The groups which possess the peculiarities in the greatest perfection are the Trogons and the Kingfishers, with which we shall commence our inquiry into the extent of the tribe. . . .
(Wallace 1856d:196–97)

As an instance how totally unable the Trogons are to use their feet for anything like climbing, we may mention that the Trogons of South America feed principally on fruit, which one would think they would get climbing or walking after if they could. But no; they take their station on a bare branch, about the middle of the tree, and having fixed their attention on some particular tempting fruit, they dart at it, seize it dexterously on the wing, and return to their original seat. . . . It is curious that this habit seems confined to the Trogons of America. In the East I have never yet observed it, and in numerous specimens I have opened, nothing has been found but insects. The Africa Trogons also appear to be wholly insectivorous. (pp. 197–98)

After pondering the position within the tribe of several families which he judged properly assigned to it and then giving the evidence for his rejection of several other families often assigned to this tribe, Wallace begins a four-page discussion of evidence for his proposed inclusion in the Fissirostres of two families usually placed in other tribes. He considers the hornbills (Bucerotidae) first, and then the hummingbirds (Trochilidae). I shall first allude briefly to the latter. The proposed assignment of this American group was not a new idea for Wallace: in the *Narrative* of his Amazonian experiences, while remarking on the habits of birds, he had said, as quoted above, "and the little hummingbirds, though they generally procure insects from the flowers, often take them on the wing, like any other fissirostral bird." But it was certainly a new idea for ornithology, and he remarks in the "birds" paper, "In this innovation we are not aware of having any support; yet we think it possible to show good reason for it." He adduces observations of their habits and anatomy in developing this position.

Thus we come to the question of the affinities of the hornbills, with which Wallace had no field experience before coming to the East. Even his initial experiences led him to separate these birds from the large-billed toucans he knew from the Amazon; as his above-quoted letter of May 1855 stated, they "take the place of the toucans of Brazil, though I believe they have no real affinity with them. . . ." He discusses the question in the "birds" paper as follows:

From an examination of the structure of the feet and toes, and from a consideration of their habits, we are led to conclude that the Hornbills are Fissirostral birds, though of a very abnormal form. Their very short legs, and united toes with a broad flat sole, are exactly similar to those of the Kingfishers. They have powerful wings, but their heavy bodies oblige them to use much exertion in flight, which is not therefore very rapid, though often extended to considerable distances. They are (in the Indian Archipelago at least) entirely frugivorous; and it is curious to observe how their structure modifies their mode of feeding. They are too heavy to dart after the fruit in the manner of Trogons; they cannot even fly quickly from branch to branch, picking a fruit here and a fruit there; neither have they strength or agility enough to venture on the more slender branches with the Pigeons and Barbets, but they alight heavily on a branch of considerable thickness, and then, looking cautiously round them, pick off any fruits that may be within their reach, and jerk them down their throat by a motion similar to that used by the Toucans, and which has been erroneously described as throwing the

fruit up in the air before swallowing it. When they have gathered all
within their reach, they move sideways along the branch by short jumps,
or rather a kind of shuffle, and the smaller species even hop across to
other branches, when they again gather what is within their reach. When
in this way they have progressed as far as the bough will safely carry
them, they take a flight to another part of the trees, where they pursue
the same course. . . . The only question that remains then is, to what
family of the Fissirostres do they most nearly approach? A careful consideration leads us to fix upon the Kingfishers. They are among the
largest birds in the group, they have the largest bills, and in the structure of the feet, the two are almost identical. The Hornbills of Africa
are said to feed principally on reptiles, as do the King-Hunters (*Dacelo*)
of Australia. We look upon Hornbills, therefore, as one of the abnormal developments of Fissirostral birds of which they are the largest,
the least elegant, and the least gifted with facilities for locomotion and
for obtaining their food; and that their nearest affinities lie in the direction of the Kingfishers. . . .   (Wallace 1856d:200–2)

Wallace expresses the interrelationships of the families within the
Fissirostres in a diagram, using a form originally suggested by Strickland (1840) (fig. 6.1). In explanation of this unusual diagrammatic
representation, Wallace says:

It is intended that the distances between the several names should
show to some extent the relative amount of affinity existing between
them; and the connecting lines show in what direction the affinities are
supposed to lie. By referring to the diagram it will be seen that there
are seven families placed close together, forming a central mass. Beyond the Trogons at some distance, come the Goatsuckers and Swallows, while at the greatest distance from each other are the Hornbills
and the Hummers, the former having a distant affinity to the Kingfishers, the latter to the Swallows.

*We may here mention that it is an article of our zoological faith, that
all gaps between species, genera, or larger groups are the result of the
extinction of species during former epochs of the world's history,* and
we believe this view will enable us more justly to appreciate the correctness of our arrangement. For instance, let us suppose that the gaps
shown in this diagram have been all filled up by genera and families
forming a natural transition from one of our groups to the other, and
we shall be able to judge whether our arrangement will agree with such

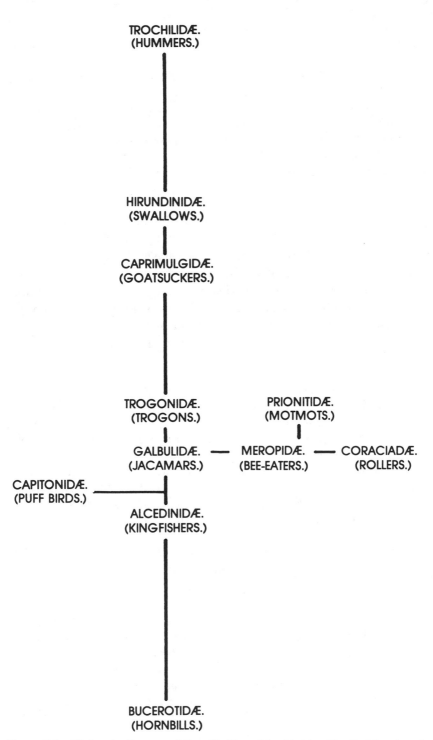

Figure 6.1. Wallace's diagram of the affinities of the bird families that he placed in the order Fissirostres. In this diagram, based on Strickland's method of diagramming, the closeness of the grouping of the families indicates his assessment of the degree of their mutual affinity. The gaps between families were, in his view, once occupied by transitional forms now extinct. See text. (From Wallace 1856d.)

a supposition. Thus, if the space between the Kingfishers and Hornbills has been filled up by a natural succession of families, we can see that the change must have been to heavier, larger, and larger-billed birds, and we see such a change begun already from the Jacamars to the Kingfishers. So, from the Goatsuckers to the Swallows the change is to smaller, stronger-winged, thicker-skinned, and brighter-coloured birds,— exactly the kind of change which continued on will lead us to the Hummers.'' (p. 206; italics added.)

The arrangement of families within the other tribe of concern, Scansores, as presented by Wallace, invites comparison with that within the Fissirostres. He begins his analysis by noting that all bird systematists, although otherwise differing, agree that four families belong in this tribe: parrots (Psittacidae), woodpeckers (Picidae), cuckoos (Cuculidae), and toucans (Rhamphastidae). These families, nonetheless, are quite distinct one from another, in contrast to the Fissirostres, in which the generally accepted families bear some affinity to each other:

> Now, though these four families [of Scansores] have evidently more connexion with each other than with any other birds, yet they present so many important points of difference, as to show that they are in reality very distant from each other, and that an immense variety of forms must have intervened to have filled up the chasms, and formed a complete series presenting a gradual transition from one to the other. . . . We should be inclined to consider therefore that they form widely distant portions of a vast group, once perhaps as extensive and varied as the whole of the existing Passeres. (p. 209)

After a careful consideration of other families for inclusion, Wallace presents a diagram of affinities for the Scansores, with the four basic families occupying peripheral positions.

> We may here remark, we can never hope to arrive at the true direction and amount of the affinities of the several families of birds, owing to our complete ignorance of the extinct forms. It is probable that in very few cases is there a direct affinity between two groups, each being more or less distantly related to some common extinct group, so that we should represent their connexion more accurately by making our

central line a blank, for the extinct portion of the group, and placing our
families right and left, at different distances from it. . . . (p. 214)

Wallace concludes his analysis with a discussion of a third group,
the "normal or typical Passeres," the songbirds, as we may call this
group, by far the largest, comprising at least half of all known species at that time. These are assigned to about thirty-five families.
"But all the families which compose this group are so intimately
connected with each other, that the limits of a great many of them
cannot be determined, and there is no family of any extent which
does not blend into others." Quite unlike the situation in the Fissirostres and Scansores, these are not isolated families; there are no
families about the limits of which there is "scarcely any doubt or
disagreement whatsoever." "Here then we have three groups, one of
which, though very much more extensive than the others, offers less
variation in the form and size of the species, and in the modifications
of their principal organs" (p. 216).

Although Wallace makes no such comparison explicit, I think that
his implicit attitude allows us to consider that these three groups may
represent stages in a group's history. The songbirds, numerous in
species, yet evincing comparatively little diversity in size and morphology, could represent a relatively recently evolved group. There
have not been sufficiently extensive extinctions within the group to
isolate families or make subdivisions manifest. The Fissirostres might
represent an older stage of a group conceivably once as extensive as
the songbirds. The diversity within the Fissirostres is greater in size,
habits, and structure. Extinction of intermediate groups makes the
remaining divergent families appear isolated; but the affinities among
these families are still more or less evident. A still older stage is
represented by the tribe Scansores. The smaller number of residual
families, even more divergent, no longer have clear linkages to each
other. But they are more like each other than they are like any other
birds.

One might wonder whether, if and when the Fissirostres reach the
stage that the Scansores are thought to represent, the affinities of
hummingbirds and hornbills will be recognizable.

This completes my summary of the major points of the first scientific paper examining bird affinities in the light of the theory of organic evolution.

In the Supplement to the Natural History Division of Knight's *English Cyclopedia,* the unsigned author of the article on birds devotes five pages to a detailed examination of Wallace's "birds" paper. The publication date for the volume is not given, but the latest classification scheme noted in the article is Owen's of 1866.

> That excellent results may be obtained from a consideration of the habits and characters of the living bird is, we think, shown in Mr. Wallace's arrangement of the order *Passeres.* His remarks were published in 1856; but, if we mistake not, many of his suggestions have been more or less adopted in that part of Professor Owen's classification which relates to the same group. His conclusions, moreover, generally harmonize with the improvements proposed by Eyton and Nitzsch before him, and Blanchard and others after him, on anatomical groups; as also with what we consider to be the best features in Bonaparte's scheme. For these reasons we do not hesitate to give a full abstract of his paper, retaining in many places his own expressions. (Knight n.d., column 114)

It should be remembered that Wallace prepared his paper without benefit of library facilities, as is implied in a sentence that must have been added after the paper was essentially completed. "The preceding deductions from the habits of these birds had been made before I became aware that Mr. Eyton had arrived at similar results from anatomical considerations alone; and I had great pleasure in finding that there was such solid support for the opinion which I had formed, entirely from my own observations" (Wallace 1856d:201).

Only two exceptions are taken in the *Cyclopedia* article to Wallace's arrangement: "It will be noticed that Mr. Wallace speaks of the *Hirundinidae;* but we think his position would be improved if the swallows were excluded and *Hirundinidae* replaced by the term Cypsalidae" (Knight n.d., column 117). It was recognized by most ornithologists by 1866 that the resemblance of swallows and swifts was due to convergence, i.e., was an analogy, not an affinity. The swallows were placed with the group that Wallace had called the "normal or typical Passeres." The article continues, "One of the defects in this arrangement is that the *Psittacidae* [parrots] are included among the Scansores; but Mr. Wallace himself now admits that the Psittacidae should form a distinct order'' (column 119).

At this point I should like to refer again to the matter of the composition of items in the Species Notebook. McKinney (1972) devotes a chapter to an interpretation of the significance of selected items in the notebook he had called Wallace's ''Species Notebook,'' a designation I have followed for clarity of reference. I believe, however, that he makes an assumption about its time of composition that is not supported by the internal evidence of the document itself. McKinney concluded that ''the undated plan and concluding remarks of his book [pages 35 to 53 of the Species Notebook] precede his 1855 Paper'' (p. 32, n. 12). He is led to this conclusion, I think, by a misinterpretation of a sentence in a letter that Wallace wrote to Henry Bates on January 4, 1858. A few months earlier Wallace had received a letter from Bates commenting on the ''law'' paper. Wallace replied, ''That paper is, of course, only the announcement of the theory, not its development. I have prepared the plans and written portions of an extensive work embracing the subject in all its bearings and endeavouring to prove what in the paper I have only indicated.'' From this McKinney concluded: ''Before he wrote his important 1855 paper in February of that year, Wallace had already written the plan and portions of a book on the species problem.'' But Wallace only states that he had ''prepared the plans. . . '' before the writing of the letter, i.e., before January 1858, three years after the ''law'' paper had been written. He does not say that he had prepared the plan before the ''law'' paper was written.

Although many of the entries in the Species Notebook are undated, they are dispersed among dated items which are in chronological sequence. The chronology begins with the first entry, dated ''March 12th, 1855,'' i.e., one month after the date of the ''law'' paper. The ''Lyell Extracts,'' to use Wallace's designation for the contents of pages 34–53, are bracketed by an earlier entry of late June 1855 and one nine months later dated March 1856. These are the items that McKinney has interpreted as having been written before February 1855.

In addition to their sequence in the Species Notebook, there is internal evidence that the undated notations on pages 34–53, the

"Lyell Extracts," were written in the interval suggested above. In the index that Wallace prepared for his manuscript notebook, the line preceding "Lyell Extracts" is "Proofs of Design—p. 12, 31, 32, 52." These entries, closely bracketing the "Lyell Extracts," are undated, but their content refers to Wallace's observations and interests of the spring and summer of 1855.

The first Proof of Design, on p. 12, is: "Extracts, of supposed proofs of design. *Knight's Cyc. Nat. Hist. Bats.* 'But it is in the bones of the metacarpus and fingers that the adaptation of the *osseus* parts of the animal to its necessities is, perhaps most strongly shown.'" Wallace's comment on this begins, "As if an animal could have necessities before it came into existence. . . ." This quotation is from the entry "Cheiroptera" in the *English Cyclopedia,* Natural History Division (Knight 1854, vol. 1, column 962). This is just one statement taken from a long account of the biology of bats. A possible date is suggested by the only reference that Wallace made to bats in that period, an entry on page 6 of the Species Notebook, for April 21, 1855, which begins, "An immense flight of the great Bat passed over us. . . ."

The second Proof is on page 31, the intervening eighteen pages all being narrative relating to orangutans, the last item of which is dated "June 27." It refers to an entry on coconuts in the *English Cyclopedia,* Natural History Division (vol. 2, column 55).

The third Proof of Design, "Skeleton of Birds," occupies pages 32 and 33. Again there is a quotation from the *Cyclopedia,* a few sentences taken out of a long account on birds (vol. 1, column 461). At the end Wallace wrote, "(See p. 53)." The pages from 34 to 53 are all "Lyell Extracts," i.e., statements by Lyell which Wallace did not accept, with his own position following each. The only exception is page 35, where there is a "Note for Organic Law Change." The last Proof of Design fills the rest of 53, at the end of the Lyell notations. It is about hornbills and, unlike the others, does not give a quote and a comment; nor does it refer to the *English Cyclopedia.* All of the notations about hornbills and trogons of Africa and India, however, refer to information given in the entry on "Hornbills" in the *Cyclopedia.*

This information on hornbills, which Wallace cannot have learned by direct observation, is included in the "birds" paper, which, as noted earlier, must have been written between July 1855 and March 1856, but most probably during his period of house confinement, July–August 1855. The conclusion I reach, therefore, is that the "Lyell Extracts" and the "Proofs of Design" were written at about the same period, which was not before the end of June 1855, so that they followed rather than preceded the composition of the "law" paper.

CHAPTER SEVEN
Asian Bali to New Guinean Aru

In early February 1856, on the very day that the ship on which Wallace returned from Borneo docked in Singapore, another left for Macassar, Celebes. When he learned of its departure, Wallace was disappointed. Passage to Macassar from Singapore was not easy to arrange. Two weeks after his arrival he wrote to his sister, "The day I arrived a vessel sailed for Macassar, and I fear that I shall not have another chance for two months unless I go a roundabout way, and perhaps not then, so I have hardly made up my mind what to do" (Marchant 1916 1:61). But he stayed with his original plan; a month later he wrote, "I believe I wrote to you last mail, and now have little to say except that I am still a prisoner in Singapore and unable to get away to my land of promise, Macassar, with whose celebrated oil you are doubtless acquainted" (p. 62). Although that proprietary name for a hair oil is now long forgotten, it has left its mark on the language: "antimacassar" denotes a piece of cloth that was, and probably still is, used to protect the upholstery of a chair back from hair oil.

Macassar, the major port of south Celebes, is situated near the tip of the south-pointing arm of the four long arms that comprise this island. Celebes is in the center of the then least-known part of the Archipelago. It lies between the two great islands of Borneo and New Guinea, with the Moluccas, or Spice Islands, between it and the latter. The Philippines are just to the north of Celebes, and while Wallace never did collect there, they had been identified as a likely possibility in his application to the Royal Geographical Society for a travel subsidy. Timor, which he was to visit twice, lies to the southwest.

This central locality seemed to Wallace a good place to start, and not merely because of future travel convenience. He had expected "that the productions of this central island in some degree represented the richness and variety of the whole Archipelago, while we should not expect much individuality in a country, so situated, that it would seem as if it were pre-eminently fitted to receive stragglers and immigrants from all around" (Wallace 1869:207).

On March 10, 1856, he completed a short summary of his endeavors over the preceding year and a half, entitled "Observations on the Zoology of Borneo" (1856c), for publication in the popular natural-history journal, the *Zoologist*. He ended with a look to the future.

I will now say a few words as to my future plans. The two years which I have now spent in the East I consider as, in a great measure, preliminary or preparatory to the main object of my journey, which is to investigate the less known islands of the Eastern part of the Archipelago—Celebes, the larger Molucca Islands, Timor, and, if possible, New Guinea. I feel myself now far better qualified than if I had gone at once to those countries. I have acquired the Malayan language, and have become acquainted with the manner, customs and prejudices of the people. I have learned much by experience in Eastern collecting, and have obtained such a knowledge of the productions of the western portion of the Archipelago as will add greatly to my pleasure and interest while exploring the Eastern.

I look forward, in fact, with unmixed satisfaction to my visit to the rich and almost unexplored Spice Islands—the land of the Lories, the cockatoos and the birds of paradise, the country of tortoise-shell and pearls, of beautiful shells and rare insects. I look forward with expectation and awe to visiting lands exposed to destruction from the sleeping volcano and its kindred earthquake; and not less do I anticipate the pleasures of observing the varied races of mankind, and of becoming familiar with the manners, customs and modes of thought of people so far removed from the European races and European civilization.

The physical privations which must be endured during such journeys are of little importance, except as injuring health and incapacitating from active exertion. Intellectual wants are much more trying: the absence of intimate friends, the craving for intellectual and congenial society, make themselves severely felt, and would be unbearable were it not for the constant employment and ever-varying interest of a collector's life, and the pleasures of looking forward to a time when the stores now amassed will furnish inexhaustible food for study and reflection, and call back to memory the strange beautiful scenes among which they have been obtained. (Wallace 1856c:5116–17)

In planning a voyage to the Spice Islands, Wallace was adding his name to a roster begun in the dimness of the unrecorded past. But he was different, in that he sought not spices but "the Lories, the cockatoos and the birds of paradise." His predecessors had been drawn by the exuberant productions of the plant world—cloves, mace, and nutmeg. Mankind had long ago learned of these potent spices: these, together with black pepper from India, Sumatra, and Java and cinnamon from Ceylon. The wealthy families of the population centers of faraway Europe and China would pay enough for them to sustain the trade that brought these spices over thousands of miles of sea and desert.

The use of spices to make food more palatable and to stimulate digestion is recorded by the Greeks and Romans, and the custom had probably reached both the Mediterranean region and the cities of China well before then. The Old Testament notes that a goodly part of King Solomon's income derived from "the traffic of spice merchants." Arab, and later Roman, traders brought the spices from India. Under the Ptolemies and the Romans, Alexandria became the principal center for the spice trade between India and the markets of Greece and the Roman Empire. As the Roman Empire declined, Arab traders reasserted their dominance over the spice trade with the East. Their dhows went beyond India, to Ceylon, and then much farther east, to Malacca on the Malay Peninsula. Early in the second millennium A.D., Malacca was probably the chief trading port for spices; Chinese and Arab traders acquired the spices brought there from their diverse sources. During the later part of this long period, Venice came to dominate the European end of the long chain of trade, and by the thirteenth century it had (with Genoa) largely monopolized the spice trade and thus could demand exorbitant prices from buyers in northern and western Europe.

The Europeans knew that the spices traded through Alexandria came from India, although the Arab traders had long concealed what knowledge they had about ultimate sources. As is well known, it was the Portuguese who in the fourteenth century began a series of voyages that probed the then-unknown coasts of Africa as they sought a sea route to India. The Portuguese and Spaniards had developed a lighter, faster ship, the caravel, for coastal trade over the rough waters of the Atlantic. With only the most primitive aids to navigation, the Portuguese reached the southwest coast of India, the Malabar coast, in the final years of the fifteenth century, some eighty years after Prince Henry the Navigator initiated this momentous series of voyages. In 1501 the first cargo—spices, porcelains, and precious stones—reached Lisbon: European sea trade in Oriental spices had begun. Throughout their effort to gain direct access to the sources of the spices, the Portuguese encountered unremitting hostility from Arab traders, who perceived this as the threat to their age-old domination of a lucrative enterprise that it was, indeed, intended to be.

Soon after establishing trade with Calicut and Cochin, the Portuguese learned that these Malabar Coast ports were not the primary center for trade in spices from the islands of the Indies. The center was Malacca, nearly two thousand miles further east, on the western shore of the Malay Peninsula, facing Sumatra across the narrow Straits of Malacca. It was unlikely that the Arab traders divulged their secret. Napier (1973) believes that the Portuguese learned of the importance of Malacca from an Italian adventurer, Ludovico di Varthema. Further, they learned about the islands where the spices actually grew. Di Varthema was the first European to have recorded a visit to the Spice Islands. He had left Italy in 1502, traveling overland to India. After traveling along both coasts of India and that of the island of Ceylon, he continued eastward into Burma and thence south to Malacca. Crossing the Straits to Sumatra, he visited the chief port (Pedir) for the export of black pepper, then sailed on a Chinese junk to the Spice Islands themselves. He saw clove trees, the dried, unopened buds of which are the precious item of trade. On the small, isolated islands of Banda further south he saw nutmeg trees, the fruit of which provides nutmeg from the seed and mace from the bright red aril wrapped around the seed.

On his return he visited Borneo and Java, then proceeded to India. In 1508 he stopped in Cochin, and it was probably here that he told the Portuguese what he had discovered. The Portuguese lost no time. In 1509 their ships joined the Chinese junks crowding the harbor at Malacca. They pushed on, exploring the islands of the Archipelago, seeking the Spice Islands. One ship reached the Banda Islands. In 1512 another ship was wrecked in the Moluccas, but the captain was rescued and taken to Ternate, which along with the neighboring volcanic island of Tidore was the principal trade source for cloves. During the next years Portuguese ships explored the surrounding islands of the Archipelago. Although this discovery enabled Portugal to dominate the spice trade to Europe, Portuguese power waned as the sixteenth century came to a close. The Dutch, having rebelled against Spanish rule, were ready to challenge Portugal for the spice trade. By 1597 a ship had returned to the Netherlands with a cargo of pepper, nutmeg, and mace. Five years later the Dutch East India Company was chartered. The Dutch presence in the Indies grew; the Portuguese were eclipsed. When Wallace sailed south from Singapore he was entering the Dutch colonial empire, which by then had 250 years of history. The Portuguese held only half of the island of Timor. But Wallace found the Portuguese had left an impression in their former colonies. The memories of Brazilian forests and trogons evoked by the Portuguese aura that Wallace felt while in the fringe of the forest in Malacca have already been mentioned.

Europe first learned of what we now refer to as birds of paradise through the Portuguese traders. The skins of these magnificently plumed birds were a minor but treasured item of trade in the Moluccan ports. The skins lacked feet and wings. The Portuguese were baffled, and named them "Pássaros de Sol," birds of the sun. The first Dutch designation was "Avis paradiseus." Linnaeus named the largest species *Paradisea apoda*, because a complete skin (with feet) had still not been seen in Europe. One of Wallace's primary objectives in visiting the Spice Islands was to learn the habits of these birds. But, as he was to find out, the birds do not live in those islands; they were brought by traders from New Guinea and islands surrounding it.

Other birds, less spectacular but more readily encountered, as well as insects and shells, were collected by the European traders and colonists. These spectacular manifestations of God's bounty found eager acceptance into the natural-history cabinets of a Europe longing for a touch of the exotic and beautiful. Many of the cultivated Europeans whom Wallace met in this island empire had splendid private collections.

These collections and the efforts of a small number of determined naturalists formed the basis of Western knowledge of the organic productions of the Malay Archipelago. Yet this body of knowledge misrepresented the nature of the region's biota for an unappreciated reason, as revealed by the following comments in a letter from Wallace to Stevens:

> In the town [Amboina] I reside with Dr. Mohinke, the chief physician of the Moluccas, a German, an entomologist, and a very learned and hospitable man; he had lived in Japan, made a voyage to Jeddo [? near Nagasaki, Japan], ascended volcanoes, and made collections: my pleasure may be imagined in looking over his superb collection of Japanese Coleoptera, large and handsome Longicornes and Lucani, tropical Buprestidae and northern Carabi: he had also an extensive collection of Coleoptera made during many years' residence in Sumatra, Java, Borneo and the Moluccas—a collection that makes me despair; such series of huge Prioni, Lamiae and Lucani, Dynastidae and Eucheirus! It is such collections that give, and have always given, such an erroneous idea of Tropical Entomology: these collections are made entirely by natives. Dr. Mohinke has resided here in Amboyna, for example, two years, and every native in the island knows that large and handsome beetles will be purchased by him; he has, therefore, hundreds of eyes spread over hundreds of square miles, and thus species which in ten years might never once occur to a single collector, are inevitably obtained by him in greater or less abundance, whilst the smaller, more active, and much more common species are never brought at all.   (Wallace 1858d:6121–23)

Earlier he had commented on the subject and on a mistaken conclusion often drawn:

> I am in hopes, therefore, that this collection may give a *true* idea of the Entomology of this country [Borneo], which can never be done when the small and obscure insects are either little sought after or en-

tirely neglected. This, however, has been generally the case in collections from tropical countries. Numbers of large and brilliant insects
have been obtained, perhaps over a large extent of country, and during
several successive seasons; and the results, exhibited in our museums,
have been too often held to give a correct idea of the Entomology of
the Tropics, and have led to hasty generalizations and very erroneous
views as to the universal characteristics of the productions of hot and
cold climates. . . .

I have made these remarks because some persons who have seen that
portion of my collections which has already arrived in Europe have
been much disappointed, and have complained (almost as if I *made* the
insects as well as collected them) that Mr. Fortunes' beetles from the
North of China, though from a comparatively cold climate, were much
finer.   (Wallace 1856b:5114–15)

The best information then available on the zoology of the eastern
part of the Archipelago derived from recent endeavors of French naturalists; witness Wallace's reliance on Boisduval's treatment of the
butterflies. These naturalists had been associated with voyages of exploration during the second decade of the nineteenth century. Their
efforts had provided descriptions of the animal life of the eastern part
of the Archipelago, New Guinea, and islands to the east. Jules Sé-
bastien César Dumont D'Urville was a leader on two of these voyages. He was second in command to Duperrey on the *Coquille,* which
sailed from Toulon in August 1822 on a voyage around the world.
After rounding South America and sailing across the Pacific, the *Coquille* reached the region of interest here—the Moluccas, New Guinea,
and Java. Dumont D'Urville was responsible for botanical and entomological collections. One of the other two naturalists, the self-taught
René-Primevère Lesson, concentrated at first on fish, mollusks, and
other invertebrates but later attended to the birds and mammals as
well. After returning to France in 1825, he spent four years studying
this material and preparing the results.

The insects of the collection were described by F. E. Guérin-
Méneville (with Lesson) in Lesson 1829. One butterfly species described in this French work, for example, was mentioned above, a
species that Boisduval placed in his genus *Ornithoptera.* This species
has a pattern in the wings of the male much like that of *O. priamus*

(then called *Papilio priamus* L.), except that the rich green is replaced by a rich blue. Guérin had named this *Papilio urvillianus* and
gave the locality as "Offack." Neither Boisduval nor George Gray,
in his catalog of butterflies in the British Museum, gives any identification of this locality; they merely repeat the word. We now know
that this blue *Ornithoptera* occurs in the Solomon Islands, to the east
of New Guinea. Wallace found this vagueness and frequent inaccu-
racy of locality in the descriptions by the French naturalists vexing,
because for him the association of specimen with locality was of paramount importance. For earlier collectors of these creatures, the exact
position where the specimen occurred had no scientific significance;
since God had created this beautiful butterfly, he could have selected
any locality that pleased Him. Lesson's observations on birds of paradise, as another example, added greatly to the meager information
available to science. But Wallace, after observing two species of birds
of paradise in Aru, regretted the want of precision that he found in
Lesson's observations when he had an opportunity to read them in
detail. Hitherto he had had to rely on the succinct summaries in Bonaparte. Wallace had added a footnote to his paper on these birds:

Since writing this paper; I have, by the kindness of a German physi-
cian residing at Macassar, Dr. Bauer, obtained a perusal of the 'Zoology' of the voyage of the 'Coquille,' containing Lesson's observations
on the Paradise Birds. There is, however, a great want of preciseness
in his account, owing to his using French trivial names, and his not
stating where and how he obtained such species. He visited, I find,
only the north coast (Dorey Harbour) and the islands of Waigiou. His
details of habits refer to, and the specimens shot by himself or companions are spoken of as, "petit Emeraude," which must be the *P. papuana* Bechst. (*P. minor* Forst.). He states, however, that he procured
from the natives at Dorey *the two species of 'Emeraude,'* the other
being, no doubt, the true *P. apoda* Linn., which I believe does not
inhabit that district. They were probably obtained from the Ceramese
traders, who had brought them from the south or from Aru, just as they
offered me at Aru specimens of the *P. papuana* which they had brought
from the north peninsula of New Guinea. He mentions the apparently
large number of females, and concludes that the bird is polygamous!
but I have no doubt that what he took for females were mostly young

males. He says nothing about the vertical expansion of the plumes,
which will form, I hope, an important addition to our knowledge of
these remarkable birds. (Wallace 1857e:415)

Dumont D'Urville was not involved with studying and describing
his collections, although his name was given to innumerable species;
the year after his return he was given command of the corvette *Astrolabe,* which set out to explore the South Pacific. After charting parts
of New Zealand, Fiji, and the adjacent Pacific, he returned to the
Eastern Archipelago and visited Amboina and Celebes. One result of
this voyage was the designation of the Indo-Pacific island groups with
terms still used—Melanesia, Micronesia, Polynesia, and Malaysia.
The *Astrolabe* returned in 1829, laden with natural-history specimens
from this vast Indo-Pacific world. Boisduval studied the new Indo-
Pacific specimens of Lepidoptera, and the knowledge of the butterflies of the Archipelago he derived from this research made his later
comprehensive treatment of all butterflies, *Espèces Générales des
Lépidoptères* (1836), especially useful to Wallace. Nevertheless,
Wallace was to find that many of the locality designations of Bois-
duval were quite inaccurate, as was the case with Lesson and Guérin-
Méneville.

A quarter of a century after the *Astrolabe* visited Amboina and
Celebes, Wallace waited in Singapore for passage to these fabled
islands. By the middle of May 1856 direct passage to Celebes was
not yet available. Wallace booked passage to Bileling (Bulaleng), on
the north coast of Bali. Bali is near the middle of the great arc of
islands, nearly 2,800 miles long, that bounds the entire Archipelago
on the south. The large island of Sumatra, just west of the Malay
Peninsula, forms the northern beginning of the arc. Next is long,
narrow Java with its nearly east-west orientation Bali is separated by
only a narrow waterway from the eastern tip of Java and is the west-
ernmost of a string of much smaller islands trending eastward, aim-
ing, it could be said, straight at New Guinea but falling well short of
it. By taking this indirect route, which he had not wanted to do,
Wallace covered four-fifths of the distance from Singapore to Macassar in southern Celebes. In Bali and Lombock, its neighbor to the

east, he was delayed for two and a half months—an unscheduled visit that proved most illuminating. A decade later, when writing *Malay Archipelago,* he said of these two islands, "Had I been able to obtain a passage to that place [Macassar] from Singapore, I should probably never have gone near them, and should have missed some of the most important discoveries of my whole expedition to the East" (1869:115–16).

With his arrival in Bali Wallace began the field narrative that chronicled the remaining six years of his Eastern wanderings. The text of that field journal, rearranged to provide geographical rather than chronological continuity, and with few alterations, was published as the narrative chapters of *Malay Archipelago.* To provide a more immediate sense of his experiences and thoughts, I shall quote letters that Wallace wrote to his agent, Samuel Stevens, with the obvious intent that they be published. Stevens read the informative ones at meetings of the Entomological Society of London. They were published in its *Proceedings* and reprinted in the *Zoologist,* and probably were widely read.

Wallace spent only two days in Bali and had some success with birds and butterflies. The intensively cultivated land with its irrigated terraces delighted Wallace with its beauty and with the ingenuity and efficiency of land use that it clearly manifested. But such cultivated landscape makes for poor collecting. He left for neighboring Lombock primarily because its port, Ampanam (Ampenan), across the strait from Bali, was judged to offer a better chance of a ship to Macassar.

Collecting right around Ampanam was also relatively poor because of intense cultivation. While waiting, Wallace hired an outrigger to take him and his assistants to an uncultivated area along the southern part of Ampanam Bay. Here the land was covered by scrubby, thorny vegetation. Wallace stayed for more than a week, because birds were plentiful. To appreciate fully the richness of Wallace's experience, only a part of which is germane to our immediate objective, one should consult *Malay Archipelago,* available in a recent paperback reprint. His journal records: "Birds very interesting, Australian forms appear. These do not pass further West to Baly and Java and many

Javanese birds are found in Baly but do not reach here'' (entry 8A).
On his return to Ampanam he wrote to Stevens:

> Ampanam, Lombock, August 21, 1856.—Another month has passed
> since I wrote to you, and there is still no chance of a passage to Ma-
> cassar; having missed one opportunity by being away from the village,
> I am afraid to go out in the country any more and here there are nothing
> but dusty roads and paddy fields for miles around, producing no insects
> or birds worth collecting: it is really astonishing, and will be almost
> incredible to many persons at home that a tropical country when culti-
> vated should produce so little for the collector: the worst collecting-
> ground in England would produce ten times as many species of beetles
> as can be found here, and even our common English butterflies are finer
> and more numerous than those of Ampanam in the present dry season;
> a walk of several hours with my net will produce perhaps two or three
> species of Chrysomela and Coccinella, and a Cicindela, and two or
> three Hemiptera and flies; and every day the same species will occur.
> In an uncultivated district which I have visited, in the south part of the
> island, I did indeed find insects rather more numerous, but two months'
> assiduous collecting have only produced me eighty species of Coleop-
> tera! why there is not a spot in England where the same number could
> not be obtained in a few days in spring. Butterflies were rather better,
> for I obtained thirty-eight species, the majority, however, being Pieri-
> dae; of the others, Papilio Peranthus is the most beautiful.
>
> The birds have, however, interested me much more than the insects,
> as they are proportionately much more numerous, and throw great light
> on the laws of geographical distribution of animals in the East. The
> Islands of Baly and Lombock, for instance, though of nearly the same
> size, of the same soil, aspect, elevation and climate, and within sight
> of each other, yet differ considerably in their productions, and, in fact,
> belong to two quite distinct zoological provinces, of which they form
> the extreme limits. As an instance, I may mention the cockatoos, a
> group of birds confined to Australia and the Moluccas, but quite un-
> known in Java, Borneo, Sumatra and Malacca; one species, however
> (Plyctolophus sulphureus), is abundant in Lombock, but is unknown in
> Baly, the island of Lombock forming the extreme western limit of its
> range and that of the whole family. Many other species illustrate the
> same fact, and I am preparing a short account of them for publication.
> My collection here consists of sixty-eight species of birds, about twenty
> of which are probably not found west of the island, being species either

found in Timor and Sumbawa or hitherto undescribed. I have here, for the first time, met with many interesting birds, whose structure and habits it has been a great pleasure to study, such as the Artamidae and the genera Ptilotis, Tropidorhynchus, Plyctolophus and Megapodius. . . . (Wallace 1857a:5414–45)

This was the first notice of the discovery that there is a sharp faunal discontinuity in the Archipelago, between islands to the north and west, dominated by animal groups with affinities to those of mainland Asia, and those to the east, where a quite distinct, Australian biota is dominant. This discovery provided another objective for further exploration in the Archipelago: identifying the locus of this discontinuity among the other island groups.

A year after his return to England in 1862, Wallace presented to the Royal Geographical Society a long analysis of his findings under the title "On the Physical Geography of the Malay Archipelago"; it examined the physical aspects primarily as determinants of the distribution of animals. He displayed a map on which he had drawn a line indicating the locus of this faunal discontinuity. Its southern end passed between Bali and Lombock, northward it ran between Borneo and Celebes, following the eastern edge of the submarine shelf that connects Borneo, Sumatra, Java, and Bali with the Malay Peninsula. That line was later referred to as "Wallace's Line," a name still in current use.

The scale, or magnitude, of the distribution pattern revealed here was quite unexpected. Wallace's intent when he first undertook his exotic collecting was to study the patterns of distribution of closely related species for evidence that might elucidate the circumstances in which new species arise. These we might call fine-scale patterns. By contrast, the discontinuity between Bali and Lombock was on a much coarser scale, for the distribution of entire families was demarcated.

Wallace landed at Macassar, his "land of promise," early in September 1856. His collections, however, did not fulfill that promise. This centrally located island, where a rich fauna had been anticipated, was surprisingly poor in both number of species and number of major groups. Several subsequent periods of collecting in the Celebes only confirmed this finding. Thus, the trend of Wallace's Line was established by the small initial sampling of the Celebes fauna, although Wallace could not have been certain of that result before completing more extensive studies. A letter to Stevens detailed the findings of his three months of collecting:

Macassar, December 1st, 1856.—After this you will probably not receive another letter from me for six or seven months, so I must give you a full one now. I am busy packing up my collections here, but have been unfortunately caught by the rains before I have finished, and I fear my insects will suffer. The last four or five days have been blowing, rainy weather, like our February, barring the cold. In a bamboo house, full of pores and cracks and crannies, through which the damp air finds its way at pleasure, you may fancy it will not do to close up boxes of insects in such weather. However, as the wet season has not regularly set in, we may expect a little sun and dry air soon, and then I am ready to pack and close everything. The neighbourhood of Macassar has much disappointed me. After great trouble I discovered a place I thought rather promising, and after more trouble got the use of a native house there, and went. I staid five weeks, and worked hard, though all the time ill (owing to bad water I think), and often, for days together, unable to do more than watch about the house for stray insects. Such weakness and languor had seized me that often, on returning with some insects, I could hardly rise from my mattress, where I had thrown myself down, to set them out and put them away. However, now that I am back at my cottage near Macassar, with a few of the comforts of civilized life, I am nearly well, and will tell you what I have done.

My collections here consist of birds, shells and insects. In none of these, I am sorry to say, have I got anything very remarkable. The birds are pretty good as containing a good many rare and some new species; but I have been astonished at the want of variety compared with those of the Malayan Island and Peninsula. Whole families and genera are altogether absent, and there is nothing to supply their place. I have found no barbets, no Eurylaimi, no Trogons, no Phyllornes; but, what is still more extraordinary, the great and varied family of thrushes, the Ixodinae and the Timalias, seem almost entirely absent; the shrikes, too, have disappeared, and of flycatchers I have only seen one small species. To supply this vast void there is not a single new group, the result of which is that in about equal time and with greater exertions I have not been able to obtain more than half the number of species I got in Malacca. Indeed, were it not for the raptorial and aquatic birds I should not have one-third. You hint that in Borneo I neglected Raptores. They are too good to neglect; but there were none. Here in two months I have got fifteen species, many more than all my collections of the two preceding years contain. Of these six are represented by single specimens only; but of the rest I send you thirty fine specimens, and they will, I doubt not, contain something new. Among my rare birds I may mention the two hornbills peculiar to Celebes (*Hydrocissa exarata*, Tem., *Buceros cassidix*. Tem.); the anomalous *Scythrops Novae-Hollandiae*, Lath.; the handsome cuckoo, *Phaenicophaus callirhynchus;* the *Pica albicollis,* Vieill.; and the remarkable *Pastor corythaix* Wag., which unites the characters of the starlings with the form and compressed crest of the Calyptomena and Rupicola. . . .

Now for the insects, which are the most interesting to so many of my friends. They will, I fear, disappoint you, as they have, with a few exceptions, disappointed me. But you must remember the circumstances. Almost all the good insects have been collected during a five weeks' stay at a tolerable place in the interior, during which time, however, I was so unwell as not to make more than five visits to the forest, to be near which was the especial purpose for which I went there. It was also the very end of the dry season, which I have always found the worst time for insects. To proceed in order, the Coleoptera shall be first considered. The number of species yet obtained is only 254, some groups being rich, others very poor. . . . I am rich in Cicindela [tiger bettles], having six species, but of Colliuris and Therates only one each. *Cicindela Heros,* Fab. (which I believe is rare) is my largest species. In Boisduval's 'Faune de l'Oceanie' it is said to come from the isles of the Pacific. *Therates flavilabris,* Fab., is also said to inhabit New Ireland, but it is found here, with the var. *T. fasciata*. The habitats given to insects in that work, indeed, from the French voyages, appear so liable to error that little dependence can be placed upon them. They seem to have been trusted altogether to memory, or perhaps ticketed on the voyage home. For example, to *Scarabaeus Atlas* is this remark, "It is noted as from Vanikoro I., but M. D'Urville is certain that it was taken at Menado in Celebes;" again, to *Tmesisternus septempunctatus*, "If there is no mistake on the ticket, this species is from Amboina;" *Lamia 8-maculata,* "It is ticketed as coming from Vanikoro, but I believe it is rather from N. Guinea or Celebes;" and *L. Hercules*, "It is found in Amboina," while on the plate it is said to be from Celebes. Other examples of a similar kind are to be found; and they lead me to

suppose that voyagers and amateur collectors seldom ticket their specimens *at the time of collection,* but trust to memory in a matter in
which no memory can be trusted. Even after making a collection at two
localities only, and of only a hundred species each, I would defy any
one to ticket the whole correctly: how, then, must it be when dozens
of places are visited in succession, and the species taken at each vary
from perhaps a dozen to a thousand. But we must return to our collections.

The Lepidoptera come last, and, though few in species, present a fair
amount of novelty. On my very first visit to the forest I took three fine
specimens of the magnificent Ornithoptera Remus, or a variety of it,
for the female does not agree with Boisduval's very imperfect description of it. This made me think it common, but I have since never taken
another, except an imperfect female. The common Ornithoptera here is
a variety of Amphrisius, with the upper wings entirely black in both
sexes. . . . I have about 35 species out of 115 butterflies, and of half
of these I have got the two sexes. With health, a better season and a
better locality, I have no doubt a very fine collection of insects might
be made in this part of Celebes, and these I hope to have next dry
season, which I have arranged, if all goes well, to spend at Bontyne,
situated at the South end of the Peninsula, and close to one of the
highest mountains in Celebes.

I must now tell you where I am off to in the mean time. I am going
another thousand miles eastward to the Arru Islands, which are within
a hundred miles of the coast of New Guinea, and are the most eastern
islands of the Archipelago. Many reasons have induced me to go so far
now. I must go somewhere to escape the terrific rainy season here. I
have all along looked to visiting Arru, as one of the great objects of
my journey to the East; and almost all the trade with Arru is from
Macassar. I have an opportunity of going in a *proa,* owned and com-
manded by a Dutchman (Java born), who will take me and bring me
back, and assist me in getting a house, &c., there; and he goes at the
very time I want to leave. I have also friends here with whom I can
leave all the things I do not want to take with me. All these advanta-
geous circumstances would probably never be combined again; and were
I to refuse this opportunity I might never go to Arru at all, which, when
you consider it is the nearest place to New Guinea where I can stay on
shore and work in perfect safety, would be much to be regretted. What
I shall get there it is impossible to say. Being a group of small islands,
the immense diversity and richness of the productions of New Guinea

will of course be wanting; yet I think I may expect some approach to the strange and beautiful natural productions of that unexplored country. Very few naturalists have visited Arru. One or two of the French discovery-ships have touched at it. M. Payen, of Brussels, was there, but stayed probably only a few days; and I suppose not twenty specimens of its birds and insects are positively known. Here, then, I shall have tolerably new ground, and if I have health I shall work it well. I take three lads with me, two of whom can shoot and skin birds.

A. R. Wallace
(Wallace 1857c:5652–57)

Wallace's statement that Aru "is the nearest place to New Guinea where I can stay on shore and work in perfect safety" was quite literally correct. Any foreigner setting foot on the shores of New Guinea at that time was likely to be met with the same murderous assault that the landing parties of the first European discoverers encountered. When the indigenous Papuans were dissatisfied with the barter offered they frequently murdered the traders. Wallace later recorded: "While I was at Goram [Gorang, east of Seran; he was there in May 1860], the crews of two prahuws, including the Rajah's son, were attacked in this part of New Guinea [the south coast of the northern peninsula], in open day, while bargaining for some trepang, and all murdered except three or four, who escaped in a small boat and brought the news. The shrieks and lamentations in the village when the news was brought was most distressing, almost every house having lost a relative or a slave" (Wallace 1862:131). The products from New Guinea most sought by the traders came from the inshore waters—trepang (bêche-de-mer), mother-of-pearl shell, and tortoise shell. As Aru was a particularly rich source of these marine products, and as the natives were not hostile and food was plentiful, it is not surprising that traders from the western islands had long flocked to its shores. This trade apparently long antedated the Europeans' knowledge of it. The bulk of the commodities were consumed in the dense settlements of the western parts of the Archipelago. The only New Guinea product to reach Europe in any quantity was mother-of-pearl shell. Only the traders seeking wild nutmegs and Mussoi bark (its pungent oil was used as a liniment in Java), products of the interior, took the high risk of landing in New Guinea itself.

The seasonal winds, monsoons, determined both the place and the time of the Macassar-Aru trade. During the northern winter the winds in the Banda Sea blow from west to east, from Macassar to Aru. During midsummer they blow in the opposite direction. The sailing vessels (varyingly referred to by Wallace as "proa," "prau," or "prahuw") traditionally used in this trade had limited maneuverability.

> The trade is mainly carried on in native prahuws, a few small schooners only being now engaged in it from Ternate, Menado, Amboyna, and Macassar. They, however, form quite an unimportant feature in the trade of New Guinea, which is essentially native.
>
> A Malay prahuw is a vessel so unique as to deserve a brief description. It is a short vessel with bow and stern nearly alike. The deck (when it has one) slopes down towards the bows. The mast is a triangle, and consequently wants no shrouds, and, being low, carries an immense yard much longer than the vessel itself, which is hung out of the centre, and the short end hauled down on deck, so that the immense mainsail slopes upwards to a considerable height. A full-rigged prahuw carries a smaller similar sail abaft, and a bowsprit and jib. It has two rudders, one on each quarter, with a window or opening on each side for the tillers considerably below the deck. These vessels can only sail 8 points from the wind (so that it is impossible to make any way by tacking when the wind is ahead), and make their voyages only with the favourable monsoon—accomplishing, therefore, generally but one voyage a year. They are of all sizes, from 1 to 100 tons' burden, and are built—some with regularly nailed planks, some fastened only with rattans—but so ingeniously and securely as very well to stand a sea-voyage. When I first went from Macassar to New Guinea, a distance of 1000 miles, a small prahuw of about 10 tons which had not a single nail in its whole structure kept company with us all the way. The largest prahuws are from Macassar and the Bugis countries of Celebes and the island of Boutong. Smaller ones in great numbers sail from Ternate, Tidore, East Ceram, and Goram. . . .   (Wallace 1862:126)

A letter to Stevens provides the only contemporary account of Wallace's Aru adventure:

> Dobbo, Arru Islands, March 10, 1857.—Here I am, alive, well, and hard at work. I have been here just two months, and as I am going into

the interior I leave this note to be sent by a vessel which returns to
Macassar in April. The country is all forest, flat and lofty, very like
the Amazonian forest. Insects, on the whole, are tolerably plentiful in
specimens, but very scarce in species. There are, however, some fine
things, and I am getting good series of several, including Ornithoptera
sp., near Priamus, perhaps O. Poseidon, or close to it, a glorious thing
but hard to get perfect; four or five other rare or new Papilios, but all
scarce; Cocytia d'Urvillei rather scarce, a lovely creature; also Hestia
d'Urvillei. For six weeks I have almost daily seen Papilio Ulysses? or
a new closely-allied species, but never a chance of him; he flies high
and strong, only swooping down now and then, and off again to the
treetops; fancy my agony and disgust; I fear I shall never get him.
There is a fine Drusilla or Hyades abundant, with numerous varieties;
but the Lycaenidae and Erycinidae are the gems; I only wish there were
more of them; there are about half-a-dozen species equal to the very
finest of the little Amazonians. The Coleoptera are far too few in species to please me: in two months' hard work I can only muster fifty
Longicornes, a number I reached in ten days in Singapore; but Lamel-
licornes are the most extraordinarily scarce; I have only nine species,
and four of them single specimens; there are, however, two fine Lo-
maptera among them, I hope new. All other groups are the same; Geo-
dephaga, scarcely more than a dozen species, and nothing remarkable;
not one Cicindela; only one Tricondyla (T. aptera) and one Theretes
(T. labiata), with not a single Colliuris; two or three fine Buprestis,
however, and some remarkable Curculionidae, with the beautiful Tmesisternus mirabilis, make a pretty good show.

On my way here we stayed six days at Ké Island, and I got there
some very fine beetles, two fine Cetonias, and a Buprestis the most
beautiful I have seen. Of the few insects I got there the greater part
were different from any I have seen here, though the distance is only
sixty miles, the mountains of Ké being visible from Arru in fine weather.
This makes me think I shall get different things at every island in this
part of the Archipelago. Arru is zoologically a part of New Guinea. Of
the birds here half are New Guinea species; in the small island where
we live many of the birds of Arru never come, such as the two species
of the birds of Paradise, the black cassowary, &c. I am going now to
the mainland, or great Island of Arru, in search of these birds, but have
had the usual difficulty about men and boats.

I have learnt here all about New Guinea; parts are dangerous, parts
not; and next year, if I live and have health, I am determined to go. I
must go either to Banda or Ternate first, I have not yet decided which,

and shall try to go to the large island of Wargion [Waigiou], at the north-east of New Guinea, where are found the Epimachus magnificus, three rare species of the Paradise birds, and the glorious Ornithoptera d'Urvilliana. The weather here is very changeable; storm, wind and sunshine alternately. I think nine-tenths of the things I am getting will be new to the English collections; with which comfort for our entomological friends,

I remain yours sincerely,

Alfred R. Wallace

Postscript—Dobbo, May 15.—I have returned from my visit to the interior, and the brig is not gone yet; so I add a postscript. Rejoice with me, for I have found what I sought; one grand hope in my visit to Arru is realized: I have got the birds of Paradise (that announcement deserves a line of itself); one is the common species of commerce, the Paradisea apoda; all the native specimens I have seen are miserable, and cannot possibly be properly mounted; mine are magnificent. I have discovered their true attitude when displaying their plumes, which I believe is quite new information; they are then so beautiful and grand that, when mounted to represent it, they will make glorious specimens for show-cases, and I am sure will be in demand by stuffers. I shall describe them in a paper for the "Annals". The other species is the king bird (*Paradisea regia,* Linn.), the smallest of the paradisians, but a perfect gem for beauty; of this I doubt if any really fine specimens are known, for I think Lesson only got them from the natives; I have a few specimens absolutely perfect. I have, besides, a number of rare and curious birds,—the great black cockatoo, racquet-tailed kingfisher, magnificent pigeons, &c.,—and a fair addition to my insects and shells. On the whole I am so much pleased with Arru that my plans are somewhat altered: on returning to Macassar I shall probably not stay more than two or three months, but get as soon as I can to Ternate, and then to the north coast of New Guinea, where all the remaining species of Paradise birds are found? I believe I am the only Englishman who has ever shot and skinned (and ate) birds of Paradise, and the first Englishman who has done so alive, and at his own risk and expense; and I deserve to reap the reward, if any reward is ever to be reaped by the exploring collector. I think there is good work for three years in N.E. Celebes, Gilolo, Ceram, north coast of New Guinea, and intermediate islands, of all of which Ternate is near the centre, and it is certainly one of the least-explored districts in the world, and one which contains some of the finest birds and insects in the world. On the whole I have had much better health here than at Macassar, but I am now, and have been a whole month, confined to the house, owing to inflammation and sores on the legs, produced by hosts of insect bites. Confinement has brought on an attack of fever, which I am now getting over. My insect collecting has suffered dreadfully by this loss of time.—A. W. (Wallace 1857d:91–93)

With a strong, steady summer monsoon Wallace's prau covered the 1,000-mile return to Macassar in nine and a half days. On his safe return he had completed his most successful collecting expedition. He brought back over 9,000 specimens of 1,600 species, "distinct species," as he noted in *Malay Archipelago*, adding, "It is still the portion of my travels to which I look back with the most complete satisfaction."

Before analyzing the significance of Wallace's six months of observations in Aru, we should briefly review his experiences in the preceding six months as well. It had been a year of surprises, of discovering unexpected patterns of geographical distribution, beginning in Lombock. There Wallace had first become aware of the astonishing differences between the bird faunas of Bali and Lombock, small islands within sight of each other. Here Asian and Australian bird faunas are separated by a strait only ten miles wide. Yet they have maintained their distinctness, even though Wallace concluded that the islands are "of nearly the same size, of the same soil, aspect, elevation, and climate. . . ." His next collecting site, Celebes, held a different surprise. He had expected that the inhabitants of this large island in the very center of the Archipelago would to some degree represent "the richness and variety of the whole Archipelago." Instead he found that Celebes was poor in both number of species and number of families. Furthermore, the affinities of many Celebes species were not with those of neighboring islands; their isolated nature was puzzling. Like Lombock, Celebes lacked a strong Asian element; but it lacked a strong Australian one as well. Then Aru; Wallace's guess, and hope, had initially been that this small group of islands, 100 miles off the coast of New Guinea, might have a somewhat impoverished representation of the "strange and beautiful productions" of that great, unexplorable island. Actuality exceeded his fondest hope and differed from his expectation. The central island of the Aru group had a rich fauna, and the specimens that he could identify were all known New Guinean species; an unmistakably distinct variety of a New Guinea butterfly was the only exception.

CHAPTER EIGHT
Aru: Glimpses of Paradise

During the Aru expedition Wallace made a series of observations that formed the basis for the eventual completion of his theory of organic evolution, including that of man:

1. Shortly after settling in at Dobbo, Aru (in Kepulauan Aru), he achieved the long-anticipated capture of a green-marked *Ornithoptera*. While quite similar to the typical *Ornithoptera priamus* from the Moluccas, it was even more similar to the New Guinean *O. poseidon*. Yet it was distinct from each.

2. This butterfly was the only animal on Aru that appeared to Wallace to be closely allied to, but distinct from, any species previously described. All other birds and insects collected were either undescribed or assignable to species described from New Guinea and adjacent islands.

3. In the exclusiveness of its faunal affinity with New Guinea, Aru stands in contrast to the Ké (Kai) Islands, sixty miles to the west. Ké is just as close to New Guinea proper as Aru is. On Ké Wallace found Moluccan as well as New Guinean species.

4. The birds and mammals of the deep forest of the large, central island of Aru were all species known from the forests of New Guinea; noteworthy are two species of birds of paradise; the great black cockatoo; a species of cassowary, which is a genus of large, flightless birds characteristically Australian; and a kangaroo, along with several species of smaller marsupials.

5. Wallace found that the narrow channels traversing the large central island of Aru closely resemble river valleys. They are of uniform width and depth, winding "through an irregular, undulating, rocky country." But they are now filled with salt water, indeed "are open at each end to the entrance of the tide" (Wallace 1857f:479).

6. On arrival in the Ké Islands Wallace was immediately struck by the distinctness of the Papuans from the Malays in physical features and behavioral traits alike.

7. The health of the Papuans living in the villages of Aru varied with the nature of their diet. In villages where the diet was irregular and nutritionally poor, Wallace found that skin diseases were common, as well as "ulcers on legs and joints." But in those villages where diligent effort ensured a stable food supply, health was superior, as Wallace had found to be true elsewhere as well.

8. Wallace learned that the dry season in Aru, while relatively short, lasting only a month or two, brings severe drought because surface water quickly percolates into the porous coralline bedrock.

The Aru Bird-wing, a Representative of the *Ornithoptera priamus* Group

Wallace had eagerly studied the specimens of *Ornithoptera* in the British Museum before venturing on his Eastern sojourn. He had observed and collected species of the yellow-marked *Ornithoptera* near Malacca, and again in Celebes. But he had never seen one of the spectacular green-marked forms alive until he saw it flying among the tree-tops in the Ké Islands. Capture of these high flyers was not possible during his short stay there.

An early delight that Aru offered was the capture of some of these giants, which were so powerful on the wing that they did, indeed, resemble birds. On the day following his arrival in Dobbo, Aru, Wallace went into the forest and was pleased with his collection of butterflies, among them the large, more dull-colored female of an *Ornithoptera*. This capture is not recorded in *Malay Archipelago,* but in the Species Registry he remarked, "O. priamus ♀—fine." The next two days have no entries—explained by the comment, "2 last days strong winds and almost continual rain." The next day weather was fine; the registry remarked, "fine, a ♂ & ♀ *Ornithoptera* near *Poseidon . . .* ♀ 8½″ ♂ 6 ½″."

It was clear to Wallace that the Aru population was very like *Ornithoptera poseidon* from New Guinea, but was it a variety of *O. poseidon* or a closely related species? Later, back in Macassar, he prepared a paper describing the details of its life history, and his title and opening line indicate that he considered the Aru form very similar both to *O. priamus* and to *O. poseidon.* The title reads: "On the habits and transformations of a species of *Ornithoptera,* allied to *O. priamus,* inhabiting the Aru Islands, near New Guinea." The first line of text reads: "This beautiful insect is very closely allied to *O. poseidon* Doub., of which it may be a variety." Wallace seemed unable to decide whether that population should be considered a species or a variety; in either case, was it closer to *O. priamus* or to *O. poseidon?* This paper was read by the Secretary to the Entomological Society of London at its meeting on December 7, 1857.

The January 1858 issue of the *Zoologist* just a month later carried a short paper by Wallace, entitled "Note on the Theory of Permanent and Geographical Varieties." This paper asks, What is the nature of the difference between a permanent variety and a species? Is this difference one of quality, or is it quantitative? His brief analysis is presented below in its entirety:

Note on the Theory of Permanent and Geographical Varieties
by Alfred R. Wallace, Esq.

As this subject is now attracting much attention among naturalists, and particularly among entomologists, I venture to offer the following observations, which, without advocating either side of the question, are intended to point out a difficulty, or rather a dilemma, its advocates do not appear to have perceived.

The adoption of permanent and geographical varieties has this disadvantage, that it leaves the question "What is a *species?*" more indeterminate than ever; for if permanent characters do not constitute one when those characters are minute, then a species differs from a variety in degree only, not in nature, and no two persons will agree as to the amount of difference necessary to constitute the one, or the amount of resemblance which must exist to form the other. The line that separates them will become so fine that it will be exceedingly difficult to prove its existence. If, however, the two things are of essentially distinct natures, we must seek a qualitative not a quantitative character to define them. This may be done by considering the permanence, not the amount, of the variation from its nearest allies, to constitute the specific character, and in like manner the instability, not the smaller quantity, of variation to mark the variety. In this way you define the two things by a difference in their nature; by the other, you assert that they are of exactly the same nature, and differ only in degree.

Now the generally adopted opinion is that species are absolute independent creations, which during their whole existence never vary from one to another, while varieties are not independent creations, but are or have been produced by ordinary generation from a parent species. There does, therefore (if this definition is true), exist such an absolute and essential difference in the nature of these two things that we are warranted in looking for some other character to distinguish them than one of mere degree, which is necessarily undefinable. If there is no other character, that fact is one of the strongest arguments against the independent creation of species, for why should a special act of creation be required to call into existence an organism differing only in degree from another which has been produced by existing laws? If an amount of permanent difference, represented by any number up to 10, may be produced by the ordinary course of nature, it is surely most illogical to suppose, and very hard to believe, that an amount of difference represented by 11 required a special act of creation to call it into existence.

Let A and B be two species having the smallest amount of difference a species can have. These you say are certainly distinct; where a smaller amount of difference exists we will call it a variety. You afterwards discover a group of individuals C, which differ from A less than B does, but in an opposite direction; the amount of difference between A and C is only half that between A and B: you therefore say C is a variety of A. Again you discover another group D, exactly intermediate between A and B. If you keep to your rule you are now forced to make B a variety, or if you are positive B is a species, then C and D must also become species, as well as all other permanent varieties which differ as much as these do: yet you say some of these groups are special creations, others not. Strange that such widely different origins should produce such identical results. To escape this difficulty there is but one way: you must consider every group of individuals presenting permanent characters, however slight, to constitute a species; while those only which are subject to such variation as to make us believe they have descended from a parent species, or that we know have so descended, are to be classed as varieties. The two doctrines, of "permanent varieties" and of "specially created unvarying species," are inconsistent with each other.

Alfred R. Wallace.
(Wallace 1858a:5887–88)

I believe that it was the attempt to assess the status and affinities of the Aru population of *Ornithoptera* that brought into sharp focus a dilemma that had long existed. I believe that the apparently hypothetical example analyzed in the last paragraph is basically the problem presented by the Aru bird-wing. For "A" read *O. priamus;* for "B" read *O. poseidon.* Clearly the difference between these two species is sufficiently slight that it can be called the "smallest." (In his description of *O. brookiana,* Wallace had expressed the opinion that most of the green-marked species of *Ornithoptera* [such as *O. poseidon*] might be considered varieties "of the original Papilio priamus of Linnaeus.") Later in the paragraph: "Again you discover another group D, exactly intermediate between A and B." That the Aru *Ornithoptera* fits the requirements of "D" can be seen in the photographs of the males of *O. priamus,* the Aru *Ornithoptera,* and *O. poseidon* (see fig. 5.1). It is almost exactly intermediate between "A" and "B."

Unquestionably, one important consequence of the discovery of the Aru bird-wing is that it challenged Wallace's understanding of the exact nature of the relationship of variety to species. His conclusion: it is a question of degree of difference. The formation of a variety is the first step in the formation of a new species.

Recent Separation of Aru from New Guinea

The observations numbered 1, 2, and 3 in the list heading this chapter indicated to Wallace that Aru (see map 1) bore a special relationship to New Guinea. Although the Aru Islands and the Ké Islands, within sight of each other on a clear day, are equidistant from the mainland of New Guinea, Aru's fauna, as far as he could determine, is entirely New Guinean, while Ké has an admixture of Moluccan bird and insect species. Further, the Aru fauna is much more representative of the New Guinean than would be expected if it had been stocked, as oceanic islands usually are, solely by occasional invaders. Their more complete representation of the New Guinean fauna suggests the possibility that the Aru Islands had once been directly connected to the larger island. This possibility became a probability—rather, a near certainty—when Wallace found that the forest

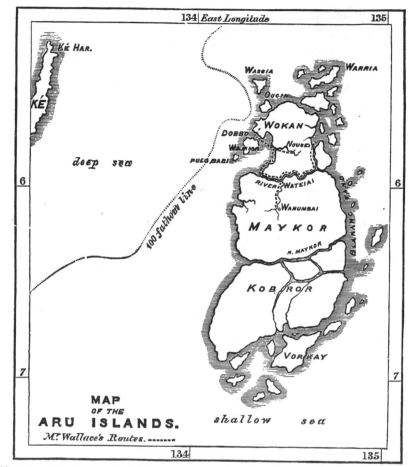

Map 1   Aru Islands with Wallace's routes. From Wallace 1869. (NOTE: The names
and configurations of the islands in the map used by Wallace differ from
those of current maps, such as those used in map 2. See text.)

of the larger central island of Aru was inhabited by many of the
larger birds and marsupial mammals known previously from the deep
forest of New Guinea proper. Denizens of deep forest are almost
never "island hoppers." The final discovery that the channels (see
map 2) traversing the main islands of Aru were river valleys led to
two conclusions about recent changes of the physiography. As sea
water now coursed along their length, one obvious conclusion was

that Aru itself had recently subsided. The other was that these valleys had once been part of the lower reaches of rivers that must have had their sources to the east and south. Not far from the west coast of Aru the sea floor drops to great depths. The source of the rivers, therefore, had to be in the direction of New Guinea. The sea floor between Aru and New Guinea is relatively shallow, less than 100 fathoms, and must have subsided even more than Aru itself.

Wallace had long sought a situation in which he could find evidence of linkage between the formation of new elements in the organic world and recent physiographic change. He had at last found it. One would expect little change following a recent physiographic alteration. According to Lyell extinctions would occur one by one. Possibly some had occurred; it was impossible to know which of the species that had lived on this terrain when it was a part of a larger New Guinea had subsequently become extinct.

But the one novel element of the fauna was predictable under Wallace's hypotheses: the new form (was it a species or a variety?) was derived from a preexisting closely allied species. The Aru bird-wing was very like the New Guinean species. Lyell, on the other hand, had said that new species were created to fit the new situation, entirely without relation to species that had existed under prior conditions.

Aru thus presented Wallace with a situation that could be used to test publicly his previously published hypothesis as opposed to Lyell's in explaining a set of observable facts. He made this comparison in an essay, "On the Natural History of the Aru Islands" (1857f), which briefly described his trip and summarized the island's fauna, with emphasis on the birds and mammals. Then:

> The Birds and Mammalia only have been used for illustration, because they are much better known than any other groups. The Insects, however, of which I have made a very extensive collection, furnish exactly similar results, and were these, particularly the Coleoptera, well known, they would perhaps be preferable to any group for such an inquiry, from the great number of their genera and species, and the very limited range which many of them attain.   (p. 483)

From this list, and the preceding observations, it will be seen that many Australian genera and some species occur in Aru; while, consid-

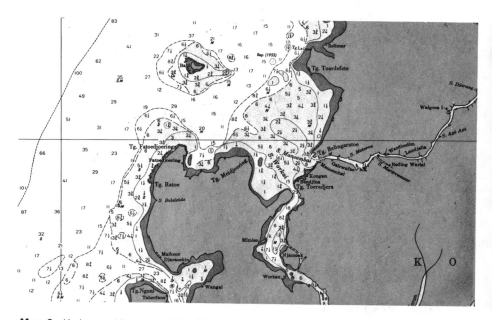

Map 2 Hydrographic chart of the River Manoembai (Wateiai) and adjacent coasts, Aru Islands.

Confirmation of Wallace's deduction that the seawater-filled channels traversing the Aru Islands are drowned rivers is provided by recent hydrographic studies. The more extensive drowning of the eastern end of the river indicates greater subsidence there, but a submarine channel extending toward New Guinea traces the probable extension of the river. Off-

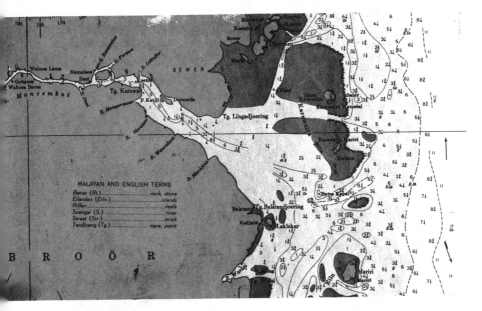

shore at the western end of the "river" another submarine channel extends westward; here also the channel is about 6 fathoms (11 meters) below sea level. The notch in the 7-fathom contour line was presumably eroded by sediment-laden river water prior to subsidence. From Defense Mapping Agency Chart 73130, Kepulauan Aru. Soundings in fathoms. Approximate scale 1:260,000.

ering the very small number of species known from New Guinea, and
the necessarily very imperfect exploration of Aru in such a short time,
the number of identical species is very remarkable. I believe that nearly
one-half of the hitherto described species of passerine birds from New
Guinea will be found in my Aru collections, a proportion of which we
could only expect if all the species of the latter country inhabit also the
former. Such an identity occurs, I believe, in no other countries separated by so wide an interval of sea, for the average distance of the coast
of Aru from that of New Guinea is at least 150 miles, and the points
of nearest approach upwards of 100. Ceylon is nearer to India; Van
Diemen's Land is not farther from Australia, nor Sardinia from Italy;
yet all these countries present differences more or less marked in their
faunas; they possess each their peculiar species, and sometimes even
peculiar genera. Almost the only islands possessing a rich fauna, but
identical with that of the adjacent continent, are Great Britain and Sic-
ily, and that circumstance is held to prove that they have been once a
portion of such continents, and geological evidence shows that the separation had taken place at no distant period. We must, therefore, suppose Aru to have once formed a part of New Guinea, in order to account for its peculiar fauna, and this view is supported by the physical
geography of the islands, for, while the fathomless Molucca sea extends to within a few miles of them on the west, the whole space eastward to New Guinea, and southward to Australia, is occupied by a
bank of soundings at the uniform depth of about 30 or 40 fathoms. But
there is another circumstance still more strongly proving this connexion: the great island of Aru, 80 miles in length from north to south, is
traversed by three winding channels of such uniform width and depth,
though passing through an irregular, undulating, rocky country, that
they seem portions of true rivers, though now occupied by salt water,
and open at each end to the entrance of the tides. This Phaenomenon
is unique, and we can account for their formation in no other way than
by supposing them to have been once true rivers, having their source
in the mountains of New Guinea, and reduced to their present condition
by the subsidence of the intervening land.

This view of the origin of the Aru fauna is further confirmed by
considering what it is not, as well as what it is; its deficiencies teach
as much as what it possesses. There are certain families of birds highly
characteristic of the Indian Archipelago in its western and better-known
portion. In the Peninsula of Malacca, Sumatra, Java, Borneo and the
Philippine Islands, the following families are abundant in species and

in individuals. They are everywhere *common birds*. They are the *Buc-eridae, Picidae, Bucconidae, Trogonidae, Meropidae,* and *Eurylaimi-dae;* but not one species of all these families is found in Aru, nor, with two doubtful exceptions, in New Guinea. The whole are also absent from Australia. To complete our view of the subject, it is necessary also to consider the Mammalia, which present peculiarities and defi-ciencies even yet more striking. Not one species found in the great islands westward inhabits Aru or New Guinea. With the exception only of pigs and bats, not a genus, not a family, not even an order of mam-mals is found in common. No Quadrumana, no Sciuridae, no Carni-vora, Rodentia, or Ungulata inhabit these depopulated forests. With the two exceptions above mentioned, all the mammalia are *Marsupials;* in the great western islands there is not a single marsupial! A kangaroo inhabits Aru (and several New Guinea), and this, with three or four species of *Cuscus,* two or three little rat-like marsupials, a wild pig and several bats, are all the mammalia I have been able either to obtain or hear of.

It is to the full development of such interesting details that the col-lector and the systematist contribute so largely. In this point of view the discovery of every new species is important, and their correct de-scription and accurate identification absolutely necessary. The most ob-scure and minute species are for this purpose of equal value with the largest and most brilliant, and a correct knowledge of the distribution and variations of a beetle or a butterfly as important as those of the eagle or the elephant. [A cryptic allusion to the significance of the Aru bird-wing?] It is to the elucidation of these apparent anomalies that the efforts of the philosophic naturalist are directed; and we think, that if this highest branch of our science were more frequently alluded to by writers on natural history, its connexion with geography and geology discussed, and the various interesting problems thence arising ex-plained, the too prevalent idea—that Natural History is at best but an amusement, a trivial and aimless pursuit, a useless accumulating of barren facts,—would give place to more correct views of a study, which presents problems as vast, as intricate, and as interesting as any to which the human mind can be directed, whose objects are as infinite as the stars of heaven and infinitely diversified, and whose field of re-search extends over the whole earth, not only as it now exists, but also during the countless changes it has undergone from the earliest geolog-ical epochs.

Let us now examine if the theories of modern naturalists will explain the phaenomena of the Aru and New Guinea fauna. We know (with a degree of knowledge approaching to certainty) that at a comparatively recent geological period, not one single species of the present organic world was in existence; while all the *Vertebrata* now existing have had their origin still more recently. How do we account for the places where they came into existence? Why are not the same species found in the same climates all over the world? The general explanation given is, that as the ancient species became extinct, new ones were created in each country or district, adapted to the physical conditions of the district. Sir C. Lyell, who has written more fully, and with more ability, on this subject than most naturalists, adopts this view. He illustrates it by speculating on the vast physical changes that might be effected in North Africa by the upheaval of a chain of mountains in the Sahara. "Then," he says, "the animals and plants of Northern Africa would disappear, and the region would gradually become fitted for the reception of a population of species *perfectly dissimilar in their forms, habits, and organization.*" Now this theory implies, that we shall find a general similarity in the productions of countries which resemble each other in climate and general aspect, while there shall be a complete dissimilarity between those which are totally opposed in these respects. And if this is the general law which has determined the distribution of the existing organic world, there must be no exceptions, no striking contradictions. Now we have seen how totally the productions of New Guinea differ from those of the Western Islands of the Archipelago, say Borneo, as the type of the rest, and as almost exactly equal in area to New Guinea. This difference, it must be well remarked, is not one of species, but of genera, families, and whole orders. Yet it would be difficult to point out two countries more exactly resembling each other in climate and physical features. In neither is there any marked dry season, rain falling more or less all the year round; both are near the equator, both subject to the east and west monsoons, but everywhere covered with lofty forest; both have a great extent of flat, swampy coast and a mountainous interior; both are rich in Palms and Pandanaceae. If, on the other hand, we compare Australia with New Guinea, we can scarcely find a stronger contrast than in their physical conditions: the one near the equator, the other near and beyond the tropics; the one enjoying perpetual moisture, the other with alternations of excessive drought; the one a vast ever-verdant forest, the other dry open woods, downs, or deserts. Yet the faunas of the two, though mostly distinct in species, are strikingly similar in character. Every family of birds (except *Menuridae*) found in Australia also inhabits New Guinea, and, when that country is better known, it is to be supposed that the number will be increased. In the Mammalia it is the same. Marsupials are almost the only quadrupeds in the one as in the other. If kangaroos are especially adapted to the dry plains and open woods of Australia, there must be some other reason for their introduction into the dense damp forests of New Guinea, and we can hardly imagine that the great variety of monkeys, of squirrels, of Insectivora, and of Felidae, were created in Borneo because the country was adapted to them, and not one single species given to another country exactly similar, and at no great distance. If there is any reason in the hardness of the woods or the scarcity of wood-boring insects, why woodpeckers should be absent from Australia, there is none why they should not swarm in the forests of New Guinea as well as in those of Borneo and Malacca. We can hardly help concluding, therefore, that some other law has regulated the distribution of existing species than the physical conditions of the countries in which they are found, or we should not see countries the most opposite in character with similar productions, while others almost exactly alike as respects climate and general aspect, yet differ totally in their forms of organic life.

In a former Number of this periodical we endeavoured to show that the simple law, of every new creation being closely allied to some species already existing in the same country, would explain all these anomalies, if taken in conjunction with the changes of surface and the gradual extinction and introduction of species, which are facts proved by geology. At the period when New Guinea and North Australia were united, it is probable that their physical features and climate were more similar, and that a considerable proportion of the species inhabiting each portion of the country were found over the whole. After the separation took place, we can easily understand how the climate of both might be considerably modified, and this might perhaps lead to the extinction of certain species. During the period that has since elapsed, new species have been gradually introduced into each, but in each closely allied to the pre-existing species, many of which were at first common to the two countries. This process would evidently produce the present condition of the two faunas, in which there are many allied species,— few identical. The great well-marked groups absent from the one would necessarily be so from the other also, for however much they might be *adapted* to the country, the law of close affinity would not allow of their appearance, except by a long succession of steps occupying an immense geological interval. The species which at the time of separation were found only in one country, would, by the gradual introduction of species allied to them, give rise to groups peculiar to that country. This separation of New Guinea from Australia no doubt took place while Aru yet formed part of the former island. Its separation must have occurred at a very recent period, the number of species common to the two showing that scarcely any extinctions have since taken place, and probably as few introductions of new species.

If we now suppose the Aru Islands to remain undisturbed during a period equal to about one division of the Tertiary epoch of geologists, we have reason to believe that the change of species of Vertebrata will become complete, an entirely new race having gradually been introduced, but all more or less closely allied to those now existing. During the same period a few fauna will also have arisen in New Guinea, and then the two will present the same comparative features that North Australia and New Guinea do now. Let the process of gradual change still go on for another period regulated by the same laws. Some species will then have become extinct in the one country, and replaced, while in the other a numerous series of modified species may have been introduced. Then the faunas will come to differ not in species only, but in generic groups. There would be then the resemblance between them that there is between the West India Islands and Mexico. During another geological period, let us suppose Aru to be elevated, and become a mountainous country, and extended by alluvial plains, while New Guinea was depressed, reduced in area, and thus many of its species perhaps extinguished. New species might then be more rapidly introduced into the modified and enlarged country; some groups, which had been early extinct in the other, might thus become very rich in species, and then we should have an exact counterpart of what we see now in Madagascar, where the families and some of the genera are African, but where there are many extensive groups of species forming peculiar genera, or even families, but still with a general resemblance to African forms. In this manner, it is believed, we may account for the facts of the present distribution of animals, without supposing any changes but what we know have been constantly going on. It is quite unnecessary to suppose that new species have ever been created "perfectly dissimilar in forms, habits, and organization" from those which have preceded them; neither do "centres of creation," which have been advocated by some, appear either necessary or accordant with facts, unless we suppose a "centre" in every island and in every district which possesses a peculiar species.

It is evident that, for the complete elucidation of the present state of the fauna of each island and each country, we require a knowledge of its geological history, its elevations and subsidences, and all the changes it has undergone since it last rose above the ocean. This can very seldom be obtained; but a knowledge of the fauna and its relation to that of the neighbouring countries will often throw great light upon the geology, and enable us to trace out with tolerable certainty its past history. (Wallace 1857f:478–83)

To my knowledge no contemporary comment on this paper has been recorded.

Distinctness of Papuans and Malays

When the prau stopped briefly in the Ké Islands, sixty miles short of Aru, Wallace's first impressions were of the people.

When the native boats arrived in the Ké Islands on December 31, 1856, I had my first view of the Papuan race in their own country. They had not been five minutes on board before I was convinced that my former ideas, derived only from the stray specimens of slaves from Timor and New Guinea, were correct. There can be no confounding them with Malays, of any variety or in any degree of degradation. Had I been blind I could have been certain they were not Malays. The loud rapid eager tones, the incessant motion, the intense vital activity manifested in their speech and actions, are totally the reverse of the quiet unimpulsive unanimated Malays. During nearly three years I have now spent in Malay countries I have had sufficient opportunities of becoming acquainted with their most striking characteristics and none is more strongly marked than that reserve and quiet which give them an appearance of having an amount of good breeding and politeness of which they are in reality totally destitute. . . . These moral features I consider more striking and more conclusive of absolute diversity of race than even the physical ones though they are sufficiently remarkable. The mop-like head of long frizzly hair, the dusky sootiness of the skin and most important of all the marked form of countenance of quite a different type to that of the Malay are what we cannot believe to result from mere climatal or other modifying influences on one and the same race. The Malay face is of the Mongolian type and essentially flat. . . . The Papuan on the other hand has a face which we may say is compressed or projecting. The forehead is rounded, the eyebrows overhanging the lips thick and whole mouth projecting, while the nose is large the apex prominent the ridge thick and the nostrils equally dilated. It is true cases are seen of a perfect mixture of the two types, but this I believe may always be referred to as a mixture of race, and does not in any way show a natural gradation from the one to the other. (FJ, entry 50)

After being in Aru for a month, Wallace again commented on this subject:

These moral traits [of Papuan as compared to Malay] are of the greatest interest when taken in connection with physical features. They do not admit of the same ready explanation by external causes which is frequently applied to the latter. Ethnologists have too often to trust to the information of travellers who passing rapidly from country to country, have too few opportunities of becoming acquainted with peculiarities of national character, and scarcely ever with those of physical conformation. Such are exceedingly apt to be deceived in places where two races have long intermingled by looking on intermediate forms and mixed habits as evidences of a natural transition from one race to the other, not an artificial intermingling of the two; and they will be the more easily led into this error if as in the present case, writers on the subject should be in the habit of classing those races as mere varieties of one stock as closely related in physical conformation as from their geographical proximity one might *a priori* suppose them to be. To me at present the Malay and the Papuan appear to be as widely separated as any two human races can be, the latter possessing the closest affinities both physical and moral to the true Negro races. It is a most interesting question and one to which I shall direct my attention in all the islands of the Archipelago I may be enabled to visit. (FJ, entry 63 [Aru, late January, 1857])

The phrase "writers on the subject" almost certainly referred primarily to his friend Dr. Robert Gordon Latham, philologist and ethnologist. Latham had consulted with Wallace on a representation of Amazonian Indians for the exhibition at the Crystal Palace in 1852 and had provided comments to accompany Wallace's notations on tribal languages in his Amazonian narrative. In 1850 he had published *The Natural History of the Varieties of Man*. Latham, like Prichard and Lawrence before him, held to the view that mankind was a single species, all of its diverse races having been derived from the single, original, divinely created stock. Ethnologists during Prichard's lifetime (he died in 1848), and even later, generally subscribed to the alternative view that mankind was originally created as a diversity of species. In terms of biological classification mankind would represent a genus comprising more than one species. The number and character of the human "species" were matters of endless dispute. Prichard, however, held firm to his belief that races are to be considered "permanent varieties." His argument focused on two interrelated points: first, that hybrids between the most diverse human races are fully fertile and can continue to propagate themselves, whereas hybrids between related species of animals or plants are not capable of reproducing themselves; second, as a result of the interfertility of the most diverse tribes, there exist all possible intermediates between adjacent races. Gradual transitions were, he believed, the universal rule. The existence of these transitions between adjacent "typical" races of man was thus Prichard's basic argument for placing all human diversity within a single species.

Prichard clearly defined his concepts of "species" and of "permanent variety":

> The meaning attached to the term *species* in natural history is very definite and intelligible. It includes only the following conditions, namely, separate origin and distinctness of race, evinced by the constant transmission of some characteristic peculiarity of organization. . . .
> (Prichard 1841 1:105)

> *Varieties* are distinguished from species by the circumstance that they are not original or primordial, but have arisen, within the limits of a particular race or stock. *Permanent varieties* are those which having once

taken place, continue to be propagated in the breed in perpetuity. . . . The
properties of species are two, viz. original difference of characters and the
perpetuity of their transmission, of which only the latter can belong to
permanent varieties. (pp. 108–9)

As it is usually impossible to know whether any particular characteristics of a group of organisms are "original" or not, this defined
difference between the categories of "species" and "permanent variety" is of no pragmatic significance. When it was necessary to make
a decision between "species" and "permanent variety" it had to be
made on the basis of the facts related to hybridity, i.e., whether or
not the population in question would interbreed with other populations and thus give rise to hybrid populations with intermediate characteristics transitional between the two original populations. On this
basis the races of man, argued Prichard, had to be permanent varieties.

Latham, who stated in his introduction that his book only brought
Prichard up to date, added definitions of his own: "Hence, *transitional forms* are of two kinds, the first indicates descent, affiliation,
and historical connexion; the second, the effect of common climato-
logical, alimentary, or social influences. This last will be called *quasi-
transitional.*" (Latham 1850:9). In his view there were only three
primary varieties of the human species, which he idiosyncratically
named Mongolidae, Atlantidae, and Iapetidae. The variety of interest
here, the Mongolidae, comprised seven Divisions, the "Oceanic
Mongolidae" being one; all peoples of "the great Oceanic area" found
their place here.

On taking the localities more in detail, we may say that from Madagascar,
on the west, to Easter Island, half way between Asia and America, and
from Formosa to the north, to New Zealand southwards, in the great islands of Borneo, Sumatra and New Guinea, in the almost continental extent of Australia, in groups like the Philippines and the Moluccas, and in
scattered clusters like the Mariannes or the other islands of the South Sea,
the race is one and the same—and that race *Oceanic*. (p. 130)

Latham then divided this Oceanic Division into two classes:

A. One class of the Oceanic islanders is yellow, olive, brunette, or brown rather than black, with long black and straight hair; and when any member of this division is compared with a native of the continental portions of the world, it is generally with the Mongol.

B. Another class of the Oceanic islanders is black rather then yellow, olive, brunette, or brown; and when any member of this division is compared with a native of the continental portions of the world, it is generally with the Negro. As to the hair of this latter group, it is always long, sometimes strong and straight; but, in other cases, crisp, curly, frizzy, or even woolly. Upon these differences, especially that of the hair, we shall see in the sequel, that subdivisional groups have been formed.

The first class Latham named "Malay," the second "Negrito." Papuans are considered a branch of the Negrito class. Later in his book, when introducing the discussion of Papuans and their relation to Malays, he stated: "Whether we take the Protonesian [Malay-inhabited] islands in the line from Timor to Moa, Sermatty, Timorlaut, the Keys, and the Arrus, or begin with the Northern Moluccas, Gilolo, and Morty, we equally reach the great island of New Guinea; and in either case the ethnological change coincides with the geographical" (p. 211). Latham earlier stated explicitly that there are transitional forms between all of his geographically continuous groups—Primary Variety, Division, and Class—and that these transitional forms a priori will occupy the areas where these groups are continuous. Latham is clearly, then, one whose a priori assumption would be that the closeness of the "physical conformation" of two human "races" would be in direct relation to their geographical position.

Soon after his return to Macassar from his Aru journey, Wallace reflected, "My residence among the natives had given me an intimate acquaintance with the moral features of the Papuan races, not hitherto attained by writers on the subject and has laid the foundation of a knowledge which may perhaps enable me to give a more probable view of their origin than those generally entertained" (FJ, entry 106). This statement indicates that after the Aru experience Wallace was thinking about the origin of human races as well the origin of

species in general. I believe that the simultaneous consideration of
these two problems was of fundamental significance for the insight
into the dynamic process of species formation that occurred to him
six months later in Gilolo. His discovery on the Ké and Aru Islands
of the distinctiveness of the Papuans from the Malays raised the possibility that there are no natural transitions between human races, as
Prichard had maintained, at least not between these two. If further
observation were to substantiate this hypothesis, then these two human races would be shown to be distinct entities in the same way
that closely related species of animals are distinct but similar entities.
There is no indication as to whether Wallace was consciously thinking of the congruence of the two problems, but there is no question
that he was consciously pondering both.

Food Provisioning and State of Health

In his search for birds of paradise and other forest denizens, Wallace went to two sites in the large central landmass of Aru. The first
trip was to a village in the northernmost island of that landmass,
which Wallace called Wokan, now Wokam. Wokan is quite close to
the small island off its western shore whereon Dobbo is located. The
second trip involved a longer boat journey. Wallace first completely
traversed the narrow channel running west to east that separates Wokan
from the landmass to the south; he called this "river" Wateiai (now
Manoembai). The second village, Wanumbai (on the island he called
Maykor, now Kobroör), was reached by ascending a tributary of the
Wateiai. Wallace stayed at Wanumbai for six weeks. His field journal
records his impressions of the differences between the conditions of
existence for these two tribes of Papuans.

[Wokan, Aru: March 13–28, 1857]

The human inhabitants of these forests are not less interesting to me
than the feathered tribes. They are on the whole a miserable set of
savages. They live much as all people in the lowest state of human

existence live and it seems to me now a more miserable life than ever
I have thought it before. To begin with the grand item of food, the Aru
natives have no regular staple, no staff of life such as bread and rice
and mandiocca and sago are to so large a proportion of mankind. They
eat various vegetables, plantains, yams, sweet potatoes and crude sago,
and they chew up vast quantities of sugar cane as well as betel and
gambir and tobacco. To those on the coast a good supply of fish renders
them far better off, but when inland as we are here they get little, but
occasionally bring up their canoes full of cockles and other shell fish.
Now and then too they get wild pig and kangaroo but too rarely to
form anything like a regular part of their diet which is essentially vegetable, and what is of more importance as affecting their health, of
green watery vegetables, roughly roasted or boiled and even this in
varying and often insufficient quantities. It is to this diet that I think
may be attributed the great prevalence of skin disease and ulcers on the
legs and joints often giving them a disgusting appearance. I have observed pretty often the connection of the scrufy skin disease so common
among all savages, with the poorness or irregularity of their living. The
Malays generally who are never without their daily rice are free from
it; the hill dyaks of Borneo who grow paddy and live well are clean
skinned, those who are less industrious and live for a part of the year
on fruits and vegetables only, are much subject to the disease. Among
the Sago eaters, the natives of Goram and Ceram who visit Aru are
stout and healthy for though they live almost entirely on Sago it is upon
the baked cakes which those countries export to all the Eastern islands
of the Archipelago and which are both more wholesome than the crude
sago fresh from the tree which many of the natives of the Sago countries eat, and more nourishing than the white pearl sago from which all
the astringent woody matter has been washed. Again most of the Indian
tribes on the Amazon who have large mandiocca fields and regular
supplies of farinha and cassava bread are far more healthy skinned than
those who feed only on fruits, fish, and vegetable with no such regular
supply of wholesome food. One tribe even derive their name from the
very great prevalence of a leprous disease, which I have suggested in
my "Travels" was probably the effect of that tribe not using the ham-
mock but sleeping on the ground generally on the sand of the river; but
more extended observation leads me to think it much more likely to be
the effect of their irregular food which in their case is usually fish and
turtle, with what roots and fruits the forest furnishes. In fact in this as
in other respects man does not seem capable of making a beast of him-

self with impunity, living from hand to mouth on the herbs and fruits of the Earth alone. He must labour and select and prepare some farinaceous product capable of being stored to give him a regular daily staple food. When this is obtained he may add vegetables and fruits with advantage, as well as animal food. . . .

Their houses and furniture are on a par with their food. A rude shed, supported on rough and slender sticks rather than posts, no walls, but the floor raised to within a foot of the eaves, is the style of architecture they usually adopt. . . . For hours or even days they sit idle in their houses, the women bringing in the vegetables or sago for their food. Occasionally they work at their fields or houses or fishing, but their life is on the whole an idle one, with the necessary accompaniments of poor and scanty food, clothing, and shelter. (FJ, entry 71)

[Wanumbai, Maykor, Aru. April 1–May 8, 1857]

I am here more among the genuine natives of Arru tolerably free from foreign admixture. Our house which is a very good one contains about four or five families and there are generally from six to a dozen visitors besides. They keep up a continual row from morning to night,— talking laughing shouting without intermission; not very pleasant, but I take it as a study of national character and submit. My boy Ali says ''Banyak quot bitchara Orang Arru'' (The Arru people are very strong talkers) never having been accustomed to such eloquence either in his own or any other Malay Country we have visited. All the men and boys are expert archers never stirring out without their bows and arrows. They shoot all sorts of birds as well as pigs and kangaroos occasionally, which gives them a pretty regular supply of meat with their vegetables. The result of this better living is superior healthiness, well made bodies and generally clear skins. (FJ, entry 77)

Here, as among the Dyaks of Borneo and the Indians of the Upper Amazon I am delighted with the beauty of the human form, a beauty of which stay at home civilized people can never have any conception. What are the finest grecian statues to the living moving breathing forms which everywhere surround me. The unrestrained grace of the naked savage as he moves about his daily occupations or lounges at his ease must be seen to be understood. A young savage handling his bow is the perfection of physical beauty. Few persons feel more acutely than myself any offense against modesty among civilized folk, but here no such ideas have a moment's place; the free development of every limb seems wholly admirable, and made to be admired. (FJ, entry 83)

In these accounts Wallace makes it quite clear that in his opinion a people must exert diligence in procuring a steady food supply to maintain a state of healthiness.

During his stay at Wanumbai Wallace learned that surface water on Aru disappeared rapidly when clear weather replaced the intermittent rain that had continued since his arrival in January.

> We have had now seven or eight days of fine hot weather which has reduced the river to a succession of shallow pools connected by the smallest possible thread of trickling water. Were there a dry season like that of Macassar, Aru would be uninhabitable, there being no part of it probably having more than a hundred feet of elevation, and the whole being a mass of porous coralline rock allows the surface water rapidly to escape. The only really dry season seems to be for a month or so about October and then there is an excessive scarcity of water, so much so that in some seasons hundreds of birds and other animals die of drought. The natives then remove to houses near the sources of the small streams where in the depths of the forests a small quantity of water remains. Even then many of them walk miles for their water which they bring in large bamboos and use very sparingly. . . .
> (FJ, entry 82 [middle of April 1857])

The developing drought appears to have focused Wallace's attention on the vicissitudes of the seasons, particularly evident in that part of the Archipelago. That seasonality was a continuing interest is seen in a field journal entry written during the prau's return to Macassar:

> The sky was continually cloudy and dark and threatening with slight drizzling showers occasionally, till we were west of the Island of Bouru when it cleared up and we enjoyed the bright sunny skies of the dry season in the western part of the Archipelago. Here, therefore, seems to be the place where the remarkable change of seasons occurs between the eastern and western districts. This difference however seems to consist rather in the gloom and dampness of the atmosphere than in the absolute quantity of rain, for the little fresh water streams in Aru were all dried up when we left while in January and February and March they were always flowing, the intervals of rainy weather being marked by heavy showers and the general temperature being higher. The dryest

time of all in Aru according to both traders and natives occurs in September and October, so that though the seasons there a[re] very different from those of Celebes and Java they cannot be said to be opposite to them. It will be interesting to trace the modifications in the various islands of the Moluccas and it is much to be wished that the Dutch government would establish simple registers of thermometer Rain and Wind in all the places where they have settlements by which in a few years data would be furnished which might enable the various anomalies of climate to be reduced to some dependence on general laws. (FJ, entry 105 [early July 1857])

This chapter began with a list of eight observations by Wallace, all significant for the development of his theory. A concluding look reveals some commonalities among these observations. Both the fauna of Aru and its indigenous human population proved quite other than expected. Wallace had expected the fauna to be largely New Guinean in character but poor in species, as would be characteristic of a group of small islands separated from that large landmass by over a hundred miles of ocean. Instead, he found a richness of animal life, even in dense forest, that was exclusively New Guinean—species for species, to the extent that he could judge. The explanation of this virtual faunal identity was revealed by the discovery of clear physiographic evidence that the sea between Aru and New Guinea had been created by recent subsidence—recent in geological time. This discovery provided Wallace with a geographic situation of the kind he had sought since his Amazonian days (see chapter 3). According to his theory, only a slight change in the organic world should be manifest following a recent physiographic change. The species of birds, mammals, and insects that he found in Aru were identical to those described for New Guinea, with the sole exception of the *Ornithoptera*. The Aru form was distinct, but minimally so, from *O. poseidon*, described from New Guinea. Observation thus confirmed the theory. Wallace used these observations in Aru to provide the basis for a public challenge to the Lyellian theory of special creation, as well as an opportunity to present his own views of how organic change followed geographic change. The Aru *Ornithoptera* also demonstrated with stunning clarity the problem of distinguishing variety from species. Was the Aru bird-wing to be considered a new variety or a new species? Wallace discussed the implications of this question in general terms in a second paper.

Not only were observations of the indigenous people of Aru at variance with the Prichard-Latham theory; they even opened to question its basic postulate, that the universal existence of transitional populations is evidence that human races are permanent varieties, not species. Latham had designated Aru as one home of peoples transitional between Malay and Papuan. (Gilolo in the Moluccas was the other.) Wallace quickly perceived that the indigenes of Aru were distinctly Papuan, without trace of Malay. On Aru, at least, there was no transition between the races. If there were no transitional populations, then Prichard's argument that races were permanent varieties was demolished. Are human races varieties or species? The same question. Observations in Aru raised the question; the answer was to come a year later, in Gilolo. Other observations in Aru, on the differing life-styles of Papuan villages and the vicissitudes of life there, helped provide the eventual answer.

CHAPTER NINE
Revelation:
How a Variety Becomes a Species

Back safely in Macassar, Wallace devoted the next month to preparing his collections for shipment to England and finishing several papers based on his Aru findings. At the end of July, this work completed, he decided on a new collecting area, at the foot of some mountains thirty miles north of Macassar. Here he experienced the rigors of a seasonal climate such as he had heard about and begun to experience in Aru. A letter to Samuel Stevens provides details:

> . . . when I arrived in August there had not been rain for two months and it was fearfully hot and parched; dead leaves strewed the ground, and a beetle of any kind was sought for in vain. After some time I found a rocky river-bed issuing from a cleft in the mountains, and though dry it still contained a few pools and damp hollows; these were the resort of numerous butterflies. . . . About the mud holes Hymenoptera were abundant and on the fallen palm stems. . . . Coleoptera were not to be found. . . . After a few weeks of this work the mud holes got baked hard, the pools of water disappeared one after another, and with them the butterflies and other insects, and for some days I got almost nothing. I now set to turning over the stones and dead leaves in sandy river-bed, and soon found that there were some minute Coleoptera under them. . . . I now turned my attention to buffalo-dung, which though very barren compared with genuine British cow-dung, would, I found, yield something to a persevering search.   (Wallace 1858d:6120–21)

For the next few weeks rotting jackfruit produced the only live animals to be found—beetles. The first rains came in late September, and over the next few weeks the weather became increasingly cloudy and wet. In early November Wallace packed up and returned to Macassar.

The year before, Wallace had escaped the rainy season at Macassar by going to Aru. Now he decided to leave on the next Dutch mail steamer—on November 19—for Ternate, the embarkation point for New Guinea. He hoped to follow the plan tentatively decided on in Aru after he had gathered all the information on New Guinea that the traders at Dobbo could offer.

En route the mail steamer made port at Coupang, the chief city of the Dutch half of Timor, at its western end, and at the Banda Islands and Amboina, a small island off the southern coast of Ceram (Seram), on which the Dutch had concentrated the cultivation of nutmegs and cloves, respectively. His field journal records preoccupation with two matters to which the Aru observations had directed his attention: climatic differences among islands in the eastern half of the Archipelago and the presence or absence of true transitions between the Malay and Papuan races. Entry 112 first notes the scrubbiness of Timor's vegetation, its lack of forest, and the barrenness of the small offshore islands visible from the steamer. It continues:

> At Coupang are Chinese, Malays, Timorese Dutch and English and every shade and mixture between them. The mass of the population are however evidently the native islanders and they have all the characteristics of the Papuan races in hair, features, colour, and stature. Many have lank hair yet they are unmistakably Papuan and cannot be taken for Malay. . . . About Coupang the loud free conversation of the women both among themselves and with the men marks them as unmistakably non-Malay. They are evidently closely allied to the people of Ké, Babber and Arru.   (FJ, entry 112)

The trip from Coupang to Banda afforded a further opportunity to compare differences in the effects of seasonal patterns of rainfall among various island groups:

> After losing sight of Timor, in two days we reached the volcanic island of Banda, whose dense and brilliant green vegetation contrasted strongly with the bare hard rugged hills of the islands adjacent to [north

of] Timor. This difference is the more remarkable from the similarity of many of the islands in their geological formation. The coralline rocks of Timor support but a scanty and scrubby vegetation which cannot be called forest. The almost identical rocks of Ké and Arru are covered with the densest and most luxuriant of forests, and even the precipices are hidden under a pendant mass of folige. The volcanic rocks of the islands from Bali to beyond Timor are all more or less bare and are in many parts absolutely destitute of vegetation; while the equally volcanic Moluccas are clothed with a bright robe of ever verdant forest. The difference may probably be due to the position of Australia with regard to them. S.E. winds after passing over the parched barren plains of the interior of that great island would strike upon the range from Timor to Bali while the Moluccas and Arru Islands are subject only to the influence of the winds which passing over the vast pacific and damp forest of N. Guinea come to them loaded with a supply of moisture highly favourable to a vigorous vegetation.   (FJ, entry 113)

The next entry is largely a description of the beautiful island of Banda [Bandaira], its volcanos, and speculation about "the lakes of molten rock whose undulations probably cause the fearful earthquakes that so frequently occur here. . . ." The entry concludes, "In Banda there is nearly the same mixture of races as Timor the Papuan element being formed by natives of Ké and Ceram with which places there is much trade."

On the last day of November, twenty-four hours after leaving Banda, Wallace disembarked for a month's stay in Amboina. He remained until the fourth of January, 1858, when the next mail steamer departed.

Dr. Mohinke, his host and an amateur entomologist, accompanied Wallace to the residence of the Dutch Governor of the Moluccas. Courtesies aside, Wallace informed the Governor of his desire to go to New Guinea. He received a promise of letters to the missionaries and "every protection the Government can afford."

This was Wallace's first opportunity to study the rich fauna of the Moluccas—his first chance to see *Ornithoptera priamus* in the locality whence had come the first specimens of this spectacular bird-wing to reach Europe, over two hundred years before. The birds and insects did not disappoint in their splendor. Yet the perspicacious Wallace found that, as elsewhere, smaller, less conspicuous species were much more numerous in nature than the collections of amateur or less discerning entomologists would lead one to believe. We have quoted (in ch. 7) Wallace's comments on the misconceptions among European biologists about the characteristics of tropical insects that had arisen from collections strongly biased in favor of the largest, and hence usually rarest, species of beetles and butterflies. Nonetheless, the Moluccan insect fauna as seen at Amboina was strikingly different in splendor of aspect as well as in richness from that which he had just left in Celebes. Many species seemed closely allied to those collected in Aru, constituting a New Guinean element which Celebes had unexpectedly lacked.

The only comment on the confused racial picture in this ancient trade center relevant to the Malay-Papuan relationship is, "The native Amboinese are a strange half civilized, half savage lazy race; who seem a mixture of at least three nations, Portuguese Malay and Papuan or Ceramese, with an occasional cross of Chinese and Dutch to give a little variety to the compound. . . ." We have elsewhere noted Wallace's discernment of the persistence of Portuguese habits among elements of this population and the inclusion of many Portuguese words in the Malay spoken there.

On January 8, after a four-day trip from Amboina, the mail steamer made port at Ternate. Ternate is the northernmost of a chain of small volcanic islands skirting the western coast of the large, irregularly shaped island of Gilolo, or Halmahera. Together with the larger, non-volcanic Batchian, just to the south, these constitute the Spice Islands, in the older sense. At present the term is applied to all of the Moluccas, the numerous islands large and small between Celebes and the western tip of New Guinea—Gilolo, Bouru (Buru), and Ceram (Seram), to name some of the largest. Wallace had a letter of introduction to Mr. Duivenboden, a Ternate native of an ancient Dutch family, who had been educated in England. Mr. Duivenboden, a rich man of property, was versed in literature and science, "a phenomenon of the region," as Wallace remarked. Among his enterprises was trade in wild nutmeg from New Guinea. Wallace arranged to accompany one of his schooners on a trading voyage along the north coast of New Guinea, leaving about the middle of March. He obtained a house near the edge of town, "ruinous" in condition but made satisfactory with a few repairs and some bamboo furniture. Here he settled down to "prepare the plan of the campaign for the ensuing year," a plan that centered on birds of paradise and other exotic novelties which the unexplored country might offer.

The two months before the planned departure left more time for collecting than the tiny island of Ternate could make profitable. On January 25 he added a postscript to a long letter to Henry Bates: "About ten miles to the east [of Ternate] is the coast of the large Island of Gilolo, perhaps the most perfect entomological *terra incognita* now to be found. I am not aware that a single insect has ever been collected there, and cannot find it given as the locality of any insects in my catalogues or descriptions. In about a week I go for a month collecting there, and then return to prepare for a voyage to New Guinea" (Marchant 1916 1:68).

The actual date of Wallace's departure for Gilolo is not clear, either from the field journal or from *Malay Archipelago*. Entry 125 of the journal begins, "After a fortnight spent in Ternate I determined to visit the island of Gilolo for a month and then return to prepare for a voyage to New Guinea. . . ." In the chapter on Ternate, *Malay Archipelago* states, "Soon after my arrival in Ternate I went to the island of Gilolo. . . ." Both are consistent in a general way with what the postscript to the Bates letter suggests, that Wallace quitted Ternate for Gilolo toward the end of January. The date of Wallace's return from Gilolo to Ternate is stated in the field journal to be March 1 (see ch. 4). I think, therefore, there can be little question that Wallace was in Gilolo during the month of February.[1]

The important fact is that Wallace was in Gilolo when he had his

1. The matter of where he spent that month has been the topic of some discussion of late, because Wallace's next paper on organic evolution, "On the Tendency of Varieties to Depart Indefinitely from the Original Type" (1858e) is signed "Ternate February, 1858." McKinney (1972), after pointing out the evidence indicating that Wallace was in Gilolo during February and wrote the paper there, suggests that Wallace was practicing a deliberate deception by indicating "Ternate" and not "Gilolo" in the signature, because Wallace, with an eye to history, deemed that well-known Ternate was a more appropriate site for a "momentous" discovery than Gilolo. As noted in chapter 4, one cannot deny that Wallace rearranged and altered some words from the field journal of his two visits to Gilolo—the second after his return from New Guinea—to form a single short chapter on "Gilolo" in *Malay Archipelago*. But I see this as merely an effort to make a readable account from sketchy and somewhat duplicative field notes on two short visits.

now-acclaimed insight into the dynamic process by which a variety
becomes a species. Wallace makes no reference to the composition
of the pivotal paper in either the field journal or *Malay Archipelago*.
His writings in the journal for that month are brief; the three entries
(125–127) total nine handwritten pages. The first entry is a description of his trip to Dodinga and procurement of adequate housing for
a month. The second describes Dodinga and its situation: "Dodinga
is at the narrowest part of the island where a narrow isthmus unites
the northern with the trifid southern peninsula. The distance across is
not more than a couple of miles and there is a good path along which
much rice and sago is brought from all the Eastern villages," and its
inhabitants: "The village was entirely occupied by Ternate men, who
are malays with an occasional admixture of papuan blood. The true
indigenes of Gilolo live on the Eastern coast or in the interior" (FJ,
entry 126).

Entry 127, the one before the entry noting the return to Ternate on
March 1, is the last before his new insight. I quote it in its entirety:

> The natives of this large and most unknown island were examined
> by me with much interest, as they would help to determine whether,
> independent of mixed races, there is any transition from the malay to
> the papuan type. I was soon satisfied by the first half dozen I saw that
> they were of genuine papuan race, lighter in colour indeed than usual
> but still presenting the marked characters of the type in features and
> stature. They are scarcely darker than dark Malays and even lighter
> than most of the coast malays who have some mixture of papuan blood.
> Neither is their hair frizzly or wooly, but merely crisp or waved, yet it
> has a roughness or slight wooliness, an appearance produced I think by
> the individual hairs not lying parallel and close together, which is very
> different from the smooth and glossy though coarse tresses, everywhere
> found in the unmixed malayan race. The stature alone marks them as
> distinct being decidedly above the average malay height, while the fea-
> tures are as palpably *unmalay* as those of the Europeans or the negro.

The question of the existence of transitional forms on Gilolo was
possibly of special interest because of a comment in Latham about
the origin of the Papuan race from the Malay. Just below a major
subheading, "The Arru Isles," Latham stated, "The probable source,

however, of the Papuan population must be sought for in the parts about Gilolo. Here the distinction between these islands which constitute the more eastern and northern portions of the Moluccas, and those which are considered to belong to New Guinea, is difficult to be drawn'' (Latham 1850:212). A brief examination by Wallace's now practiced eye convinced him that these "Galela men," as he later referred to the indigenes, were unmistakably Papuan, with an admixture of Malay suggested by the lighter skin color. They were definitely not transitional forms.

A letter that Wallace wrote to his friend George Silk the following October makes it clear that Latham's views were uppermost in his mind in relation to his observation of the nontransitional nature of the Gilolo indigenes. In September, recall (see ch. 4), Wallace had revisited the island and recorded in his narrative that further examination had reaffirmed his conviction that the "Galela men" were a recently mixed race and were not transitional in the sense of Prichard and, of course, Latham. The letter to George Silk appears to give a meaning to a cryptic notation in *Malay Archipelago* (1869:243) that he had made a significant ethnological discovery that September:

> If I live to return I shall come out strong on Malay and Papuan races, and shall astonish Latham, Davis, and Co. By-the-by, I have a letter from Davis; he says he sent my last letter to you, and it is lost mysteriously. Instead, therefore, of sending me a reply to my "poser," he repeats what he has said in *every* letter I have had from him, that "myriads of miracles are required to people the earth from one source." I am sick of him. You must read "Pritchard" through, and Lawrence's "Lectures on Man" carefully; but I am convinced no man can be a good ethnologist who does not travel, and not *travel* merely, but reside, as I do, months and years with each race, becoming well acquainted with their average physiognomy and their character, so as to be able to detect cross-breeds, which totally mislead the hasty traveller, who thinks they are transitions! (Wallace 1905 1:366)

The question for us now to consider is whether this observation of the nature of the "Galela men" was an element leading to his insight about the formation of animal species. As I have noted, there are no clues either in the field journal, other than entry 127, or in *Malay*

Archipelago that help determine this. Fortunately, there are several much later reminiscences about the circumstances of this intellectual event. Between 1898 and 1908, largely as the result of the interest of others, Wallace prepared five versions of this reminiscence; the last was on the occasion of the fifty-year celebration of the joint Darwin-Wallace publication. The crucial elements of all are, naturally, the same. McKinney (1972) quotes from all five. Parts of two, written in 1903 and 1905, respectively, provide the most complete description of the course of his thoughts, in complementary fashion:

> In February, 1858, I was living at Ternate, one of the Moluccas Islands and was suffering from a sharp attack of intermittent fever, which obliged me to lie down every afternoon during the cold and subsequent hot fits which lasted together two or three hours. It was during one of these fits, while I was thinking over the possible mode of origin of new species, that somehow my thought turned to the "positive checks" to increase among savages and others described in much detail in the celebrated *Essay on Population,* by Malthus, a work I had read a dozen years before. These checks—disease, famine, accidents, wars, &c.—are what keep down the population, and it suddenly occurred to me that in the case of wild animals these checks would act with much more severity, and as the lower animals all tended to increase more rapidly than man, while their population remained on the average constant, there suddenly flashed upon me the idea of the survival of the fittest—that those individuals which every year are removed by these causes,—termed collectively the "struggle for existence"—must on the average and in the long run be inferior in some one or more ways to those which managed to survive.
>
> The more I thought of this the more certain it appeared to be; while the only alternative theory—that those who succumbed to enemies, or want of food, or disease, drought, or cold, were in every way and always as well constituted as those that survived—seemed to me impossible and unthinkable. . . . (Wallace 1903:78)
>
> Then it suddenly flashed upon me that this self-acting process would necessarily *improve the race,* because in every generation the inferior would inevitably be killed off and the superior would remain—that is, the *fittest would survive.* Then at once I seemed to see the whole effect of this, that when changes of land and sea, or of climate, or of food supply, or of enemies occurred—and we know that such changes have

always been taking place—and considering the amount of individual variation that my experience as a collector has shown me to exist, then it followed that all the changes necessary for the adaptation of the species to the changing conditions would be brought about; and as great changes in the environment are always slow, there would be ample time for the change to be effected by the survival of the best fitted in every generation. In this way every part of an animal's organization could be modified exactly as required, and in the very process of this modification the unmodified would die out, and thus the *definite* characters and the clear *isolation* of each new species would be explained. The more I thought it over the more I became convinced that I had at length found the long-sought-for law of nature that solved the problem of the origin of species. For the next hour I thought over the deficiencies in the theories of Lamarck and of the author of the "Vestiges," and I saw that my new theory supplemented these views and obviated every important difficulty. I waited anxiously for the termination of my fit so that I might at once make notes for a paper on the subject. The same evening I did this pretty fully, and on the two succeeding evenings wrote it carefully in order to send it to Darwin by the next post, which would leave in a day or two. (Wallace 1905 1:361–63)

Before considering the content of these remarks, I must call attention to an obvious error in the recollection of the locality. Wallace must have relied on the date on his paper, i.e., "Ternate, February 1858." As noted, this is confusing because the field narrative clearly places Wallace on Gilolo in February. Further evidence that the event occurred on Gilolo is a sentence in the "Gilolo" chapter of *Malay Archipelago:* "I got some very nice insects here, though, owing to illness most of the time, my collection was a small one" (Wallace 1869:241). "Most of the time" must have been two or three weeks, since the activities recorded in the field journal account for about two weeks at the most. The sentence at the end of entry 126, which was altered to the final form given above, read: "In my first walk I obtained a few insects quite new to me and was very well pleased with my prospects of making a fine collection." This and remarks relating to his second visit to Gilolo, in September 1858, indicated that he had been unable to do any other collecting during his February visit. The later recollections suggest that the period of intense intellectual activity had occupied only a few days. But the field journal indicates that the idleness enforced by the malarial attack (for such it almost certainly was) probably lasted a few weeks—time for long reflection on problems of interest, and probably opportunity to observe the villages and the "Galela men" bringing "much sago and rice."

The content of the last narrative entry made on Gilolo, and the later recollection about "savages," reinforces my speculation that Wallace was thinking about the origin of human races, especially Papuans. His discovery that there was no transitional population on Gilolo bridging the gap between Malay and Papuan must have seemed like a validation of his tentative conclusion reached in Aru. What had before seemed a possibility had become a revealing reality. If human races were entities as distinct as animal species, possibly their modes of origin were similar.

In his 1855 paper Wallace had demonstrated that affinity gaps in species clusters were due to the extinction of intermediates. Was extinction of intermediate human populations the explanation for the distinctiveness of races? As a preamble to the recollection of his insights of February 1858, as given in his autobiography, Wallace remembered his frame of mind:

> My paper written at Sarawak rendered it certain to my mind that the change had taken place by natural succession and descent—one species becoming changed either slowly or rapidly into another. But the exact process of change and the causes which led to it were absolutely unknown and appeared almost inconceivable. The great difficulty was to understand how, if one species was gradually changed into another, there continued to be so many quite distinct species, so many which differed from their allies by slight yet perfectly definite and constant characters. . . . The problem then was, not only how and why do species change, but how and why do they change into new and well-defined species, distinguished from each other in so many ways; why and how do they become so exactly adapted to distinct modes of life; and why do all intermediate grades die out (as geology shows they have died out) and leave only clearly defined and well-marked species, genera, and higher categories.   (Wallace 1905 1:360–61)

If, as I have speculated, he was also ruminating on the origin of the Papuan race from the Malay, the dying out of "intermediate grades'' of people might present itself as a mechanism accounting for the present distinctness of the two races, a distinctness that had been forcefully impressed on Wallace's mind. Famine, drought, war, and natural disasters such as earthquakes presented themselves as agents for such extinctions. If, indeed, he was thinking of circumstances that might lead to the dying out of human populations, his recall both of Malthus and of the concept of ''survival of the fittest'' becomes more understandable. Let us first consider the relevance of Malthus.

For his presentation at the fifty-year celebration of the Darwin-Wallace publication (in 1908), Wallace reexamined Malthus' *Essay on Population* (sixth edition). He concluded that there were no specific passages that he could select as having been especially influential on his thinking; rather that it was the ''cumulative effect'' of those chapters which ''comprised very detailed accounts from all available sources, of the various causes which keep down the populations of savage and barbarous nations, in America, Africa, and Asia, notwithstanding that they all possess a power of increase sufficient to produce a dense population of any of the continents in a few centuries.''

The passages he chose as ''fairly illustrative of the whole'' are of interest here, not because they necessarily are the passages that came to mind fifty years earlier, but merely because he selected them. The first two short passages refer to American Indians:

> We may next turn our view to the vast continent of America, the greater part of which was found to be inhabited by small independent tribes of savages, subsisting nearly like the natives of New Holland, on the productions of unassisted nature. . . . The produce of a most rude and imperfect agriculture, known to some of the tribes of hunters, was so trifling as to be considered only as a feeble aid to the subsistence acquired by the chase. The inhabitants of this new world therefore might be considered as living principally by hunting and fishing. . . . The supplies derived from fishing could reach only those who were within a certain distance of the lakes, the rivers, or the sea-shore; and the ignorance and indolence of the improvident savages would frequently prevent him from extending the benefits of these supplies much beyond the time when they were actually obtained. . . .
>
> . . . It cannot escape observation, that an insufficient supply of food to any people does not show itself merely in the shape of famine, but in other more permanent forms of distress, and in generating certain customs, which operate sometimes with greater force in the prevention of a rising population than in its subsequent destruction. (Malthus 1872 1:35–37)

In every part of the world, one of the most general characteristics of the
savage is to despise and degrade the female sex. Among most of the tribes
in America their condition is so peculiarly grievous, that servitude is a
name too mild to describe their wretched state. A wife is no better than a
beast of burden. While the man passes his days in idleness or amusement,
the woman is condemned to incessant toil. Tasks are imposed upon her
without mercy, and services are received without complacence or gratitude. There are some districts in America, where this state of degradation
has been so severely felt, that mothers have destroyed their female infants,
to deliver them at once from a life in which they were doomed to such a
miserable life of slavery. (1:39)

These two passages are similar in both content and attitude to Wallace's comments on the Wokan tribe in Aru (see above). Wallace
makes no mention of infanticide in that account, but his selection of
this passage is noteworthy.

His third selection from Malthus begins with quotations from Bruce
about his travels in mid-Africa–Ethiopia.

Bruce says, "we arrived at Garigana, a village whose inhabitants had all
perished with hunger the year before; their wretched bones all being un-
buried and scattered upon the surface of the ground where the village formerly stood. . . .

". . . There is no water between Teawa and Beyla. Once Indedidema
and a number of villages were supplied with water from wells, and had
large crops of Indian corn sown about their possessions. The curse of that
country, the Daveina Arabs, have destroyed Indedidema and all the villages about it; filled up their wells, burnt their crops, and exposed all the
inhabitants to die by famine.

". . . We began to see the effects of rain having failed. There was little
corn sown, and that so late as to be scarcely above ground. . . . Many
people were here employed in gathering grass-seeds to make a very bad
kind of bread. These people appear perfect skeletons, and no wonder, as
they live upon such fare. . . ."

Under such circumstances of climatic and political situation, though a
greater degree of foresight, industry and security, might considerably better
their condition and increase their population, the birth of a greater number
of children without these concomitants would only aggravate their misery,
and leave their population where it was. (1:158–70)

Malthus continued with a discussion of the "once flourishing and
populous country of Egypt. Its present depressed state has not been

caused by the weakening of the principle of increase, but by the weakening of the principle of industry and foresight, from the insecurity of property, consequent on a most tyrannical and oppressive government. . . ." He indicated that in ancient times constant maintenance of "vast lakes, canals, and large conduits" not only retained the annual flood waters of the Nile but also provided water for the years when the flood should fail. He concluded that subsequent neglect of these water-works has diminished the population's means of subsistence. Periodic epidemics and famine have taken a frightful toll in this populace leading a marginal existence.

The content of the three citations from Malthus recalls Wallace's observations and experiences in Aru and subsequently in Celebes—the first two quite similar to situations that Wallace observed in Wokan, and the third relating to drought. This fact, I think, provides a degree of support for my earlier speculation that Wallace was pondering the reasons for the "dying out" of intermediate human tribes as a step leading to the formation of the distinct Papuan race. In the course of reflection on the drastic circumstances that might lead to the extinction of a tribe, one might well be reminded of Malthus, with his images of populations in dire straits. When the name "Malthus" came to mind, his *Essay*'s main thesis—"positive checks" by an inadequate food supply—should have followed. A statement in the first selection from the *Essay,* that "an insufficient supply of food . . . does not show itself merely in the shape of famine, but in other more permanent forms of distress, . . . which operate sometimes with greater force in the prevention of a rising population than in its subsequent destruction," links the concept of famine, a catastrophic event, with other less dramatic but continuing effects of food shortage. The drought described in the third selection from Malthus might have been called to mind in 1858 by what Wallace had learned of the drought in Aru. While it created hardships for the Papuans of the area, the drought caused the deaths of hundreds of animals. These interrelated elements could have led to the conclusion that positive checks act on animal populations with even greater force than they do on humans.

We now come to the second insight—the relevance of the concept of "survival of the fittest." I think that this insight possibly had its origin in Wallace's observation of the superiority of the Gilolo indigenes in food provisioning. This is an aspect of that "nontransitional population" alluded to only on that February visit. But the reports on a subsequent visit speak of superlative qualities, undoubtedly obvious to Wallace during times in February when he was not confined to bed but lacked the strength to continue his narrative. Two separate sentences in entry 126 of the field journal allude briefly to the prowess of the Gilolo indigenes as cultivators: "The true indigenes of Gilolo live in the Eastern coast or in the interior." "There is a good path [on the isthmus] along which much rice and sago is brought from all the Eastern villages." Later comments expand on this. On his second visit to Gilolo, in September, Wallace tried collecting first at Sahoe (Sahu), on the west coast of the northern peninsula, and then at the village of Jilolo (Djailolo), further inland. Entry 154 of the field journal notes, "I was much interested in the indigenes or *alfuros* of this part of Gilolo, of which a large population are settled in the neighboring interior and numbers are daily seen in the villages, either bringing their produce for sale or engaged by the Chinese or Ternate traders." After completing his travels in the Archipelago Wallace presented the results of his ethnological researches in "On the Varieties of Man in the Malay Archipelago" (1865a) and therein gave a more complete assessment of these "Galela men":

> The islands of Obi and Batchian, and the three southern peninsulas of Gilolo possess no true indigenous population. The northern peninsula, however, is inhabited by a native race, whose principal tribes are the so-called Alfurus of Sahoe and Galela. These people are quite distinct from the Malays, and almost equally so from the Papuan. They are tall and well-made, with Papuan features, curly hair, bearded and hairy bodied, but quite as light in colour as the Malays. They are an industrious and enterprising race, cultivating largely, and indefatigable in their search after the natural productions of sea and land. They are very intelligent and improvable, and on the whole seem one of the best races in the archipelago. . . ." (Wallace 1865a:207)

While Wallace probably did not gain this complete an appreciation during the February 1858 visit, it seems likely that he would have perceived, and been impressed by, the industriousness of these people and their obvious success as cultivators and gatherers. As food-provisioners they were superior to the better of the two tribes on Aru, the Wanumbai, and far superior to the Wokan, who lived chiefly, and poorly, on "watery green vegetables." In fact, on the occasion of discussing the Wokan, Wallace contrasted their health with that of the Malay sago- and rice-producers he had studied. But here on Gilolo was a tribe that excelled at cultivation of sago and rice. Could the obvious differences among these Papuan tribes in effecting an adequate and regular food supply have suggested different probabilities of surviving a natural disaster? Surely the people of Galela would survive a prolonged drought or general famine better than the vegetable-eaters of Wokan.

"Survival of the fittest" might well have come to mind in this regard. Herbert Spencer had used the phrase while writing of mankind in his 1852 essay "Theory of Population." But Spencer, seeking "the proximate cause of progress," was looking to the differential survival of the individual of a race:

> For as those prematurely carried off must, in the average of cases, be those in whom the power of self-preservation is the least, it unavoidably follows, that those left behind to continue the race must be those in whom the power of self-preservation is the greatest—must be the select of their generation. So that, whether the dangers to existence be of the kind produced by excess of fertility, or of any other kind, it is clear that by the ceaseless exercise of the faculties needed to contend with them, and by the death of all men who fail to contend with them successfully, there is ensured a constant progress towards a higher degree of skill, intelligence, and self-regulation—a better coordination of actions—a more complete life. (Spencer 1852b:34)

It is unlikely that Wallace recalled the details of Spencer's essay. There is nowhere any mention of Spencer in relation to the 1858 formulations, but Wallace often wrote in admiration of Spencer's works, with which he first became acquainted in 1852 after his return from the Amazon (Wallace 1898).

If my conjectures are correct, Wallace was thinking about which kinds of human tribes, i.e., populations, might survive a severe general food shortage. The "survival of the fittest," then, probably referred to the fittest population. But as Spencer had been considering individuals, human individuals to be sure, the application of the concept to animal populations (varieties) and individual animals within those populations could follow readily. Wallace's thinking also linked Malthus' "positive checks," a concept originally used in relation to human populations, first to animal populations, and then to individuals. Thus the "positive checks," such as an inadequate and uncertain food supply, which Malthus had believed kept down the size of human populations, were applied to individuals of animal populations that were conceived by Wallace as variable in their inherent ability to sustain life.

The last step for Wallace was to postulate that the varietal populations that had arisen from the "typical" population would vary in their fitness to survive, such that some were superior, some inferior, to the typical population.

The clarity and logic with which Wallace developed these ideas is evident in the "Ternate" essay, given below in its entirety. Though I risk painting the lily, I shall venture to give a brief, stepwise analysis of his dynamics of species formation and continued divergence.

1. Varieties can be expected to differ in organization and habits from each other and from the "parent species," and hence in their ability to gather food.
2. Even slight differences will make a variety "inferior" or "superior" to the parent species *under a given set of conditions*.
3. The size of any population is the reflection of its food-gathering ability, not of its reproductive capacities.
4. Suppose, then, that a "parent species" is represented in different geographical areas by an "inferior" and a "superior" variety. If the general circumstances should worsen, as in a prolonged drought, making basic food scarce, the populations of all three will dwindle.
5. But the variety "inferior" in its food-gathering abilities and the consequent size of its population will be the first to dwindle to extinction, followed by the parent species. At that point only the "superior" variety, initially most numerous, will survive.
6. If conditions ameliorate, the basic food (plants) will again become abundant, and the population of the only surviving population, the "superior" variety, will increase its numbers and extend its range, alone attaining the size and range of the three former populations.

7. Thus the "superior" variety has replaced the parent species, becoming what must be called a new species and in time becoming a "parent," geographical representatives of which may become new varieties.
8. Repetition of the process results in progressive development (progression of types) and continued divergence from the original type.

On the Tendency of Varieties to Depart Indefinitely
from the Original Type
By Alfred Russel Wallace

One of the strongest arguments which have been adduced to prove the original and permanent distinctness of species is, that *varieties* produced in a state of domesticity are more or less unstable, and often have a tendency, if left to themselves, to return to the normal form of the parent species; and this instability is considered to be a distinctive peculiarity of all varieties, even of these occurring among wild animals in a state of nature, and to constitute a provision for preserving unchanged the originally created distinct species.

In the absence or scarcity of facts and observations as to *varieties* occurring among wild animals, this argument has had great weight with naturalists, and has led to a very general and somewhat prejudiced belief in the stability of species. Equally general, however, is the belief in what are called "permanent or true varieties,"—races of animals which continually propagate their like, but which differ so slightly (although constantly) from some other race, that the one is considered to be a *variety* of the other. Which is the *variety* and which the original *species,* there is generally no means of determining, except in those rare cases in which the one race has been known to produce an offspring unlike itself and resembling the other. This, however, would seem quite incompatible with the "permanent invariability of species," but the difficulty is overcome by assuming that such varieties have strict limits, and can never again vary further from the original type, although they may return to it, which, from the analogy of the domesticated animals, is considered to be highly probable, if not certainly proved.

It will be observed that this argument rests entirely on the assumption, that *varieties* occurring in a state of nature are in all respects analogous to or even identical with those of domestic animals, and are governed by the same laws as regards their permanence or further variation. But it is the object of the present paper to show that this assumption is altogether false, that there is a general principle in nature which will

cause many *varieties* to survive the parent species, and to give rise to
successive variations departing further and further from the original type,
and which also produces, in domesticated animals, the tendency of varieties to return to the parent form.

The life of wild animals is a struggle for existence. The full exertion
of all their faculties and all their energies is required to preserve their
own existence and provide for that of their infant offspring. The possibility of procuring food during the least favourable seasons, and of
escaping the attacks of their most dangerous enemies, are the primary
conditions which determine the existence both of individuals and of
entire species. These conditions will also determine the population of a
species; and by a careful consideration of all the circumstances we may
be enabled to comprehend, and in some degree to explain, what at first
sight appears to be inexplicable—the excessive abundance of some species, while others closely allied to them are very rare.

The general proportion that must obtain between certain groups of
animals is readily seen. Large animals cannot be so abundant as small
ones; the carnivora must be less numerous than the herbivora; eagles
and lions can never be so plentiful as pigeons and antelopes; the wild
asses of the Tartarian deserts cannot equal in numbers the horses of the
more luxuriant prairies and pampas of America. The greater or less
fecundity of an animal is often considered to be one of the chief causes
of its abundance or scarcity; but a consideration of the facts will show
us that it really has little or nothing to do with the matter. Even the
least prolific of animals would increase rapidly if unchecked, whereas
it is evident that the animal population of the globe must be stationary,
or perhaps, through the influence of man, decreasing. Fluctuations there
may be; but permanent increase, except in restricted localities, is almost impossible. For example, our own observation must convince us
that birds do not go on increasing every year in a geometrical ratio, as
they would do, were there not some powerful check to their natural
increase. Very few birds produce less than two young ones each year,
while many have six, eight, or ten; four will certainly be below the
average; and if we suppose that each pair produce young only four
times in their life, that will also be below the average, supposing them
not to die either by violence or want of food. Yet at this rate how
tremendous would be the increase in a few years from a single pair! A
simple calculation will show that in fifteen years each pair of birds
would have increased to nearly ten millions! whereas we have not reason to believe that the number of the birds of any country increases at

all in fifteen or in one hundred and fifty years. With such powers of increase the population must have reached its limits, and have become stationary, in a very few years after the origin of each species. It is evident, therefore, that each year an immense number of birds perish— as many in fact as are born; and as on the lowest calculation the progeny are each year twice as numerous as their parents, it follows that, whatever be the average number of individuals existing in any given country, *twice that number must perish annually*—a striking result, but one which seems at least highly probable, and is perhaps under rather than over the truth. It would therefore appear that, as far as the continuance of the species and the keeping up the average numbers of individuals are concerned, large broods are superfluous. On the average all above *one* become food for hawks and kites, wild cats and weasels, or perish of cold and hunger as winter comes on. This is strikingly proved by the case of particular species; for we find that their abundance in individuals bears no relation whatever to their fertility in producing offspring. Perhaps the most remarkable instance of an immense bird population is that of the passenger pigeon of the United States, which lays only one, or at most two eggs, and is said to rear generally but one young one. Why is this bird so extraordinarily abundant, while others producing two or three times as many young are much less plentiful? The explanation is not difficult. The food most congenial to this species, and on which it thrives best, is abundantly distributed over a very extensive region, offering such differences of soil and climate, that in one part or another of the area the supply never fails. The bird is capable of a very rapid and long-continued flight, so that it can pass without fatigue over the whole of the district it inhabits, and as soon as the supply of food begins to fail in one place is able to discover a fresh feeding ground. This example strikingly shows us that the procuring a constant supply of wholesome food is almost the sole condition requisite for ensuring the rapid increase of a given species, since neither the limited fecundity, nor the unrestrained attacks of birds of prey and of man are here sufficient to check it. In no other birds are these peculiar circumstances so strikingly combined. Either their food is more liable to failure, or they have not sufficient power of wing to search for it over an extensive area, or during some season of the year it becomes very scarce, and less wholesome substitutes have to be found; and thus, though more fertile in offspring, they can never increase beyond the supply of food in the least favourable seasons. Many birds can only exist by migrating, when their food becomes scarce, to regions pos-

sessing a milder, or at least a different climate, though, as these migrating birds are seldom excessively abundant, it is evident that the
countries they visit are still deficient in a constant and abundant supply
of wholesome food. Those whose organization does not permit them to
migrate when their food becomes periodically scarce, can never attain
a large population. This is probably the reason why woodpeckers are
scarce with us, while in the tropics they are among the most abundant
of solitary birds. Thus the house sparrow is more abundant than the
redbreast, because its food is more constant and plentiful,—seeds of
grasses being preserved during the winter, and our farm-yards and stub-
ble-fields furnishing an almost inexhaustible supply. Why, as a general
rule, are aquatic, and especially sea birds, very numerous in individuals? Not because they are more prolific than others, generally the contrary; but because their food never fails, the sea-shores and river-banks
daily swarming with a fresh supply of small mollusca and crustacea.
Exactly the same laws will apply to mammals. Wild cats are prolific
and have few enemies; why then are they never as abundant as rabbits?
The only intelligible answer is, that their supply of food is more precarious. It appears evident, therefore, that so long as a country remains
physically unchanged, the numbers of its animal population cannot materially increase. If one species does so, some other requiring the same
kind of food must diminish in proportion. The numbers that die annually must be immense; and as the individual existence of each animal
depends upon itself, those that die must be the weakest—the very young,
the aged, and the diseased,—while those that prolong their existence
can only be the most perfect in health and vigour—those who are best
able to obtain food regularly, and avoid their numerous enemies. It is,
as we commenced by remarking, "a struggle for existence," in which
the weakest and least perfectly organized must always succumb.

Now it is clear that what takes place among the individuals of a
species must also occur among the several allied species of a group,—
viz. that those which are best adapted to obtain a regular supply of
food, and to defend themselves against the attacks of their enemies and
the vicissitudes of the seasons, must necessarily obtain and preserve a
superiority in population; while those species which from some defect
of power or organization are the least capable of counteracting the vicissitudes of food, supply, &c., must diminish in numbers, and, in
extreme cases, become altogether extinct. Between these extremes the
species will present various degrees of capacity for ensuring the means
of preserving life; and it is thus we account for the abundance or rarity

of species. Our ignorance will generally prevent us from accurately tracing the effects to their causes; but could we become perfectly acquainted with the organization and habits of the various species of animals, and could we measure the capacity of each for performing the different acts necessary to its safety and existence under all the varying circumstances by which it is surrounded, we might be able even to calculate the proportionate abundance of individuals which is the necessary result.

If now we have succeeded in establishing these two points—1st, *that the animal population of a country is generally stationary, being kept down by a periodical deficiency of food and other checks;* and, 2nd, *that the comparative abundance or scarcity of the individuals of the several species is entirely due to their organization and resulting habits, which, rendering it more difficult to procure a regular supply of food and to provide for their personal safety in some cases than in others, can only be balanced by a difference in the population which have to exist in a given area*—we shall be in a condition to proceed to the consideration of *varieties*, to which the preceding remarks have a direct and very important application.

Most or perhaps all the variations from the typical form of a species must have some definite effect, however slight, on the habits or capacities of the individuals. Even a change of colour might, by rendering them more or less distinguishable, affect their safety; a greater or less development of hair might modify their habits. More important changes, such as an increase in the power or dimensions of the limbs or any of the external organs, would more or less affect their mode of procuring food or the range of country which they inhabit. It is also evident that most changes would affect, either favourably or adversely, the powers of prolonging existence. An antelope with shorter or weaker legs must necessarily suffer more from the attacks of the feline carnivora; the passenger pigeon with less powerful wings would sooner or later be affected in its powers of procuring a regular supply of food; and in both cases the result must necessarily be a diminution of the modified species. If, on the other hand, any species should produce a variety having slightly increased powers of preserving existence, that variety must inevitably in time acquire a superiority in numbers. These results must follow as surely as old age, intemperance, or scarcity of food produce an increased mortality. In both cases there may be many individual exceptions; but on the average the rule will invariably be found to hold good. All varieties will therefore fall into two classes—those which under the same conditions would never reach the population of the parent species, and those which would in time obtain and keep a numerical superiority. Now, let some alteration of physical conditions occur in the district—a long period of drought, a destruction of vegetation by locusts, the irruption of some new carnivorous animal seeking "pastures new"—any change in fact tending to render existence more difficult to the species in question, and tasking its utmost powers to avoid complete extermination; it is evident that, of all the individuals composing the species, those forming the least numerous and most feebly organized variety would suffer first, and, were the pressure severe, must soon become extinct. The same causes continuing in action, the parent species would next suffer, would gradually diminish in numbers, and with a recurrence of similar unfavourable conditions might also become extinct. The superior variety would then alone remain, and on a return to favourable circumstances would rapidly increase in numbers and occupy the place of the extinct species and variety.

The *variety* would now have replaced the *species*, of which it would be a more perfectly developed and more highly organized form. It would be in all respects better adapted to secure its safety, and to prolong its individual existence and that of the race. Such a variety *could not* return to the original form; for that form is an inferior one, and could never compete with it for existence. Granted, therefore, a "tendency" to reproduce the original type of the species, still the variety must ever remain preponderant in numbers, and under adverse physical conditions *again alone survive*. But this new, improved, and populous race might itself, in course of time, give rise to new varieties, exhibiting several diverging modifications of form, any of which, tending to increase the facilities for preserving existence, must, by the same general law, in their turn become predominant. Here, then, we have *progression and continued divergence* deduced from the general laws which regulate the existence of animals in a state of nature, and from the undisputed fact that varieties do frequently occur. It is not, however, contended that this result would be invariable; a change of physical conditions in the district might at times materially modify it, rendering the race which had been the most capable of supporting existence under the former conditions now the least so, and even causing the extinction of the new and, for a time, superior race, while the old parent species and its first inferior varieties continued to flourish. Variations in unimportant parts might also occur, having no perceptible effect on the life-preserving powers; and the varieties so furnished might run a course parallel with the parent species, either giving rise to further variations or returning to the former type. All we argue for is, that certain varieties have a tendency to maintain their existence longer than the original species, and this tendency must make itself felt; for though the doctrine of chances or averages can never be trusted to on a limited scale, yet if applied to high numbers, the results come nearer to what theory demands, and, as we approach to an infinity of examples, become strictly accurate. Now the scale on which nature works is so vast—the numbers of individuals and periods of time with which she deals approach so near to infinity, that any cause, however slight, and however liable to be veiled and counteracted by accidental circumstances, must in the end produce its full legitimate results.

Let us now turn to domesticated animals, and inquire how varieties produced among them are affected by the principles here enunciated. The essential difference in the condition of wild and domestic animals is this,—that among the former, their well-being and very existence depend upon the full exercise and healthy condition of all their senses and physical powers, whereas among the latter, these are only partially exercised, and in some cases are absolutely unused. A wild animal has to search, and often to labour, for every mouthful of food—to exercise sight, hearing, and smell in seeking it, and in avoiding dangers, in procuring shelter from the inclemency of the seasons, and in providing for the subsistence and safety of its offspring. There is no muscle of its body that is not called into daily and hourly activity; there is no sense or faculty that is not strengthened by continual exercise. The domestic animal, on the other hand, has food provided for it, is sheltered, and often confined, to guard it against the vicissitudes of the seasons, is carefully secured from the attacks of its natural enemies, and seldom even rears its young without human assistance. Half of its senses and faculties are quite useless; and the other half are but occasionally called into feeble exercise, while even its muscular system is only irregularly called into action.

Now when a variety of such an animal occurs, having increased power or capacity in any organ or sense, such increase is totally useless, is never called into action, and may even exist without the animal ever becoming aware of it. In the wild animal, on the contrary, all its faculties and powers being brought into full action for the necessities of existence, any increase becomes immediately available, is strengthened by exercise, and must even slightly modify the food, the habits, and the whole economy of the race. It creates as it were a new animal, one of superior powers, and which will necessarily increase in numbers and outlive those inferior to it.

Again, in the domesticated animal all varieties have an equal chance of continuance; and those which would decidedly render a wild animal unable to compete with its fellows and continue its existence are no disadvantage whatever in a state of domesticity. Our quickly fattening pigs, short-legged sheep, pouter pigeons, and poodle dogs could never have come into existence in a state of nature, because the very first steps toward such inferior forms would have led to the rapid extinction of the race; still less could they now exist in competition with their wild allies. The great speed but slight endurance of the race horse, the unwieldy strength of the ploughman's team, would both be useless in a state of nature. If turned wild on the pampas, such animals would probably soon become extinct, or under favourable circumstances might each lose those extreme qualities which would never be called into action, and in a few generations would revert to a common type, which must be that in which the various powers and faculties are so proportioned to each other as to be best adapted to procure food and secure safety,—that in which by the full exercise of every part of his organization the animal can alone continue to live. Domestic varieties, when turned wild, *must* return to something near the type of the original wild stock, *or become altogether extinct.*

We see, then, that no inferences as to varieties in a state of nature can be deduced from the observation of those occurring among domestic animals. The two are so much opposed to each other in every circumstance of their existence, that what applies to the one is almost sure not to apply to the other. Domestic animals are abnormal, irregular, artificial; they are subject to varieties which never occur and never can occur in a state of nature: their very existence depends altogether on human care; so far are many of them removed from that just proportion of faculties, that true balance of organization, by means of which alone an animal left to its own resources can preserve its existence and continue its race.

The hypothesis of Lamarck—that progressive changes in species have been produced by the attempts of animals to increase the development of their own organs, and thus modify their structure and habits—has been repeatedly and easily refuted by all writers on the subject of varieties and species, and it seems to have been considered that when this was done the whole question has been finally settled; but the view here developed renders such an hypothesis quite unnecessary, by showing

that similar results must be produced by the action of principles constantly at work in nature. The powerful retractile talons of the falcon-
and the cat-tribes have not been produced or increased by the volition
of those animals; but among the different varieties which occurred in
the earlier and less highly organized forms of these groups, *those always survived longest which had the greatest facilities for seizing their
prey*. Neither did the giraffe acquire its long neck by desiring to reach
the foliage of the more lofty shrubs, and constantly stretching its neck
for the purpose, but because any varieties which occurred among its
antitypes with a longer neck than usual *at once secured a fresh range
of pasture over the same ground as their shorter-necked companions,
and on the first scarcity of food were thereby enabled to outlive them.*
Even the peculiar colours of many animals, especially insects, so closely
resembling the soil or the leaves of the trunks on which they habitually
reside, are explained on the same principle; for though in the course of
ages varieties of many tints have occurred, *yet those races having colours best adapted to concealment from their enemies would inevitably
survive the longest.* We have also here an acting cause to account for
that balance so often observed in nature,—a deficiency in one set of
organs always being compensated by an increased development of some
others—powerful wings accompanying weak feet, or great velocity
making up for the absence of defensive weapons; for it has been shown
that all varieties in which an unbalanced deficiency occurred could not
long continue their existence. The action of this principle is exactly like
that of the centrifugal governor of the steam engine, which checks and
corrects any irregularities almost before they become evident; and in
like manner no unbalanced deficiency in the animal kingdom can ever
reach any conspicuous magnitude, because it would make itself felt at
the very first step, by rendering existence difficult and extinction almost
sure soon to follow. An origin such as is there advocated will also
agree with the peculiar character of the modifications of form and structure which obtain in organized beings—the many lines of divergence
from a central type, the increasing efficiency and power of a particular
organ through a succession of allied species, and the remarkable persistence of unimportant parts such as colour, texture or plumage and hair,
form of horns or crests, through a series of species differing considerably in more essential characters. It also furnishes us with a reason for
that "more specialized structure" which Professor Owen states to be a
characteristic of recent compared with extinct forms, and which would

evidently be the result of the progressive modification of any organ applied to a special purpose in the animal economy.

We believe we have now shown that there is a tendency in nature to the continued progression of certain classes of *varieties* further and further from the original type—a progression to which there appears no reason to assign any definite limits—and that the same principle which produces this result in a state of nature will also explain why domestic varieties have a tendency to revert to the original type. This progression, by minute steps, in various directions, but always checked and balanced by the necessary conditions, subject to which alone existence can be preserved, may, it is believed, be followed out so as to agree with all the phenomena presented by organized beings, their extinction and succession in past ages, and all the extraordinary modfiications of form, instinct, and habits which they exhibit.

Ternate, February, 1858.

CHAPTER TEN
As Told to Mr. Wallace

This chapter and the next examine the activities of Charles Darwin and two close associates of his in response to receipt of Wallace's manuscript "On the Tendency of Varieties to Depart Indefinitely from the Original Type." These activities culminated in the publication by Darwin of the *Origin of Species* in November 1859. The present chapter examines the nature of three successive sources of information received by Wallace concerning the results of these activities. All the while he was, of course, studying natural history and collecting on the other side of the earth. He did not return to England until the spring of 1862.

Wallace had watched the Dutch mail steamer depart from Ternate on March 9, 1858, with the letter enclosing his manuscript, while he was in a flurry of preparation for imminent departure on a trading schooner bound for the north coast of New Guinea. On his return to Ternate in mid-August 1858 a five-month accumulation of mail awaited him. Wallace might have had a reply from Darwin, had Darwin responded immediately. The twenty-three elapsed weeks would be about the absolute minimum for such a turnaround. Wallace knew that ten weeks was the usual transit time for a letter carried between Ternate and London by the quickest means available—"overland" and "via Marseilles." Since the mail left England every two weeks on the P & O ship carrying the India and China mails, the quickest turnaround time for a letter from Ternate to England and back was twenty-two or twenty-three weeks. But there was no answer from Darwin in that batch of accumulated mail. A letter from Darwin must have arrived by the next mail about September 21, ten weeks later, because the earliest mention of its receipt is in a letter Wallace wrote to his mother, dated October 6, 1858. "I have received letters from Mr. Darwin and Dr. Hooker, two of the most eminent naturalists in England, which has highly gratified me. I sent Mr. Darwin an essay on a subject on which he is now writing a great work. He showed it to Dr. Hooker and Sir C. Lyell, who thought so highly of it that they immediately read it before the Linnean Society. This assures me the acquaintance and assistance of these eminent men on my return home'' (Marchant 1916 1:71).

Neither Darwin's nor Hooker's letter is known to exist. Their absence is exceptional, because Wallace carefully saved all of the other Darwin letters. On an envelope containing them he had, at some unknown time, written, "The first 8 letters I received from Darwin— (while in the Malay Archipelago)'' (Marchant 1916 1:128). The first two were written in 1857 and the third extant one in January 1859. The missing letter of July 13, 1858, was actually the third.

The missing Darwin letter might explain a puzzling, undated entry in one of Wallace's field notebooks. Under the heading "Sketch of Mr. Darwin's 'Natural Selection' '' is a list (given later in this chapter) of fourteen chapters. Since the complete texts of the Darwin letters were published (see Marchant 1916; F. Darwin 1887), it is clear that none of the others conveyed that information. A letter from England that reached Ternate on September 21 must have been mailed by mid-July. Such a date for Darwin's sending the Table of Contents to Wallace is credible because Darwin's priority vis-à-vis Wallace had by then been publicly proclaimed; Darwin might be more forthcoming with information than he had been in the previous two letters. In the first, after he had read Wallace's 1855 paper, he had said, "This summer will make the twentieth year (!) since I opened my first note-book on the question how and in what way do species and varieties differ from each other. I am now preparing my work for publication, but I find the subject so very large, that though I have many chapters, I do not suppose I shall go to press for two years. . . .'' (Marchant 1916 1:129–130). Eight months later, in December 1857: "My work, on which I have now been at work more or less for twenty years, will *not* fix or settle anything; but I hope it will aid by giving a large collection of facts with one definite end. . . . I have got about half written; but I do not suppose I shall publish under a couple of years. I have now been three whole months on one chapter on hybridism! . . ." (Marchant 1916 1:133). Since the letter of January 1859 mentions the "Abstract" on which Darwin was by then working, I think it can be tentatively concluded that Darwin had provided the Table of Contents of his "Natural Selection" manuscript in his mid-July 1858 letter.

The second source of information came with the next arrival of mail from England. Wallace learned then the details of events at the Linnean Society—from a copy of the *Journal* itself. In his autobiography Wallace quoted a letter to George Silk, his oldest friend, written from the island of Batchian late in November 1858, "You cannot, perhaps, imagine how I have come to love solitude. I seldom have a visitor but I wish him away in an hour. I find it very favourable to reflection; and if you have any acquaintance who is a fellow of the Linnean Society, borrow the *Journal of Proceedings* for August last, and in the last article you will find some of my latest lucubrations, and also some complimentary remarks thereon by Sir Charles Lyell and Dr. Hooker, which (as I know neither of them) I am a *little* proud of. . . ." (Wallace 1905 1:366).

The mail steamer did not touch at Batchian itself, but government boats traveled with some regularity back and forth to Ternate, a regular mail port, about a hundred miles to the north. With regard to the Silk letter Wallace noted that he had written it in anticipation of the departure of a "Government boat" for Ternate. A month earlier (October 29), in a letter from Batchian, Wallace had written to his agent, Stevens, "As there is now a boat going which may just catch the mail at Ternate. . . ." (Wallace 1859:6546). If the Dutch mail steamer was on its established schedule, it should have arrived at Ternate about the first of November, forty days after the preceding call, which we have concluded must have been about September 21. The mail would have included letters from England for the first half of August. Apparently it did, because Wallace noted in the Silk letter that "I have just received yours of August 3. . . ."

One can only wonder whether Wallace, despite his expressions of pride and pleasure, had been prepared by Hooker's letter for the title and order of presentation of the "joint" contribution. Wallace had mailed to Darwin a manuscript with the title "On the Tendency of

Varieties to Depart Indefinitely from the Original Type.'' The title he read from the page of the *Journal of Proceedings* was ''On the Tendency of Species to Form Varieties; and on the Perpetuation of Varieties and Species by Natural Selection. By Charles Darwin, Esq. F.R.S., F.L.S., & F.G.S., and Alfred Wallace, Esq. Communicated by Sir Charles Lyell, F.R.S., F.L.S. and J. D. Hooker, M.D., V.P.R.S., F.L.S. &c.''

This title had quite a different message from that of his own contribution. He had presented a concept of how a variety could become a new species through the action of natural selection. The printed title spoke to the formation of varieties from species, and to the perpetuation of these varieties and species by natural selection. A drastic shift in emphasis! The body of this contribution comprised four elements: an introductory letter, signed by Lyell and Hooker and read by J. J. Bennett, Secretary of the Linnean Society; an extract from an unpublished work on species by Darwin; an abstract of a letter from Darwin to ''Prof. Asa Gray, Boston, U.S.,'' dated September 5, 1857; and last, Wallace's essay. It can probably be said that most scientists feel strongly that a complete manuscript, prepared for publication, should receive prior place. Certainly Lyell and Hooker's letter and Darwin's manuscript excerpts should, at best, have been appended. Even adding fragments from Darwin's papers—fragments which he had never intended for publication—would have been a quite exceptional action; to have assigned priority to his manuscript excerpts was an action difficult to justify.

The introductory letter by Lyell and Hooker notes, ''Two indefatigable naturalists, Mr. Charles Darwin and Mr. Alfred Wallace, . . . having, independently and unknown to one another, conceived the same very ingenious theory to account for the appearance and perpetuation of varieties and of specific forms on our planet, may both fairly claim the merit of being original thinkers in this important line of inquiry. . . .'' The remainder of that paragraph might well have puzzled Wallace. For Lyell to have written, ''neither of them having published his views'' was contrary to what Wallace knew was a fact. Lyell was acquainted with his 1855 essay. Darwin had written so in his second letter to Wallace. Darwin, of course, had indeed never published his views.

While that departure from the truth was likely deliberate, justifying their action in publishing bits from Darwin's private papers, the erroneous dating of one of those items might well have been unwitting on the part of Lyell and Hooker.

Lyell and Hooker listed the parts of the "joint" Wallace-Darwin contribution by their dates of composition, using these to justify the order of presentation without consideration of other aspects of the documents that might reasonably have been taken into account.

> 1. Extracts from a MS. work on Species, by Mr. Darwin, which was sketched in 1839, and copied in 1844, when the copy was read by Dr. Hooker, and its contents afterwards communicated to Sir Charles Lyell. The first part is devoted to "The Variation of Organic Beings under Domestication and in their Natural State;" and the second chapter of that Part, from which we propose to read to the Society the extracts referred to, is headed, "On the variation of Organic Beings in a state of Nature; on the Natural Means of Selection; on the Comparison of Domestic Races and true Species."
>
> 2. An abstract of a private letter to Professor Asa Gray, of Boston, U.S., in October 1857, by Mr. Darwin, in which he reports his views, and which shows that these remained unaltered from 1839 to 1857.
>
> 3. An Essay by Mr. Wallace, entitled "On the Tendency of Varieties to depart indefinitely from the Original Type." This was written at Ternate in February, 1858, for the perusal of his friend and correspondent Mr. Darwin, and sent with the express wish that it should be forwarded to Sir Charles Lyell, if Mr. Darwin thought it sufficiently novel and interesting. . . .

The first Darwin manuscript document occupies four pages, in comparison to Wallace's ten. Darwin's exposition begins with a reference to "the doctrine of Malthus," stating that it applies to animals, most of which have a greater potential for increasing their numbers than does "slow-breeding mankind." Thus every species tends to produce far more offspring than can find adequate food or other vital necessities. Many of each generation must therefore perish. It is evident, then, that there is an incessant struggle to survive, a struggle with other individuals of either the same or different species.

But should the "external condition of a country alter," in an isolated population "the original inhabitants must cease to be as perfectly adapted to the changed conditions as they were originally."

Darwin postulated that the change in external conditions would act on the reproductive system and would "probably cause the organization to become, as under domestication, plastic." Any variation, even a minute one, adapting that individual better to the new conditions would tell upon its vigor and health. "In the struggle it would have a better *chance* of surviving; and those of its offspring which inherited the variation, be it ever so slight, would also have a better *chance*." Urging the reader to recall the changes that man's selection has achieved in domesticated animals, Darwin asks, if selection and death "go on for a thousand generations, who would pretend to affirm that it would produce no effect . . . by this identical principle of selection?"

Darwin's extract concludes with a paragraph on sexual selection: "The struggle of males for females. . . . The most vigorous and healthy males, implying perfect adaptation, must generally gain the victory in their contests. This kind of selection, however, is less rigorous than the other; it does not require the death of the less successful, but gives to them few descendants."

This concluding paragraph revealed an idea new to Wallace. It must, however, have been a conclusion quite different from the one he expected from the foregoing argument. Darwin had outlined a concept of natural selection promoting the differential survival of better-adapted *individuals*. But he adduced only the formation of natural varieties as the result of this selection. There was no mention of how this might lead to the origin of new species.

The second Darwin manuscript document, nearly three printed pages in length, was copied from a letter of September 1857 to Asa Gray. At its conclusion Darwin said, "This sketch is *most* imperfect. . . . Your imagination must fill up very wide blanks," implying that it covered his entire concept. In the first of six numbered paragraphs, he begins his argument with the changes in the nature of domesticated animals that animal breeders have achieved in even so short a time as half a century. This selection acts by "slight or greater variations," and by this means man "adapts living beings to his wants. . . ."

The second paragraph asks what a "being" might not be able to achieve in millions of generations if he selected natural variations for one object alone. As any geologist knows, "We have almost unlimited time."

The third paragraph, answering this query, corresponds to the first half of the preceding extract from the Darwin manuscript. "I think it can be shown that there is such an unerring power at work in *Natural Selection* (the title of my book), which selects exclusively for the good of each organic being." He again refers to De Candolle but this time includes Lyell as well, for their excellent writings about the struggle for existence. This, together with the fourth paragraph, rehearses the argument of the extract. But in the 1857 letter the argument is carried further. In the earlier version the argument for natural selection, by analogy with human selection, concluded, "I can see no more reason to doubt that these causes [natural selection] in a thousand generations would produce a marked effect, and adapt the form of the fox or dog to the catching of hares instead of rabbits than that greyhounds can be improved by selection and careful breeding." The 1857 argument, less tentative throughout about the existence of natural selection, goes a step further, concluding: "The variety thus formed will either co-exist with, or, more commonly, will exterminate its parent form."

The short paragraph that follows merely states that "multiform difficulties will occur to every one, with respect to this theory" but that Darwin believes that many can be satisfactorily answered. But the concluding paragraph is quite without counterpart in the earlier extract. It begins, "Another principle, which may be called the principle of divergence, plays, I believe, an important part in the origin of species." Note that this is the first use of this term in these Darwin manuscript documents. Darwin then presents an argument to account for the final step in his argument of paragraph four, namely the extermination of the "less well-fitted parent by the new variety or species." But the logic is flawed. The initial assertion is that "the same spot will support more life if occupied by very diverse forms." Then he states, "The offspring of any species after it has become diversified into varieties, or subspecies, or true species" is, like every living being, "striving its utmost to increase in numbers." Then comes the biologically dubious "And it follows, I think, from the foregoing facts, that the varying offspring of each species will try (only a few will succeed) to seize on as many and as diverse places in the economy of nature as possible.'' Wallace, who had closely observed varieties of many species of birds and insects, would have been in a position to question this postulate. Certainly the members of most varieties, while they may differ slightly in color, pattern, or size, usually occupy quite similar ''places in the economy of nature,'' not diverse ones. And it is hardly a cogent explanation for extermination of ''the less well-fitted parent.'' The leap to the following sentence must cross one of the ''very wide blanks'' to which Darwin alluded, for he continues: ''This I believe to be the origin of the classification and affinities of organic beings at all times; for organic beings always *seem* to branch and sub-branch like the limbs of a tree from a common trunk, the flourishing and diverging twigs destroying the less vigorous—the dead and lost branches rudely representing extinct genera and families.''

This concluding statement must have seemed oddly familiar to Wallace. He had used the tree simile in his 1855 essay, published two years to the month before the Asa Gray letter. The reader is referred to chapter 5 of this book for a quotation in which Wallace used a tree as a model for understanding the ''origin of the classification and affinities of living beings at all times.''

Reading his own essay, Wallace could not have avoided being struck by some other surprising similarities and some distinct differences between the theory he proposed and that revealed in Darwin's manuscripts.

Wallace, as we have shown in a preceding chapter, had introduced his argument by stating his belief that varieties produced in a state of domestication are quite different from those occurring in a state of nature, because domesticated varieties if left to themselves have a tendency to revert to the ''normal form of the parent species.'' In the absence of a knowledge of varieties in wild animals, naturalists had concluded by analogy that varieties in a state of nature also revert. Wallace firmly rejected the validity of this analogy. Darwin, like other naturalists, had begun with a consideration of domestic animals and an analogy to the state of nature. But Darwin analogized the known results of human selection in domesticated forms to possible results of a more potent selective force acting in nature.

Wallace began the next step of his argument with the statement, "The life of wild animals is a struggle for existence." All must exert their faculties and energies to the fullest to preserve their own existence and that of dependent offspring. Depending on the degree of a species' success, its members will be more or less numerous. "The general proportion that must obtain between certain groups of animals is readily seen. Large animals cannot be so abundant as small ones; the carnivora must be less numerous than the herbivora. . . ." Yet despite fecundities that would enable each species to expand its numbers greatly, "it is evident that the animal population of the globe must be stationary, or perhaps, through the influence of man, decreasing," although fluctuations are everywhere evident. After a simple calculation based on bird fecundity, Wallace concluded, "It is evident, therefore, that each year an immense number of birds must perish—as many in fact as are born," if the population is to remain stationary.

In the next reasoned step, Wallace stated, "The numbers that die annually must be immense; and as the individual existence of each animal depends upon itself, those that die must be the weakest—the very young, the aged, and the diseased,—while those that prolong their existence can only be the most perfect in health and vigour— those who are best able to obtain food regularly, and avoid their numerous enemies. It is, as we commenced by remarking, 'a struggle for existence,' in which the weakest and least perfectly organized must always succumb."

To this point the arguments of Darwin and Wallace are remarkably similar, but Wallace's next logical steps lack clear counterparts in Darwin's earlier (1844) formulation and in the abbreviated, but quite different, concept expressed in his 1857 letter to Asa Gray.

Wallace stated next, "Now it is clear that what takes place among the individuals of a species must also occur among the several allied species of a group,—viz. that those which are best adapted to obtain a regular supply of food, and to defend themselves against the attacks of their enemies and the vicissitudes of the seasons, must necessarily obtain and preserve a superiority in population. . . ." Conversely, those suffering a defect of power or organization are least able to cope with the vicissitudes of life and "must diminish . . . and, in extreme cases, become altogether extinct.'' Species with capacities between these extremes will be proportionately abundant.

These considerations, Wallace concludes, also apply to varieties as well as to individuals and species.

''Most or perhaps all the variations from the typical form of a species must have some definite effect, however slight, on the habits or capacities of the individuals. Even a change of colour might, by rendering them more or less distinguishable, affect their safety. . . . It is also evident that most changes would affect, either favourably or adversely, the powers of prolonging existence. . . . If . . . any species should produce a variety having slightly increased powers of preserving existence, that variety must inevitably in time acquire a superiority in numbers,'' and the converse. In general, then, ''All varieties will therefore fall into two classes—those which under the same conditions would never reach the population of the parent species, and those which would in time obtain and keep a numerical superiority. Now, let some alteration of physical conditions occur in the district . . . any change [sufficiently severe to render existence precarious, and] . . . it is evident that, of all the individuals composing the species, those forming the least numerous and most feebly organized variety would suffer first, and, were the pressure severe, must soon become extinct.'' Should this extreme environmental stress continue, the individuals of the parent species would also die, thus diminishing that typical, ''species'' population to the point of extinction. ''The superior variety would then alone remain, and on a return to favourable conditions would rapidly increase in numbers and occupy the place of the extinct species and variety.''

Darwin's 1844 statement falls far short of an indication of how new species arise. Even about the formation of varieties in a state of nature he said only, ''Who will pretend to affirm that it [natural selection] would produce no effect . . . ?'' Wallace must have wondered why Darwin did not carry his argument further, if, as Lyell and Hooker had assessed it, both Darwin and Wallace had independently ''conceived the same very ingenious theory to account for the appearance and perpetuation of varieties and of specific forms on our planet. . . .'' Could it be that Darwin's concept in 1844 had not extended to explaining the origin of new species? Certainly the last part of the title of the second chapter ("on the Comparison of Domestic Races and true Species") suggests that the omitted remainder of the chapter of the 1844 manuscript did not advance toward an account of the formation of "true Species."

It might well have been further perplexing for Wallace to read that Lyell and Hooker had included Darwin's 1857 letter to Asa Gray to demonstrate that Darwin's views had "remained unaltered from 1839 to 1857," because the Gray letter was quite definite about the role of natural selection in the formation of varieties, and even suggested in two separate sentences (one in paragraph 4, one in paragraph 6) a mechanism by which a variety might become a species. The first stated, "The variety thus formed ["by the accumulative action of natural selection"] will either coexist with, or, more commonly, will exterminate its parent form." But this mechanism for the replacement of a parental species by a superior variety, postulated by Darwin in 1857, was entirely different from that propounded in Wallace's essay. Darwin's mechanism was biological competition carried to its extreme result—the elimination of the parental population, that is, the original species. Wallace, on the other hand, envisioned differential survival of varietal and the parental or "species" populations at a time of general extreme environmental stress. There was no direct competition between varietal and parental populations; if the parental "species" population became extinct, then, when environmental conditions were more favorable, the surviving (superior) variety would spread and occupy not only the place of the "species" population but also those of any less well-adapted varieties that had also perished.

The sentence in paragraph 6 of the letter to Gray makes Darwin's idea even clearer: "Each new variety or species, when formed will generally take the place of, and thus exterminate its less well-fitted parent." The difference between the concepts of the two "indefatigable naturalists" is clear: Wallace postulated that the superior variety expanded to occupy the place of the parental species after that population had succumbed to some environmental stress. Darwin postulated direct biological competition between the superior variety and the parental "species" population, ending in the elimination of the parental or "species" population.

A third noteworthy aspect of Darwin's exposition in the Gray letter was the concept he referred to as the "principle of divergence." Any theory of organic change must account for divergence in the history of life on earth. The term, in the usage of 1839, meant "continuous deviation from a standard or norm," and the fossil record as it was being revealed at that time made evident the divergence of the later representatives from the forms of the earlier ones in group after group of organisms. Another aspect of the history of life generally accepted by the middle of the last century was that many forms of life show a progression from a lower to a higher state of organization through geological time. Wallace's theory had provided a mechanism to account for both phenomena. The reader will recall that as the last stage of his theory Wallace reasoned, "The *variety* would now have replaced the *species*, of which it would be a more perfectly developed and more highly organized form. . . . But this new, improved, and populous race might itself, in course of time, give rise to new varieties, exhibiting several diverging modifications of form, any of which, tending to increase the facilities for preserving existence, must, by the same general law, in their turn become predominant. Here, then, we have *progression and continued divergence* deduced from the general laws which regulate the existence of animals in a state of nature, and from the undisputed fact that varieties do frequently occur."

Darwin's "principle of divergence," however, provides no explanation for "continuous deviation." Rather, it makes a statement about the composition of natural communities—"The same spot will support more life if occupied by very diverse forms"—and then concludes, "And it follows, I think, from the foregoing facts, that the varying offspring of each species will try (only a few will succeed) to seize on as many and as diverse places in the economy of nature as possible." This conjectured result would be quite contrary to Wallace's conclusion after a decade of experience in studying the attributes of natural varieties of thousands of insects and birds. While varieties usually occur in localities distinct from the "species," the differences he had observed were all slight, and both varieties and the typical species occupied the same "place in the economy of nature," not different ones. Darwin's conjecture could only have been seen by Wallace as the speculation of one who knew little of variation as it occurs in nature.

In view of these differences between Darwin's theory, as revealed in selected manuscripts, and his own, Wallace might well have wondered whether Lyell and Hooker understood what each man's theory stated. If they had, they surely would not have said that the theories of Wallace and Darwin were the same.

Most people would express more of a mixed emotional response to being presented with evidence that two of England's most eminent naturalists were convinced that you had been one of two people to discover "the same ingenious theory" but had been anticipated by fifteen years. Surely the initial reaction for most would be chagrin, frustration, anger, and despair, particularly after toiling essentially alone for ten years in the rain forests on two sides of the earth gathering evidence to test and develop an idea. If Wallace had any such emotions, there is no record of them. Wallace was a reticent man. It is possible, however, although I suggest this with diffidence, that an unusual response to collecting a most beautiful male bird-wing butterfly (*Ornithoptera*) a month later might, and I emphasize "might," have had some of that emotion attached to it:

> During my very first walk into the forest at Batchian, I had seen sitting on a leaf out of reach, an immense butterfly of a dark colour marked with white and yellow spots. I could not capture it as it flew away high up into the forest, but I at once saw that it was a female of a new species of Ornithoptera or "bird-winged butterfly," the pride of the Eastern tropics. I was very anxious to get it and to find the male, which in this genus is always of extreme beauty. . . . I had begun to despair of ever getting a specimen, as it seemed so rare and wild; till one day, about the beginning of January, I found a beautiful shrub with large white leafy bracts and yellow flowers, a species of Mussaenda, and saw one of these noble insects hovering over it, but it was too quick for me, and flew away. The next day I went again to the same shrub and succeeded in catching a female, and the day after a fine male. I found it to be as I had expected, a perfectly new and most magnificent species, and one of the most gorgeously coloured butterflies in the world. Fine specimens of the male are more than seven inches across the wings, which are velvety black and fiery orange, the latter colour replacing the green of the allied species. The beauty and brilliancy of this insect are indescribable, and none but a naturalist can understand the intense excitement I experienced when I at length captured it. On taking it out of

my net and opening the glorious wings, my heart began to beat vio-
lently, the blood rushed to my head, and I felt much more like fainting
than I have done when in apprehension of immediate death. I had a
headache the rest of the day, so great was the excitement produced by
what will appear to most people a very inadequate cause.
(Wallace 1869:257–58)

Compare this with the reaction Wallace had recorded following his
first capture of a male bird-wing. He had said that soon after arriving
in Aru, "I had the good fortune to capture one of the most magnificent insects the world contains, the great bird-wing butterfly, Ornithoptera poseidon. I trembled with excitement as I saw it coming
majestically toward me and could hardly believe I had really succeeded in my stroke till I had taken it out of the net and was gazing,
lost in admiration. . . . The village of Dobbo held that evening at
least one contented man." (Wallace 1869:378–89).

At the end of January or early in February of 1860, just a year
after his first capture of the male *Ornithoptera croesus,* the third and
final communication arrived from London—his copy of Charles Darwin's *On the Origin of Species by Means of Natural Selection; or,
the Preservation of Favoured Races in the Struggle for Life.* The
Origin had been published on November 24, 1859. Murray, the publisher, must have mailed Mr. Wallace's copy promptly. The quickest
mail from London, as noted, would reach Amboina in about nine
weeks, since at that time of year the Dutch mail steamer from Batavia
(Djakarta) visited Amboina just before its call at Ternate. The earliest
it could possibly have arrived was about sixty-three days after November 24, or January 26, 1860. Darwin acknowledged receipt of a
letter from Wallace "dated February 16, 1860, Amboina, . . . containing some remarks and your too high approbation of my book
. . ." (Marchant 1916 1:141). Whenever it actually arrived, further
details in Darwin's reply make it clear that Wallace had read the
entire book by February 16.

Wallace had been given notice of Darwin's progress in the preparation of his book in the letters Darwin had sent, as indicated above.
The reader will recall that Darwin's letter of July 13, 1858, is missing but that it was the most likely vehicle for notice of the title and

table of contents of Darwin's "Natural Selection" manuscript. The next extant Darwin letter (January 25, 1859) provided information from which Wallace might have inferred that the manuscript of the book in its final form (the "abstract") was begun about the time that Darwin wrote the July 13, 1858, letter: ". . . I owe indirectly much to you and them; for I almost think that Lyell would have proved right and I should never have completed my larger work; for I have found my abstract hard enough with my poor health; but now, thank God, I am in my last chapter but one. My abstract will make a small volume of 400 or 500 pages. . . ." Darwin's pace of writing had certainly accelerated. He had nearly completed the "abstract" in six or seven months, while the antecedent "larger work," never completed, had occupied nearly twenty years, according to Darwin's letters.

Darwin had written two letters while at work on his "abstract" that apprised Wallace of what he would, or would not, find as notice of his contributions. The comments in the first letter concern Wallace's "law" paper (1855c), to which Darwin referred as "your paper on Distribution," and Wallace's essay in their joint Linnean Society contribution. The second letter related to a second Wallace manuscript ("memoir"), "On the Zoological Geography of the Malay Archipelago" (1860), receipt of which was noted, along with several comments it evoked.

Down, Bromley, Kent

April 6, 1859

My dear Mr. Wallace—I this morning received your pleasant and friendly note of Nov. 3rd [with Wallace's comments on their joint paper in the Proceedings of the Linnean Society]. The first part of my MS is in Murray's hands. . . . There is no Preface, but a short Introduction, which must be read by everyone who reads my book. The second paragraph in the Introduction I have had copied *verbatim* from my foul copy, and you will, I hope, think that I have fairly noticed your papers in the *Linnean Transactions*. You must remember that I am now publishing only an Abstract, and I give no references. I shall of course allude to your paper on Distribution; and I have added that I know from correspondence that your explanation of your law is the same as that which I offer.

(Marchant 1916 1:136–37)

Down, Bromley, Kent

August 9, 1859

Mr Dear Mr. Wallace,—I received your letter and memoir on the 7th, and will forward it to-morrow to the Linnean Society. . . . Had I read it some months ago I should have profitted by it for my forthcoming volume. But my two chapters on this subject are in type; and though not yet corrected, I am so wearied out and weak in health that I am fully resolved not to add one word, and merely improve style. So you will see that my views are nearly the same with yours, and you may rely on it that not one word shall be altered owing to my having read your ideas. Are you aware that Mr. W. Earl published several years ago the view of distribution of animals in the Malay Archipelago in relation to the depth of the sea between the islands? I was much struck with this, and have been in the habit of noting all facts on distribution in the Archipelago and elsewhere in this relation. . . .   (Marchant 1916 1:137–38)

This could hardly have been read by Wallace without consternation. Had he been anticipated by Darwin again? Had Darwin been able to piece together from the literature a view of distribution in the Archipelago similar in detail to the one he had arrived at from his own observations in travels through the eastern islands? If he had not, then what did he mean, after saying their views were "nearly the same," by continuing, "and you may rely on it that not one word shall be altered owing to my having read your ideas"?

When the book was finally in Wallace's hands, in early 1860, he must first have observed that the title was different from the one Darwin had given him earlier. "Natural Selection"—also stated as the title in the Asa Gray letter—had become *On the Origin of Species by Means of Natural Selection; or, the Preservation of Favoured Races in the Struggle for Life.* The chapters, too, were different. The table of contents earlier provided to Wallace (see ch. 4) read:

Sketch of Mr. Darwin's "Natural Selection"

Chap. I.   On variation of animals and plants under domestication, treated generally

"   II.   do. do. treated specifically, external and internal structure of Pigeons   history of changes in them

"   III.   On intercrossing, principally founded on original observations on plants

"   IV.   Varieties under Nature

"   v.   Struggle for existence, malthusian doctrine, rate of in-
           crease,—checks to increase etc.

"   vi.   "Natural Selection" manner of its working

"   vii.   Laws of Variation, Use and Disuse reversion to ancestral
           type etc. etc.

"   viii. Difficulties in theory. Gradation of characters

"   ix.   Hybridity

"   x.   Instinct

"   xi.   Paleontology and geology

      xii.

and xiii. Geog. distribution

"   xiv.   Classification, Affinities, Embryology

Fourteen chapters had also been listed, but with differences: the first three of the original book, all on aspects of plants and animals under domestication, had been compressed to one, while two had been added near the end—a second on geology, and a final recapitulation and conclusion.

The list of chapters was as follows:

  i.   Variation under domestication
  ii.   Variation under Nature
 iii.   Struggle for Existence
  iv.   Natural Selection
  v.   Laws of Variation
  vi.   Difficulties on Theory
 vii.   Instinct
viii.   Hybridism
  ix.   On the Imperfection of the Geological Record
  x.   On the Geological Succession of Organic Beings
  xi.   Geographic Distribution
 xii.   Geographic Distribution—con't.
xiii.   Mutual Affinities of Organic Beings; Morphology; Embryology:
       Rudimentary Organs
xiv.   Recapitulation and Conclusion

The introduction, to which Wallace's attention had been directed by Darwin, stated in the first two paragraphs:

On my return home [from the *Beagle* voyage] it occurred to me, in 1837, that something might perhaps be made out on this question by patiently accumulating and reflecting on all sorts of facts which could possibly have any bearing on it. After five years' work I allowed myself to speculate on the subject, and drew up some short notes; these I enlarged in 1844 into a sketch of the conclusions, which then seemed to me probable: from that period to the present day I have steadily pursued the same object. I hope that I may be excused for entering on these personal details, as I give them to show that I have not been hasty in coming to a decision.

My work is now nearly finished; but as it will take me two or three more years to complete it, and as my health is far from strong, I have been urged to publish this Abstract. I have more especially been induced to do this, as Mr. Wallace, who is now studying the natural history of the Malay archipelago, has arrived at almost exactly the same general conclusions that I have on the origin of species. Last year he sent to me a memoir on this subject, with a request that I would forward it to Sir Charles Lyell, who sent it to the Linnean Society, and it is published in the third volume of the Journal of that Society. Sir C. Lyell and Dr. Hooker, who both knew of my work—the latter having read my sketch of 1844—honoured me by thinking it advisable to publish, with Mr. Wallace's excellent memoir, some brief extracts from my manuscripts.   (Darwin 1859:1–2)

Most interesting to Wallace would have been the indication, in the first paragraph, that Darwin had written the sketch of his ideas in 1844, not five years earlier. Hooker and Lyell had stated in their letter introducing the joint Darwin-Wallace paper that the Darwin "extract" "was sketched in 1839, and copied . . . in 1844. . . ." Now Darwin said that he had drawn up "some short notes" in 1842 (i.e., five years after a 1837 beginning) and "these I enlarged in 1844 into a sketch of the conclusions, which then seemed to me probable. . . ." If indeed Darwin had first formulated his ideas on the subject of the origin of species in 1844, this was only about two years before Wallace himself first formulated his own initial hypothesis of the conditions for the origination of new species.

Whether or not Wallace felt that his ideas in "On the Tendency of Varieties to Depart Indefinitely from the Original Type" had been "fairly noticed," as Darwin hoped, he would have soon found that it was the only mention of that paper anywhere in the book. So much for "joint" contributions!

His paper of four years earlier, "On the Law Which Has Regulated the Introduction of New Species,'' received a similar passing reference, the nature of which Darwin had already imparted in his letter of April 6, 1859. This reference, however, is not in Darwin's introduction; it falls on page 355 in chapter XI, the first of two on ''Geographical Distribution.'' A pertinent paragraph presents the fact that the inhabitants of volcanic islands are similar to, but somewhat modified from, stocks on the neighboring continent. Such facts, Darwin concludes, ''are inexplicable on the theory of independent creation'' but are in accordance with ''my theory'':

> This view of the relation of species in one region to those in another, does not differ much (by substituting the word variety for species) from that lately advanced in an ingenious paper by Mr. Wallace, in which he concludes, that ''every species has come into existence coincident both in space and time with a pre-existing closely allied species.'' And I now know from correspondence, that this coincidence he attributes to generation with modification.   (p. 355)

The third and last citation of ''Wallace'' in the index of the *Origin* is in reference to page 395, and Wallace must have turned to it with anxious curiosity over what Darwin actually had said about distribution in the Malay Archipelago. This was the passage that must have elicited Darwin's disavowal of any use of Wallace's ideas. The topic under discussion, beginning on page 393 (in the second chapter on ''Geographical Distribution''), was the distribution of mammals on oceanic islands. The final paragraph on mammals reads as follows:

> Besides the absence of terrestrial mammals in relation to the remoteness of islands from continents, there is also a relation, to a certain extent independent of distance, between the depth of the sea separating an island from the neighbouring mainland, and the presence in both of the same mammiferous species or of allied species in a more or less modified condition. Mr. Windsor Earl has made some striking observations on this head in regard to the great Malay Archipelago, which is traversed near Celebes by a space of deep ocean; and this space separates two widely distinct mammalian faunas. On either side the islands are situated on moderately deep submarine banks, and they are inhabited by closely allied or identical quadrupeds. No doubt some few anomalies occur in this great archipelago, and there is much difficulty in forming a judgment in some cases owing to the probable naturalisation of certain mammals through man's agency; but

we shall soon have much light thrown on the natural history of this archipelago by the admirable zeal and researches of Mr. Wallace. I have not as
yet had time to follow up this subject in all other quarters of the world;
but as far as I have gone, the relation generally holds good.   (p. 395)

Any concern Wallace had over possible anticipation of his detailed
conclusions on patterns of geographical distribution would have evap-
orated. Darwin had not even specified the nature of the mammalian
fauna on either side of this "space of deep ocean." Not only had
Wallace himself detailed the distribution of the marsupials peculiar to
the Australian region, but he had compared their distributions with
all other mammals of that part of the world. He had included examination of the differences in the patterns for different major kinds of
organisms—plants and insects, birds and mammals. In place of his
anxiety, there must have been growing puzzlement. Why Darwin's
disclaimer "that not one word shall be altered owing to my having
read your ideas," when Darwin's published words bore no relation
to Wallace's detailed analysis of distribution in the Archipelago and
its possible origins?

Quite probably the first chapter Wallace would have opened to
would have been the fourth, "Natural Selection." The first thirty
pages of this fifty-page chapter embellish and provide examples for
the ideas of the origin and consequences of natural selection as they
are stated in the four pages of Darwin's extract from his 1844 manuscript, published in the "joint" paper. The conclusion of this part
of the *Origin*'s chapter IV is headed "Illustrations of the Action of
Natural Selection" (pp. 90–95). Darwin here uses as an example a
population of wolves that prey on various animals, including deer.
The reader will recall that in the extract from the 1844 manuscript,
Darwin had used a "canine" animal that preys on rabbits, or sometimes swifter hares. In the *Origin* Darwin supposes that deer, the
"fleetest prey," become more numerous at a time when the other
prey become less numerous. Then, surely the "swiftest and slimmest
wolves would have the best chance of surviving, and so be preserved
or selected. . . ." Darwin then analogized this result of natural selection with the result of man's selection of greyhounds for fleetness.
This is followed by a more complex supposition involving nectar for-

mation and its role in the pollination of plants by bees. He concludes this section with much the same thought expressed in the Extract: "Slow though the process of selection may be, if feeble man can do much by his powers of artificial selection, I can see no limit to the amount of change, to the beauty and infinite complexity of the co-adaptations between all organic beings, one with another and with their physical conditions of life, which may be effected in the long course of time by nature's power of selection."

The final twenty pages of the chapter are devoted to what Darwin called the "principle of divergence" and bear the heading "Divergence of Character." Such a "principle" was not mentioned in the extract from the 1844 essay but was included in the 1857 letter to Gray, where discussion of his "principle of divergence" had been Darwin's final subject. Wallace was probably quite interested to learn how Darwin would expand this paragraph-long mention.

The twenty-page expansion in the *Origin of Species* begins with the statement that, according to his view, "varieties are species in the process of formation, or are, as I have called them, incipient species" (p. 111). With recourse first to domesticated animals, Darwin supposes that early in history man had selected some horses for swiftness, others for bulk and strength. As man's selection continued in these divergent directions,

> the inferior animals with intermediate characters, being neither very swift nor very strong, will have been neglected, and will have tended to disappear. Here, then, we see in man's productions the action of what may be called the principle of divergence, causing differences at first barely appreciable, steadily to increase, and the breeds to diverge in character both from each other and from their common parent.
>
> But how, it may be asked, can any analogous principle apply in nature? I believe it can and does apply most efficiently, from the simple circumstance that the more diversified the descendants from any one species become in structure, constitution, and habits, by so much will they be better enabled to seize on many and widely diversified places in the polity of nature, and so be enabled to increase in numbers. . . . (p. 112)

Darwin, in the following three pages, suggests how this might apply to animals and then to plants. Take the case, he says, of a carnivorous quadruped:

> If its natural powers of increase be allowed to act, it can succeed in increasing (the country not undergoing any change in its conditions) only by its varying descendants seizing on places at present occupied by other animals: some of them, for instance, being enabled to feed on new kinds of prey, either dead or alive; some inhabiting new stations, climbing trees, frequenting water, and some perhaps becoming less carnivorous. The more diversified in habits and structure the descendants of our carnivorous animals become, the more places they would be enabled to occupy. . . .
> (p. 113)

This was similar to the statement of his "principle of divergence" presented in the Gray letter. Wallace, who had collected and attempted to classify myriad varietal populations of birds and insects in their natural situations, would probably have questioned Darwin's assumptions even more on the basis of this fuller account. For Darwin was assuming that what might happen to the descendants of a species after countless generations would happen to naturally occuring varieties. Varieties are never that different from each other, or from the original species, as Darwin himself notes at the beginning of the section on divergence. Varieties and their original species all occupy essentially the same role in the "polity of nature," not widely diversified roles. Darwin makes it quite clear that the diversification he is discussing applies to an organic stock as it changes over eons of time. "In the Australian mammals, we see the process of diversification in an early and incomplete stage of development (p. 116)." But his conclusion that they represent an "early and incomplete stage" could have been reached only by comparing their diversification with that of mammals in the rest of the world, the clear result of millions of years of divergence. The inappropriateness of evoking such phenomena to explain the differential survival of relatively insignificant varietal differences would probably have been more evident to Wallace than to any other person then alive.

At this point Darwin introduces a diagram, the only one in the book, to aid the reader to understand "how this great principle of great benefit being derived from divergence of character, combined with the principles of natural selection and extinction, will tend to act" (p. 116)." The following ten pages of the *Origin* describe what might happen to the species "of a genus large in its own country."

These species are represented in the diagram by an array, (A) to (L), across the bottom of the page. From (A) and (I) small lines fan upward. These represent the diverging varieties of the two species. From each of the other species, (B) through (H), (K), and (L), a single line proceeds upward. Twelve equidistant horizontal lines each represent one thousand generations. Not all of the divergent varieties arising from (A) and (I) persist for one thousand generations; two from (A) persist and only one from (I). Darwin repeats this device for each thousand generations to illustrate various patterns of survival among the varieties of (A) and (I).

> After ten thousand generations, species (A) is supposed to have produced three forms, a^{10}, f^{10}, and m^{10}, which, from having diverged in character during the successive generations, will have come to differ largely, but perhaps unequally, from each other and from their common parent. If we suppose the amount of change between each horizontal line in our diagram to be excessively small, these three forms may still be only well-marked varieties; or they may have arrived at the doubtful category of sub-species; but we have only to suppose the steps in the process of modification to be more numerous or greater in amount, to convert these three forms into well-defined species: thus the diagram illustrates the steps by which the small differences distinguishing varieties are increased into the larger differences distinguishing species. (p. 120)

The diagram also shows two "forms" derived from the initial species (I) after ten thousand generations. (F) is the only one of the other species represented at the ten thousandth generation, and that by a single "form."

Thus it is clear that in Darwin's mind the same processes led to the formation of both varieties and species. In Wallace's theory the processes were seen as quite different. Wallace saw varieties forming as the result of the natural selection of naturally occurring variant individuals in different parts of a species' total range. Species formation, on the other hand, he saw as the result of the extinction of the parent or "species" population and of any less well adapted varieties at the time of a general environmental stress; a stress not so severe and prolonged, however, that a "superior" variety could not survive. Thus, Darwin's concept was of continual slow change from ill-defined variety to subspecies to species. Wallace viewed species formation as an occasional process by which extinction, through elimination of all but the superior variety, left a population with attributes slightly different from, and superior to, those of its parent population.

Darwin next discusses how the process of extinction, as he saw it, is represented in the diagram.

> As . . . natural selection necessarily acts by the selected form having some advantage in the struggle for life over other forms, there will be a constant tendency in the improved descendants of any one species to supplant and exterminate in each stage of descent their predecessors and their original parent. For it should be remembered that the competition will generally be most severe between those forms which are most closely related to each other in habits, constitution, and structure. Hence all the intermediate forms between the earlier and later states, that is between the less and more improved state of a species, as well as the original parent-species itself, will generally tend to become extinct. . . .   (p. 121)

After reading this discussion of "divergence of character" Wallace might well have been struck by the similarity of Darwin's conception of divergence with the one he himself had presented in his 1855 "law" paper, in which, after enunciating his "law," he proceeded to show how it

> explains and illustrates . . . the natural system of affinities. . . . The effect of this would be, that so long as each species has had but one new species formed on its model, the lines of affinities will be simple, and may be represented by placing the several species in direct succession in a straight line. But if two or more species have been independently formed on the plan of a common antitype, then the series of affinities will be compound, and can only be represented by a forked or many branched line.   (1855c:186)

Applying this model to the natural system of affinities makes it evident that both of these relationships between closely related species are commonly seen. But the lines of affinity in essentially every group quickly become complex and obscure. Wallace decided that a gnarled tree was the most understandable analogy for the complex affinities of living species to each other and to their extinct progenitors.

The similarities in the ways in which he and Darwin represented lineages must have been apparent to Wallace. Darwin's diagram could be seen as a schematic representation and elaboration of the text of Wallace's 1855 paper, quoted above. Yet there were sharp differences in the natural dynamics postulated by the two men to account for the complexities of the observed affinity pattern. For example, although each had stressed the importance of the extinction of intermediate species, each employed the phrase in quite a different way.

For Wallace, aside from the "law" itself, the principal theoretical contribution of his 1855 paper was the examination of the consequences of the extinction of intermediate forms. Wallace had said that the extinction of intermediate members of series of species derived one from another will be evident from, and account for the gaps in, the distribution pattern of the surviving members of the series. This is equally true of series extending through geological time and in space (geographic distribution). The extinction of the most divergent member or members of a series, on the other hand, would be undetectable because it would have had no effect upon the pattern of the survivors. Darwin also stressed the importance of the extinction of intermediate forms, but he asserted that their very intermediacy was responsible for their extinction. The divergent forms, he said, survived by seizing upon diverse roles in the natural economy. Thus the two men stressed the significance of the same phrase—the extinction of intermediates—but identified quite different attributes of the "intermediacy" as responsible for that significance. This identity of phrase, with quite different connotations, is reminiscent of the use of the same word, "divergence," by Darwin in the 1857 Gray letter and by Wallace in his 1858 paper, for entirely different natural dynamics.

As Wallace read the summary at the end of chapter IV, immediately following Darwin's account of the roles of extinction and divergence in the generation of the natural system of affinities, another striking similarity to his 1855 paper would have been evident. Darwin, as Wallace had in his "law" paper, used a tree as a simile. Such a simile was not altogether unexpected, but the details of expression were remarkably similar to those used by Wallace in two separate places in his "law" paper. Darwin wrote:

The affinities of all the beings of the same class have sometimes been represented by a great tree. I believe this simile largely speaks the truth. The green and budding twigs may represent existing species; and those produced during each former year may represent the long succession of extinct species. At each period of growth all the growing twigs have tried to branch out on all sides, and to overtop and kill the surrounding twigs and branches, in the same manner as species and groups of species have tried to overmaster other species in the great battle for life. The limbs divided into great branches, and these into lesser and lesser branches, were themselves once, when the tree was small, budding twigs; and this connexion of the former and present buds by ramifying branches may well represent the classification of all extinct and living species in groups subordinate to groups. Of the many twigs which flourished when the tree was a mere bush, only two or three, now grown into great branches, yet survive and bear all the other branches; so with the species which lived during long-past geological periods, very few now have living and modified descendants. From the first growth of the tree, many a limb and branch has decayed and dropped off; and these lost branches of various sizes may represent those whole orders, families, and genera which have now no living representatives and which are known to us only from having been found in a fossil state. As we here and there see a thin straggling branch springing from a fork low down in a tree, and which by some chance has been favoured and is still alive on its summit, so we occasionally see an animal like the Ornithorhynchus or Lepidosiren, which in some small degree connects by its affinities two large branches of life, and which has apparently been saved from fatal competition by having inhabited a protected station. As buds give rise by growth to fresh buds, and these, if vigorous, branch out and overtop on all sides many a feebler branch, so by generation I believe it has been with the great Tree of Life, which fills with its dead and broken branches the crust of the earth, and covers the surface with its ever branching and beautiful ramifications.   (1859:129–130)

In the 1855 paper Wallace had written:

We are also made aware of the difficulty of arriving at a true classification, even in a small and perfect group;—in the actual state of nature it is almost impossible, the species being so numerous and the modifications of form and structure so varied, arising probably from the immense number of species which have served as antitypes for the existing species, and thus produced a complicated branching of the lines of affinity, as intricate as the twigs of a gnarled oak or the vascular system of the human body. Again, if we consider that we have only

fragments of this vast system, the stem and main branches being represented by extinct species of which we have no knowledge, while a
vast mass of limbs and boughs and minute twigs and scattered leaves
is what we have to place in order, and determine the true position each
originally occupied with regard to the others, the whole difficulty of
the true Natural System of classification becomes apparent to
us.   (1855c:186–87)

Returning to the analogy of a branching tree, as the best mode of
representing the natural arrangement of species and their successive
creation, let us suppose that at an early geological epoch any group
(say a class of the Mollusca) has attained to a great richness of species
and a high organization. Now let this great branch of allied species, by
geological mutations, be completely or partially destroyed. Subsequently a new branch springs from the same trunk, that is to say, new
species are successively created, having for their antitypes the same
lower organized species which had served as the antitypes for the former group, but which have survived the modified conditions which destroyed it. This new group being subject to these altered conditions,
has modifications of structure and organization given to it, and becomes
the representative group of the former one in another geological formation. It may, however, happen, that though later in time, the new
series of species may never attain to so high a degree of organization
as those preceding it, but in its turn become extinct, and give place to
yet another modification from the same root, which may be of higher
or lower organization, more or less numerous in species, and more or
less varied in form and structure than either of those which preceded
it. Again, each of these groups may not have become totally extinct,
but may have left a few species, the modified prototypes of which have
existed in each succeeding period, a faint memorial of their former
grandeur and luxuriance. Thus every case of apparent retrogression may
be in reality a progress, though an interrupted one: when some monarch
of the forest loses a limb, it may be replaced by a feeble and sickly
substitute.   (pp. 191–92)

Other than in chapter III, "Struggle for Existence," and the following one, "Natural Selection," Wallace would have found no
marked coincidences. On the other hand, he would likely have been
disappointed with the chapters on geographical distribution, for they
did not even present as succinct a summary as he had in his 1855

paper. They also made no mention of the strong arguments that a comparison of the biotas of Borneo, New Guinea, Aru, and Australia makes in favor of a theory of organic change, such as those he himself had developed in his "Aru" paper. But Wallace would probably have been impressed with the evidence amassed on subjects on which he was little informed—hybridism, instincts, and the nature and extent of variety formation in plants, to name a few.

Viewing the book as a whole, he could not fail to see that the two chapters exhibiting the greatest similarities to his own writings were the heart of Darwin's theory. The dynamics of survival in natural populations (ch. III) had clearly been developed by both men in almost exactly the same manner from the basic Mathusian premise. The similarities in chapter IV would have been more puzzling. The two men had used the same words to denote central concepts (for example, "divergence," "extinction of intermediate forms"); yet there were differences in the natural dynamics to which these words were applied. In the *Origin* Darwin had used the word "divergence" in two ways, one of them the same as in the 1857 Gray letter. The other was similar to concepts Wallace had developed in the 1855 "law" paper. Finally, Darwin used a tree as a model for the natural system of affinities, with language very similar to that of Wallace writing in 1855 to the same end.

After Wallace's first reading of the *Origin* and his letter to Darwin, he left on his last, and what proved to be a most difficult and hazardous, exploration of the eastern Spice Islands. In March 1861, several months after his eventual safe return, he wrote to his brother-in-law, Thomas Sims, from Delli (Dili), Timor. The long letter delved into a variety of subjects in response to an accumulation of three letters, in one of which Sims must have commented on the *Origin of Species:*

> Now for Mr. Darwin's book. You quite misunderstand Mr. D.'s statement in the preface and his sentiments. I have, of course, been in correspondence with him since I first sent him my little essay. His conduct has been most liberal and disinterested. I think anyone who reads the Linnean Society papers and his book will see it. I *do* back him up in his entire round of conclusions and look upon him as the *Newton* of *Natural History.*

You begin by criticising the *title*. Now, though I consider the title admirable, I believe it is not Mr. Darwin's but the Publisher's, as you are no doubt aware they *will* have a taking title, and authors must and do give way to them. Mr. D. gave me a quite different title before the book came out. . . .   (Marchant 1916 1:76)

By the end of June Wallace had begun a slow voyage homeward, through Sumatra and Java. On April 1, 1862, he arrived in London, nearly two and a half years after Darwin had published *On the Origin of Species*.

CHAPTER ELEVEN
How Darwin Completed His Theory

In this last chapter and the Epilogue the point of view differs from that in the early chapters. These pages relate the attempts of a twentieth-century biologist to comprehend the events in England that followed Wallace's mailing of his 1858 manuscript at Ternate in the Moluccas. My interest was aroused in the 1960s during preparations for giving an undergraduate seminar course on evolution organized around the study of original scientific contributions on this subject. Each year began with a reading of Wallace's 1855 "law" paper, the joint Darwin-Wallace papers, and Darwin's *On the Origin of Species*. Over several annual cycles the similarities between the concepts, even the wording, in Wallace's papers and several chapters, but especially chapter IV, in Darwin's 1859 book became increasingly apparent and disturbing. Were these really coincidences of two totally independent conceptions? Or did Darwin somehow profit from Wallace's papers and manuscript?—a possibility to which Darwin gave no recognition, not even a hint. A nagging doubt remained; there were too many similarities.

How does one start toward resolving these doubts? The first question obviously was, When did Darwin formulate the concepts of chapter IV, "Natural Selection," of the *Origin of Species?* The entire manuscript of the *Origin* was written after July 1, 1858, at which time both of Wallace's papers had been made public (the second by oral presentation), but, as noted in the preceding chapter, there is no mention of Wallace's work anywhere in chapter IV. The manuscript of the *Origin* was written comparatively rapidly, for it was an "abstract" of a long manuscript, Darwin's "big species book," on which he had been laboring since 1857 (although he had led Wallace to believe that he had been working on it for twenty years). Darwin had revealed to Asa Gray that the title of the "big species book" was "Natural Selection," and more than half of the Asa Gray letter presented Darwin's views of the significance of natural selection. Fortunately, a few years before I began my inquiry, many of Charles Darwin's manuscript documents were published by Sir Gavin De Beer. Relevant among them is Darwin's private diary, published by De Beer (1959) as "Darwin's Journal"; I shall use the more traditional designation "diary." In this, entered under March 31, 1857, is a notation, "Finished Ch. 6 Nat: Selection."

But an entry a year later makes a second mention of chapter VI. "April 14th Discussion on large genera & small & on Divergence & correcting Ch. 6 (Moor Park) finished June 12th & Bee Cells." (De Beer 1959:14) A more personal item for 1858 recorded that Darwin had stayed from April 20 to May 4 at Moor Park, a hydrotherapy establishment in Surrey. (Darwin, in those years, had occasional recourse to hydrotherapy.) A letter to Joseph Hooker, his close friend and botanical advisor, two days after his return to Down from Moor Park enclosed the manuscript on species in large, as opposed to small, genera (F. Darwin 1887 1:465). This would indicate that "Divergence" and corrections to chapter VI were written between May 6 and June 12, 1858. This entry, therefore, establishes the dates of composition.

Since most of the troubling similarities to Wallace's work center around "divergence," the next question to be answered was, How extensive were the additions made in May–June 1858? While the diary entry identifies "Divergence" as the subject of the 1858 addition, the reader will recall that the Gray letter of September 1857 identifies a "principle of divergence," which Darwin regarded as important. That letter was written six months after the initial completion of chapter VI. I therefore had another question to resolve. Did the chapter as first written discuss a "principle of divergence"? Or had this concept occurred to Darwin while composing the Gray letter, six months after he finished chapter VI? If the latter, why had Darwin not added this new idea, obviously considered important, to his completed chapter then and there, in the fall of 1857?

It was clear that questions such as these could be answered only by an examination of the manuscript of "Natural Selection." But did that manuscript still exist? I remembered that Dr. Robert Stauffer (1959) had published a short paper in *Science* a few years before which discusses the newly discovered manuscript of "Natural Selection." The article indicates that the manuscript had actually come to light during the Second World War and that its existence had been announced by a note in *Nature* in 1942. Stauffer remarks, "The fact that the manuscript has survived seems even less well known than that of its original existence. . . ." (p. 1449). The article, " 'On the Origin of Species': An Unpublished Version," indicates that chapter VI, "On Natural Selection," was included in the manuscript. A further point of immediate interest was in the article's final footnote: Stauffer had a microfilm of the manuscript at the University of Wisconsin, at Madison, where he was on the staff of the history of science department. Students of aquatic biology sooner or later visit Madison, on Lake Mendota, and I now had another reason to visit.

One evening in January 1967 Stauffer and I renewed our acquaintance over dinner. I had been introduced to him by a mutual friend years before when he had been at the Woods Hole Oceanographic Institution doing ecological research. Stauffer reminded me that evening that his interest in learning more of Darwin's ecological insights had induced him to examine the manuscript of "Natural Selection" at the University Library, Cambridge. He had gone on to his current endeavor, the monumental task of transcribing and annotating the 125,000- to 130,000-word Darwin manuscript, eleven chapters of which are preserved. Then I asked the question that had prompted me to seek this meeting—Were insertions into the text usually identifiable? Stauffer promptly replied yes, that single folios were designated by an asterisk following the folio number; if the insertion was lengthy, the subsequent folios were designated by small letters after the number. Thus, three folios added after folio 10, for example, would be 10*, 10a, 10b. Should an insertion be longer than twenty-seven folios, the twenty-eighth would be designated "10aa," etc. Heartened by his answer, I told Stauffer the nature of my interest and expressed my desire to learn the extensiveness of the additions to chapter VI, on "divergence." I interpreted a slight hesitation to mean that Stauffer was not altogether happy with the direction of my interest, but he agreed that we examine the photocopy. There were only brief insertions to the first twenty-five folios, but the bottom quarter of the text of folio 26 was lined through, and the following folio was 26*, followed by 26a, then 26b, all the way to 26nn. A forty-one–page insert! Was it about divergence? The answer was quick to come.

A heading in the middle of folio 26 was "Extinction." Near the top of folio 26b appeared "Principle of Divergence." There was also a diagram of lineages like that in the *Origin,* the first reference to it being on folio 26s. The contents of the inserted material at first glance appeared quite similar to the content of the last twenty pages of chapter IV of the *Origin.* I was delighted. Stauffer kindly offered to lend me his transcript of chapter VI for a brief study. A careful examination verified my initial impression; the last twenty pages of chapter IV of the *Origin* had unquestionably been based on this forty-one–folio insertion into chapter VI of the long "Natural Selection" manuscript, but shortened by half.

This discovery made the "coincidences" even more remarkable. Darwin had completed the forty-one–folio addition to his chapter VI on June 12, 1858—six days before the date usually assigned for the arrival of the mail bearing Wallace's Ternate manuscript. Darwin's additional text bore similarities to the Ternate manuscript—yet to arrive—but also to Wallace's 1855 "law" paper, which Darwin had already examined several years earlier. The question now seemed clearly worth pursuing.

The next step, firsthand examination of the manuscript, would involve a trip to the library of Darwin documents in the University Library, Cambridge.

A brief stay at Cambridge that summer revealed much, as only a firsthand study can. The first obvious feature of the sheath of folios was that the inserted material was on stock of a distinctly different color from that bearing the original text, just as Stauffer had indicated in our earlier conversation. In his completed work, Stauffer (1975:213) describes the sheets originally used in 1857 as "gray wove foolscap"; all later additions (1858) are on "bluish gray" paper. Folios 26*–26nn are, of course, on bluish gray stock, but so is almost the entire remainder of the chapter, folios 51 to 76. Only the last two folios, 77 and 78, are on the original gray stock. Here, then, was yet another long addition, totaling some twenty-five pages. The heading on folio 53 is "On the Absence of Intermediate Forms or Links between Species of the Same Genus." A footnote to the last line on folio 53, placed on a separate sheet, begins, "June 1858 I doubt whether I have got intermediate links yet clear. . . ." The final folios with new material provide a summary that begins on folio 68.

Another question was, What of the original text did the forty-one–folio insert replace? The replaced material was obviously short; only one folio, 27, has been discarded, a fact alluded to by Darwin at the top of folio 28. The lines of the original text at the bottom of folio 26 have been lined through but are legible. The same is true for the lines at the top of folio 28. Examination of the beginning and the ending of the canceled portion might provide a clue to the text that had been written on the folio now missing.

To place the deleted material in its original context, we must examine the first part of folio 26. This carries the conclusion of a section on "Comparison of Nature's Selection with Man's Selection" (cf. p. 83 of the *Origin*). Its message is conveyed by these quotations:

> The forms produced by natural selection, if quite modified, will be called species, if only slightly different, will be called varieties; if no further variation occurs in the right direction by which the variety may be further profitted, I can see no reason why a variety may not remain in that state during an enormous lapse of years. . . . (end of fol. 25)
> But that a variety should remain constant during whole geological periods is excessively improbable; . . . [for] if one variety be so fixed as not to vary at all in a fitting direction, and so become through natural selection adapted to those other changing organic forms to which it is related in the polity of nature, it will be exterminated. (fol. 26)

The next heading and the next seven lines have been crossed out but are quite legible.

> Extinction
> Forms produced by natural selection if considerably different will be called species, if still more different, genera and so on. But in these cases besides inheritance and modification, extinction which will always play a

part, will here have played a very important part in the destruction at some
period of intermediate forms. To win. . . .

A new subject must have been introduced on the now-missing folio
27, because the four lines at the top of folio 28 conclude discussion
of a different topic. They too, though crossed out, are legible:[1]

a small and a very large scale. The principle of divergence, I believe, plays
an important part in the affinities or classification of all organic beings.

It might be noted here that while the crossed-out heading in the
text is simply "Extinction," Darwin had stated in the original table
of contents for the chapter: "26 Extinction and Divergence plays part"
(Stauffer 1975:213). It seems clear, then, that whatever discussion of
the "principle of divergence" was in the original text, it was not
longer than 250–300 words. This is the approximate length of the
last section of Darwin's letter to Asa Gray, written in September
1857, six months after the original text of chapter VI was completed.
One may observe the similarity of the wording crossed out at the top
of folio 28 to Darwin's lines in the Gray letter following a presentation of his "principle of divergence": "This I believe to be the origin
of the classification and affinities of organic beings at all times. . . ."
(Darwin 1858:53).

I think it reasonable to assume that most of the text of folio 27
was essentially similar to the treatment of the "principle of divergence" in the Gray letter.

With the reconstruction of the deleted portion of the original text
in mind, I now turn to a consideration of what the forty-one folios of
new text said about "divergence." In brief, this long insert is a re-
petitive and wordier version of the material presented in the final
twenty pages of chapter IV, "Natural Selection," of the *Origin of
Species*. With the exception of the first two folios, headed "Extinction," all of the text follows the heading "Divergence of Character"
without any subdivisions (Stauffer 1975:28). In the final table of contents that Darwin prepared, however, he identified a series of topics.

1. The deletion of the first four lines of fol. 28 of ch. VI has not been noted in Stauffer's
Appendix, where he placed retrievable crossed-out passages in Darwin's manuscript.

In the following list each topic follows its folio designation. The third column lists the page of the *Origin* on which this subject matter can be found. In most cases the cross-identification is obvious.

26c	Principle of Divergence: in domestic animals	(111)
d	Amount of life due to diversity shown by culture & natural distribution	(112)
h	Shown by naturalisation	(114)
l	Shown by physiological division of labour	(115)
p	Divergence acting in nature on large genera	(?)
s	Diagram of	(116)
w	Varieties how supplant parents	(121)
aa	Varietal differences become specific	(123)
cc	Bears on Classification	(?)
gg	Limit to total number of species in any country	(125)
mm	Classification compared to Tree of Life	(129)

Queries in the last column indicate exceptions. The content of pages 109 to 125 of the *Origin* quite faithfully follows the text of the added folios, through 26gg. Stauffer's associates (Stauffer 1975:640) identify (I believe correctly) Stauffer's page 247 (a transcription of Darwin's fol. 26hh and 26ii) with page 313 of the *Origin*. This is the second page of chapter IX, "On the Geological Succession of Organic Beings." This is the only bit of the text of the forty-one new folios to be incorporated in a chapter of the *Origin* other than that on "Natural Selection."

The text of fifteen of the new folios (26s to 26ff) refers to a diagram of lineages, just as some nine pages of chapter IV of the *Origin* (pp. 116–125) refer to another diagram of lineages. Comparison of the two diagrams shows that the relations delineated in the two are essentially the same but that the manner of presentation differs. Two separate panels (or separate diagrams of the "Natural Selection" manuscript, as Darwin heads them) are combined, more succinctly, into one. But the primary difference is that in the manuscript the initial species are arrayed across the top of the sheet and the lines of descent go toward the bottom of the page. In the *Origin* this vertical orientation is reversed. The initial species are arranged along the bot-

(a)

(b)

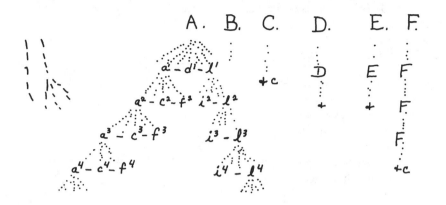

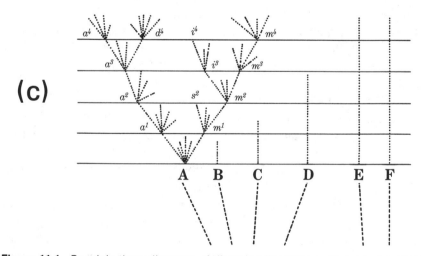

Figure 11.1 Darwin's three diagrams of diverging lineages: a. Diagram drawn in the margin of page 186 of his copy of Wallace's 1855 paper (see fig. 11.2); b. Portion of the manuscript diagram of simple and diverging lineages that accompanies the long manuscript "Natural Selection"; c. The corresponding portion (now inverted) printed as the only illustration in *Origin of Species*. The intent here is to demonstrate similarities of presentation, not details of information to be conveyed.

tom of the sheet, with the lines of descent ascending to the top (see fig. 11.1).

The remaining aspect of the disposition in the *Origin* of the content of the new folios inserted into chapter VI of the "Natural Selection" manuscript is that the "tree of life" simile, which concludes the new section (fol. 26mm, 26nn), appears as the last two pages of the three-and-a-half-page summary of chapter IV of the *Origin*.

I have alluded to the fact that the last twenty-five folios (with one or two original pages intercalated) concluding chapter VI are on "bluish gray" paper and therefore were written later than the originals, presumably in May–June 1858. This presumption is almost certainly correct, as attested by Darwin's footnote date "June 1858." The first question that suggests itself is, What did this replace? Fortunately, the original table of contents, canceled by Darwin, tells us (the reader is reminded that the new material begins on fol. 51):

49 Intermediate varieties rare
     —50 why not met with over continents
54 Large number of individuals favourable for selection
56 Summary on causes fav. & unfav. —57 Malay
59 Slowness of Selection
63 [pencil addition] Theory applied to Races of Man
(Stauffer 1975:213)

Darwin designated the items as follows in his new table of contents:

51 Slowness of selection [original 59?]
53 Absence of intermediate links; nature of such   [ch. IX, p. 280]
     links
54 Links chiefly extinct   [ch. IX, p. 284]
57 Links generally absent now when species min-   [ch. IX, p. 297]
     gle in border regions
58 Areas perhaps not formerly continuous   [ch. VI, p. 174]
60 Conditions of continuous areas do not really   [ch. VI, p. 175]
     graduate insensibly
62 Intermediate varieties rare   [ch. VI, pp. 176–78]
64 Intermediate varieties tend to be easily exter-   [ch. VI, pp. 176–78]
     minated
68 Summary—illustrated by Malay Archipelago   [ch. IV, pp. 127–28]

(Chapter and pages of the *Origin* with the equivalent text are given in brackets.)

Two aspects of this second block of new material are immediately apparent: first, it largely concerns intermediate forms; second, most of its content is dispersed to chapters of the *Origin* other than chapter IV, "Natural Selection." Only three folios of a new summary[2] (68, 73, and 74) are included in chapter IV of the *Origin;* they occupy the two pages in the summary of that chapter that precede the "tree of life" analogy.

Whereas in the original manuscript one, or probably two, folios (old 49, 50) concern intermediates ("Intermediate varieties rare"), fourteen new folios (53–67) address various aspects of their significance. While the interested reader can refer to the indicated pages of the first edition of the *Origin of Species* for details of this block of new material, a brief summary of its use elsewhere in the *Origin* than chapter IV seems in order.

The first of four classes of "difficulties" that Darwin lists at the beginning of chapter VI, "Difficulties on Theory," is "Why, if species have descended from other species by insensibly fine gradations, do we not every where see innumerable transitional forms? Why is not all nature in confusion instead of the species being, as we see them, well defined?" (p. 171). This question is addressed in the first section, "On the Absence or Rarity of Transitional Varieties"; about half of the five pages of text (174–78) are based on the folios indicated in the list above. The concluding paragraph of that section bears a notable similarity to the penultimate paragraph of Wallace's 1855 "law" paper (see ch. 5, this volume):

> Lastly, looking not to any one time, but to all time, if my theory be true, numberless intermediate varieties, linking most closely all the species of the same group together, must assuredly have existed; but the very process of natural selection constantly tends, as has been so often remarked, to exterminate the parent-forms and the intermediate links. Consequently evidence of their former existence could be found only amongst fossil remains, which are preserved, as we shall in a future chapter attempt to show, in an extremely imperfect and intermittent record.   (p. 179)

2. Most of the new summary is written in a hand other than that of Charles Darwin. While the first seven lines are in his hand, the completion of line seven and all of the following folios are written in a hand distinctly different—possibly that of one of his children?

In his stance of 1858, so similar to that of Wallace in 1855, Darwin was taking a position completely the reverse of that stated in an equivalent part of the Darwin manuscript sketch of 1844, which may be considered the first version of the *Origin of Species*.

> What evidence is there of a number of intermediate forms having existed, making a passage in the above sense [those between domesticated varieties], between the species of the same groups? Some naturalists have supposed that if every fossil which now lies entombed, together with all existing species, were collected together, a perfect series in every great class would be formed. Considering the enormous number of species requisite to effect this, . . . I think this supposition highly improbable. . . . (Darwin and Wallace 1958:154)

Equivalents to the content of the remainder of the new folios are to be found in three chapters of the *Origin* for which there are no corresponding chapters in "Natural Selection." The reader will recall that in late summer of 1858 Darwin abandoned that long manuscript and began writing his "Abstract." The three chapters referred to are chapters IX and X, both on geology, and chapter XIII, "Mutual Affinities of Organic Beings: Morphology: Embryology: Rudimentary Organs." Chapter IX, "On the Imperfections of the Geological Record," begins with a three-page discussion, "On the Absence of Intermediate Varieties at the Present Day;—on the Nature of Extinct Intermediate Varieties;—on Their Number." The subject of these pages (279–81) can be equated with that of folios 53 and 54, which fall under the manuscript heading "On the Absence of Intermediate Forms or Links Between Species of the Same Genus." (Stauffer [1975:640] also makes this textual identification.) Parts of the text of a later section of the same chapter, "On the Absence of Intermediate Varieties in Any One Formation," seem similarly derived from the May–June 1858 emendations to chapter VI. Stauffer (1975:640) identifies page 297 of the *Origin* with folio 56; I believe that the two pages following should be included in that derivation.

The next chapter (X) of the *Origin* is entitled "On the Geological Succession of Organic Beings." Toward the end of it there is an eight-page section, "On the Affinities of Extinct Species to Each Other, and to Living Forms." The central three pages refer to the lineage diagram. The content of the adjacent pages makes it quite clear that this section is based on the beginning of the second block of 1858 folios in chapter VI of the "Natural Selection" manuscript— folios 53–56. A footnote to folio 56 is the earliest reference in the second block of new material to the diagram first introduced on folio 26s of the first block. But the content of the first pages of the section on affinities (329–30) is of even greater interest. Stauffer and his associates (1975:640) identify the content of the first of these pages with Stauffer's page 384. This page transcribes a folio of chapter VIII of the "Natural Selection" manuscript, "Difficulties on the Theory of Natural Selection in Relation to Passages from Form to Form." The identification with that folio is clear, based on the subject. But our interest is in the quite different interpretation of the subject that the *Origin,* published in 1859, presents from that of chapter VIII of the original manuscript text, completed in September 1857.

In September 1857 Darwin had written,

> Before summing up this chapter, I may remark that if theory be extended to the utmost limits, which facts of any kind permit, nothing is easier than to make the whole appear to oneself quite ridiculous;—namely by asking whether a rhinoceros & gazelle, an elephant & mouse, a frog & fish, a bird, lizard & mammal could possibly have descended from a common progenitor. Involuntarily one immediately looks out for a chain of animals *directly* connecting these extreme forms. One forgets for the moment, that these great groups have been perfectly distinct for enormous geological periods; some of them, almost if not quite as distinct at the earliest period of which we possess any fossil records, as at the present day; & therefore if intermediate forms ever did exist, they would all, or nearly all be, assuredly now utterly lost. To lessen in some degree the ridiculous impression of the foregoing question, one ought to think of such animals as the Ornithorhynchus, which though an indisputed mammal presents in its skeleton & other parts some few plain resemblances to reptiles & birds. When mentally comparing a rhinoceros & gazelle, one ought to bear in mind that Cuvier & all our elder naturalists considered the Pachyderms & ruminants as the two most distinct orders of Mammalia; but now Owen has so connected them by Eocene forms, that he has made them into one great group. (fol. 97, 98; transcribed in Stauffer 1975:384)

Compare, now, Darwin's later views in the *Origin of Species:*

Let us now look at the mutual affinities of extinct and living species. They all fall into one grand natural system; and this fact is at once explained on the principle of descent. The more ancient any form is, the more, as a general rule, it differs from living forms. But, as Buckland long ago remarked, all fossils can be classed either in still existing groups or between them. That the extinct forms of life help to fill up the wide intervals between existing genera, families, and orders cannot be disputed. For if we confine our attention either to the living or to the extinct alone, the series is far less perfect than if we combine both into one general system. With respect to the Vertebrata, whole pages could be filled with striking illustrations from our great paleontologist, Owen, showing how extinct animals fall in between existing groups. Cuvier ranked the Ruminants and Pachyderms, as the two most distinct orders of mammals; but Owen has discovered so many fossil links, that he has had to alter the whole classification of these two orders; and placed certain pachyderms in the same sub-order with ruminants. . . .   (1859:329)

Darwin's view in the *Origin of Species* of affinities within the natural system had become remarkably like the view that Wallace expressed at the close of his 1855 "law" paper (see ch. 5, this volume).

In chapter XIII, the last but one of the *Origin of Species,* reference is again made to the lineage diagram in the section "Extinction separates and defines groups." No clear identification with any folio of the "Natural Selection" manuscript is evident.

In summary, then, the treatment of the subjects of extinction, intermediates, and the natural system of affinities in the later chapters of the *Origin of Species* can in large part be identified with the material that Darwin added to chapter VI of the "Natural Selection" manuscript in May–June 1858. In all, the concepts and approaches are remarkably similar to Wallace's views as expressed in 1855.

I shall now summarize briefly what I believe were Darwin's uses of the Wallace 1855 "law" paper, especially of the section in which Wallace had demonstrated how his law "explains and illustrates" all of the known facts of the system of natural affinities. I think that the evidence indicates that Darwin comprehended only some of the implications in, or by, 1857. He apparently did not grasp the significance of other passages until May–June 1858.

As stated earlier, a complete theory of organic change must account for the divergence evident in the history of life. The fossil record clearly demonstrates that some groups, vertebrates in particular, have unquestionably become more divergent with the passage of time. In other words, more recent species tend to become increasingly different from one another and from their ancestors. When Darwin wrote his manuscript sketch of 1844 he had not been aware, apparently, even of the necessity of dealing with divergence. At the end of that manuscript, in chapter VII, "On the Nature of the Affinities and Classification of Organic Beings," he had concluded, "Finally, then, we see that all the leading facts in the affinities and classification of organic beings can be explained on the theory of the natural system being simply a genealogical one" (Darwin and Wallace 1958:219). Obviously a genealogical analogy is inadequate, because in a human family tree the individuals currently representing the family are basically no more unlike each other than were those that lived as far back as the lineage can be traced. There has been no divergence, just descent.

The next two statements that Darwin made about divergence came thirteen years later, in 1857. The first (March 1857), in the original text of chapter VI, "Natural Selection," of the long "Natural Selection" manuscript, began on folio 26 and ended on folio 28, but the middle—folio 27—is, of course, missing. Yet we know that Darwin referred to the content of these folios thus: "Extinction and Divergence plays part." Crossed-out lines at the top of folio 28 concluded that section with, "The principle of divergence, I believe, plays an important part in the affinities or classification of all living beings." The second statement was in the letter of September 1857, in which Darwin summarized his theory for Asa Gray. There, as we have several times noted, he set forth a "principle of divergence" and stated: "This I believe to be the origin of the classification and affinities of organic beings at all times. . . ." He then presented the tree simile with "diverging twigs" and dead branches representing extinct groups.

Each of the 1857 statements is similar to passages in Wallace's "law" paper that had indicated the importance of extinction in producing "the complicated branching of the lines of affinity." For Wallace, a tree analogy helped in understanding the "true Natural System of classification." He wrote of a "gnarled oak" in which the twigs and leaves are the living species, while the "stem and main branches" represent the extinct species. (See ch. 5 for a full discussion.) I conclude that both of Darwin's 1857 statements about extinction and divergence as explanations of the natural system of affinities and classification are based on the same last part of Wallace's first long paragraph on the relevance of his law to the system of natural affinities.

Before returning to the spring of 1858, we must consider another aspect of this formulation of the significance of extinction and diversity. Wallace in 1855 had worked out the parts played by the processes of divergence and extinction, respectively, in creating the natural system. But he had said nothing about the natural dynamics that lead to either extinction or divergence. On the other hand, Darwin in 1857 proposed natural dynamics to account for extinction and divergence, saying that diverging offspring populations would survive best if they seize on "as many and as diverse places in the economy of nature as possible." Divergence thus caused extinction, Darwin said, because the new variety (or species) will "take the place of and thus exterminate its less well-fitted parent," as he stated in the Gray letter. Because folio 27 is missing from the original text of chapter VI of the "Natural Selection" manuscript, we do not know precisely when in 1857 Darwin had actually developed his concept of natural dynamics. Certainly later folios of the original chapter VI of the long manuscript present an obscure account of the significance of diversity in "the polity of nature" (see fols. 34–50, in the section headed "Causes Favourable & Unfavourable to Natural Selection"; Stauffer 1975:251–61). But I can find no statement in the March 1857 account that explicitly mentions the extermination of the parent by the new variety. It should be emphasized here that Darwin's view of the significance of ecological diversity in causing divergence and then extinction is entirely his own; it has no counterpart in Wallace's conceptions, either in 1855 or in 1858.

Now we can proceed to the spring of 1858 and the two blocks of additional material, over sixty pages in all, whose contents appear to have antecedents in other passages of Wallace's 1855 "law" paper. I have already discussed (p. 235) the manuscript diagram and its explanation (beginning on folio 26s). I shall now examine the possible genesis of that diagram in the first several sentences in Wallace's long paragraph in explanation of the natural system. The subject of the second block of new material, the significance of the extinction of intermediate forms, is, as I have detailed in chapter 5, one of the most important contributions of that 1855 paper.

I have, then, concluded that Darwin comprehended the significance of Wallace's "law" paper in two steps. Is there any evidence to test this hypothesis? Darwin, if he did make use of Wallace's paper, would likely have made marginal notations in his copy of the *Annals and Magazine of Natural History* for 1855. Francis Darwin has recorded that it was his father's habit to mark with vertical pencil lines in the margin any passages of a book or "pamphlet" that caught his attention; sometimes he would add a brief comment; and he would note at the end of the publication the numbers of all the pages so marked. Later Darwin would write a short summary by reexamining the marked passages and selecting those he thought might be useful (F. Darwin 1887 1:128).

Examination of Darwin's copy of Wallace's paper in the *Annals* reveals, as McKinney (1972:117–20) has noted, thirty-five vertical pencil markings and a few marginal notations. Most of the pencil lines are relatively heavy, indicating a soft lead. These extensive "heavy" markings, as we shall see, were the ones on which the summary of that volume of the *Annals* was based.

The relevant part of Darwin's summary reads:[3]

185 Wallace's paper: Law of Geograph. Distrib Nothing very new—186 His general summary "Every species has come into existence coincident in time and space with pre-existing species"—Uses my simile of tree. It seems all creation with him—alludes to Galapagos 189 on even adjoining species being closest—(It is all creation but why does (is) his law hold good. he puts the facts in striking point of view—194 argues against our supposed geological perfect knowledge—Explains rudimentary organs on same idea (I should state put generation for creation and I quite agree.) (from Charles Darwin's copy, *Ann. Mag. Nat. Hist.*, vol. 16. University Library, Cambridge)

3. It is a pleasure to acknowledge help given to me in the Anderson Room of the University Library at Cambridge in deciphering some words and phrases of Darwin's handwriting. Frederick Burkhardt, Peter Gautry, and David Kohn are masters of that art.

Each of these comments has a corresponding text marked with a heavy vertical line, but Darwin has obviously selected only a few of the marked passages for comment. I think it can be concluded from the description of Darwin's working habits that these heavy pencil lines were the original marginalia.

Let us examine the heavy markings of the text of Wallace's explication of the system of natural affinities using his "law" (Wallace 1855c:186, 187).

On page 186 (see fig. 11.2) during his earlier reading he had marked the following two passages:

It is evidently possible that two or three distinct species may have had a common antitype, and that each of these may again have become the antitypes from which other closely allied species were created. . . . But if two or more species have been independently formed on the plan of a common antitype, then the series of affinities will be compound, and can only be represented by a forked or many-branched line.

On page 187, these two longer passages are marked:

for the existing species, and thus produced a complicated branching of the lines of affinity, as intricate as the twigs of a gnarled oak or the vascular system of the human body. . . .

stem and main branches being represented by extinct species of which we have no knowledge, while a vast mass of limbs and boughs and minute twigs and scattered leaves is what we have to place in order, and determine the true position each originally occupied with regard to the others, the whole difficulty of the true Natural System of classification becomes apparent to us.

But Darwin's sole comment in the summary on the slip of blue paper was, "Uses my simile of tree." These markings are consonant with our earlier conclusion that Darwin had in 1857 utilized both the concepts and the tree simile from the text on page 187 about the natural system of affinities.

Are there also any marginal notations that substantiate my second conclusion, namely, that Darwin reread this paragraph, probably in May or June 1858? There appear to be, in the form of three marginal notations made with a relatively hard lead pencil, producing a line easily distinguishable from the earlier heavy marks. The only such narrow-line markings in the entire paper are the three that occur on these two pages.

The first (see fig. 11.2) is a phrase in the margin opposite one of Wallace's geological propositions, which had been marked earlier with a heavy vertical line (but not selected for later comment). "Can this be followed"[4] is written opposite the eighth proposition:

8. Species of one genus, or genera of one family occurring in the same geological time are more closely allied than those separated in time.

The last marginal notation, which we shall consider out of sequence, is on page 187, beside the long paragraph before the two long marked passages earlier indicated. There is a short vertical line with a small horizontal tick, and a question mark—all in a thin pencil line opposite the following text:

[It is thus difficult to determine in] every case whether a given relationship is an analogy or an affinity, for it is evident that as we go back along the parallel or divergent series, toward the common antitype, the analogy which existed between the two groups becomes an affinity.

The third and remaining notation is the most relevant to our argument. As figure 11.2 shows, there is a straight dotted line alongside another dotted line which splits into three diverging lines toward the bottom. And it can be seen from the figure that this diagram is opposite the text in which Wallace describes these two possible kinds of lineages. Note, too, that this passage had been marked by Darwin earlier but that the concept of simple and diverging lineages apparently had made no lasting impression, for it was not selected for the summary on the blue slip at the end of the *Annals* for 1855. Nor are the ideas detectable in Darwin's 1857 writings.

To conclude this analysis of Darwin's marginal comments on Wal-

4. The last word of Darwin's notation is difficult to read. Peter Gautry of the Anderson Room, an expert in deciphering Darwin's hand, kindly examined it and decided it was "followed." McKinney (1972:118) and Brackman (1980:30) concluded it was "true."

one are often represented by closely allied families, genera and species peculiar to the other.

Geology.

5. The distribution of the organic world in time is very similar to its present distribution in space.
6. Most of the larger and some small groups extend through several geological periods.
7. In each period, however, there are peculiar groups, found nowhere else, and extending through one or several formations.
8. Species of one genus, or genera of one family occurring in the same geological time are more closely allied than those separated in time.
9. As generally in geography no species or genus occurs in two very distant localities without being also found in intermediate places, so in geology the life of a species or genus has not been interrupted. In other words, no group or species has come into existence twice.
10. The following law may be deduced from these facts :—*Every species has come into existence coincident both in space and time with a pre-existing closely allied species.*

This law agrees with, explains and illustrates all the facts connected with the following branches of the subject :—1st. The system of natural affinities. 2nd. The distribution of animals and plants in space. 3rd. The same in time, including all the phænomena of representative groups, and those which Professor Forbes supposed to manifest polarity. 4th. The phænomena of rudimentary organs. We will briefly endeavour to show its bearing upon each of these.

If the law above enunciated be true, it follows that the natural series of affinities will also represent the order in which the several species came into existence, each one having had for its immediate antitype a closely allied species existing at the time of its origin. It is evidently possible that two or three distinct species may have had a common antitype, and that each of these may again have become the antitypes from which other closely allied species were created. The effect of this would be, that so long as each species has had but one new species formed on its model, the line of affinities will be simple, and may be represented by placing the several species in direct succession in a straight line. But if two or more species have been independently formed on the plan of a common antitype, then the series of affinities will be compound, and can only be represented by a forked or many-branched line. Now, all attempts at a Natural classification and arrangement of organic beings show, that both

Figure 11.2. Charles Darwin's marginalia on page 186 of his copy of the 1855 issue of *Annals and Magazine of Natural History* that carried Wallace's article "On the Law Which Has Regulated the Introduction of New Species." Note that the markings appear to have been made with two different pencils; see text for interpretation. Note also the simple diagram of divergence beside Wallace's textual account of simple and diverging lineages.

lace's paper, we can see that these marginalia were made with two different pencils. It is apparent that the heavier markings throughout the article correspond to and were the basis for the abstracted summary comments on the blue paper pinned at the end of the book. This correspondence, along with knowledge of Darwin's work habits, suggests that these were the earlier annotations. The three notations made with a harder lead, all on the facing pages 186 and 187, were likely made at a later time. Of the three, two relate to the paragraph on the system of natural affinities. The one on page 187 marks a text passage that includes the words ''parallel or diverging series.'' The other, on page 186, is a simple diagrammatic representation of Wallace's description of straight-line and diverging lines of descent. This, I believe, substantiates the conclusion that on rereading Wallace's 1855 paper in May or June 1858 Darwin grasped the fuller significance of Wallace's statements. Further, I believe that the marginal diagram on page 186 is the prototype of the sole diagram of Darwin's ''Natural Selection'' manuscript, and therefore the prototype of the sole diagram in the *Origin of Species*.

Yet another question now emerges: What was it that prompted Darwin in May or June 1858 to reread the section of Wallace's 1855 account of his explanation of the role of extinction and divergence in creating the natural patterns of affinity? The most likely stimulus would be Wallace's second manuscript on his theory, written in February of that year and mailed from Ternate on March 9. In that manuscript Wallace presented simple natural dynamics accounting for extinction, divergence, and the origin of new species. Darwin had been struggling for several years to formulate dynamics to account for the same phenomena, but with varying—one might say indifferent—success (see Browne 1980). By September of 1857 he had formulated possible dynamics to account for extinction and divergence and sent them in a letter to Asa Gray. To reiterate these, Darwin postulated that extinction resulted from the extermination of the parent ''species'' population by a better-adapted variety—through biological competition. Darwin could not, therefore, have profited from Wallace's view that extinction of the parental ''species'' population resulted from prolonged environmental stress, because he had established a different position in the Gray letter. His 1857 ''principle of divergence,'' on the other hand, was less definitely formulated than that of the May–June 1858 addition. He had postulated that since a plot of land will support more life if the forms of life are diverse, variant populations would seize the most divergent ecological roles they possibly could. One can infer, I think, that Darwin would not have been totally satisfied with this postulation, for it is obvious to any biologist that variant populations are so little different from each other and from the parent ''species'' population that the ecological roles they could ''seize'' would be very little different from that of the parental species.

Browne (1980) suggests that Darwin had spent much time and effort, especially after midsummer 1857, in trying to achieve a firmer understanding of why species have diverged in the course of time. After completing, in early 1858, a recalculation of a persistent line of reasoning, based on ''botanical arithmetic'' (a search for quantitative rules for the appearance of varieties in nature), he prepared an addition to be inserted into the text of chapter IV, ''Variation Under Nature,'' of his long manuscript. The original text had already presented some discussion of variation based on botanical arithmetic. The 1858 addition dealt with variation in large genera as compared with small ones. Darwin, to judge from the concluding sentence of this addition (fol. A43; see Stauffer 1975:164), interpreted the fact that the species of large genera had relatively more varieties to mean that the number of species in large genera was increasing more rapidly.

> [this conclusion] when taken in connexion with a large amount of extinction & with a principle, hereafter to be explained, which may be called that of divergence—taken together throw a clear light on the affinities of all organic beings within the same great classes; for we invariably see organic beings related to each other in groups within groups—or somewhat like the branches of a tree sub-dividing from a central trunk.

This addition to the manuscript chapter on ''Variation Under Nature'' was completed in mid-April of 1858, as noted above.

Why, then, just a month or so later, did Darwin return to the subject of divergence? Browne (1980:84) has stated a belief that the May–June addition to chapter VI was a continuation of that theme; that the insertion of material on divergence into chapter VI, "Natural Selection," was the addition of the "principle of divergence" to a "later" chapter to which Darwin alluded in the addition to manuscript chapter IV. But Browne has, I think, been misled by Stauffer's omission of the lines that Darwin had crossed out at the top of folio 28, for that is the only clue to the content of folio 27. Those folios bore the only mention in the original text of the "principle of divergence." Because the original text of chapter VI had already discussed that principle, no addition was necessary.

We are left, I believe, with the most likely stimulus for Darwin's restudy of Wallace's 1855 paper, namely, Wallace's concept of the dynamics of the origin of species as elaborated in his Ternate manuscript. This included explicit explanations for extinction and divergence. Darwin's marginal drawing on Wallace's 1855 paper, of simple and divergent lines of descent, is, I believe, the early result of that reexamination. It suggests the genesis of the diagram and text of the inserted folios, 26* through 26nn. This new construction of Wallace's ideas about diverging lineages and the significance of extinction was called by Darwin "Divergence of Character." While the elaboration of "Divergence of Character" occupied essentially all of the insert, it was introduced by mention of the relatively greater amount of variation in the species of larger genera as compared with smaller ones, followed by a rehearsal of the Gray letter's "principle of divergence."

The new treatment of divergence in the "Natural Selection" manuscript provided an ecological context for the diagram, a context that the *Origin* totally lacks. This was an obvious effort to bridge or amalgamate the principle from the Gray letter with the Wallace-inspired diagram. In the manuscript diagram, Darwin had postulated that his initial array of species, A through M, were disposed along what would now be called an ecological gradient. On folio 26t, at the opening of the discussion of the diagram, he said, "Suppose A the most moisture-loving & M the least moisture-loving species." In the following paragraph he wrote of the differential responses of the varieties of A and M to drought. But in the equivalent text in the *Origin,* no ecological context was offered.

The role of Wallace's 1858 manuscript in providing one source of

Darwin's new thoughts, however, is not a real possibility at all if the presumed receipt date for the Ternate manuscript is correct. Darwin is said to have received it on June 18, six days after he had recorded in his diary that he had completed "Divergence" and the corrections to chapter VI. If one is unable to dismiss as coincidental the extraordinary similarities between the new folios and Wallace's two relevant essays, then one is forced to ask, How firm is the evidence that Wallace's Ternate manuscript was received on June 18, 1858? The earliest indication of a date of receipt is by Francis Darwin (F. Darwin 1887 1:473). Charles Darwin's letter to Lyell relating the crushing news of the arrival of Wallace's manuscript was dated only "Down 18th"; but his son, as editor, added "June 1858" in brackets. Although the attribution of a month was his own, Francis Darwin, when describing the long manuscript that he referred to as "The Unfinished Book," stated without a caveat that his father's writing was interrupted by the receipt of Wallace's manuscript in "June, 1858" (p. 427).

Examination of the autograph letter was obviously necessary.[5] It is the first of three letters written to Sir Charles Lyell just prior to the reading of the joint contribution before the Linnean Society on July 1, 1858. The first letter is plainly dated "18th" in ink, in Darwin's hand. But after the numeral, "June" has been written in pencil and "1858," also in pencil, just below the day and month, in a hand other than Darwin's. On the second letter, dated just "Friday" in ink, the same hand has written in pencil, "received June 1858," but in this case the penciling is at the left-hand side of the top of the letter, not in juxtaposition to Darwin's indication of a date. The third letter bears the heading "Down 26th" in ink, in Darwin's hand. Here again "June 1858" is written in pencil, in a hand clearly distinct from Darwin's but quite like the penciled writing on the earlier letters. I interpret the pencil marking on all three letters as having been added at the home of the recipient (Lyell). Other Darwin letters to Lyell have had their dates similarly completed. (For example, on a letter that Darwin had dated "May 5th," someone in Lyell's house-

5. The letters are in the possession of the Library of the American Philosophical Society, Philadelphia. Photocopies are on file with the Darwin Collection at University Library, Cambridge.

hold had added ''1856.'') But the indication that the letter acknowledging receipt of Wallace's manuscript, dated ''18th'' by Darwin,
was probably received by Lyell in June does not constitute proof that
it was written in June. It could have been written on May 18 but not
mailed until June. Is there a possibility that Darwin could have received Wallace's letter on May 18?

When would a letter mailed on March 9, 1858, at Ternate, Moluccas, Dutch East Indies, be likely to have arrived in London? An
answer, if there is any evidence now available, would certainly have
to come from a knowledge of how the mails from the Dutch East
Indies reached the Netherlands, and indeed all of Europe, in 1858.
Officials at the Postmuseum in The Hague kindly described the system to me and supplied details through archivists at the Algemeen
Rijksarchief, also in The Hague. Dr. R. E. J. Weber, Director of the
Postmuseum, explained that beginning in 1846 the Netherlands Post
began to make official use of the overland mail service provided to
the British Government on contract by the P & O Steamship Navigation Company. This dependence on the P & O service continued
until 1870, after the Suez Canal was opened, when the Royal Dutch
Mail was established to carry the mails between Batavia (Djakarta)
and the Netherlands. Starting in 1846 the mail was carried twice a
month from Batavia to Singapore. There it was picked up by the
P & O packet sailing from Hong Kong to Singapore to Galle, Ceylon,
where it was transshipped to the Calcutta-Ceylon-Suez leg. From Suez
the mails were carried overland in Egypt to Alexandria and transferred to the Mediterranean section of the P & O. The letters were
taken to Marseilles and carried by train to Paris and then to Rotter-
dam.

Information about the interisland mail system that collected mail at
a series of colonial ports and carried it back to Batavia was supplied
by Mr. J. Giphart of the Postmuseum through the kind offices of Dr.
A. E. M. Ribberink, Chief Archivist (Second Section) of the General States Archives. Mail was collected at approximately forty-day
intervals. (This schedule was evident in the events detailed in ch.
10.)

The route of the Dutch mail steamer, with transit times, was as
follows:

Dutch Interisland Mail Route

Port	Transit Time
Batavia (Java)	
Semarang (Java)	36 hours
Surabaya (Java)	24–25 hours
Macassar (Celebes)	4–5 days
Timor	5–6 days
Banda	2 days
Amboina	15–20 hours
Ternate	1.5–2 days
Menado (Celebes)	1.5 days
Macassar (Celebes)	7 days
Surabaya (Java)	4–5 days
Batavia (Java)	2.5 days

(from E. H. Boon's traveler's guide to Netherlands East Indies, 1863, in Dutch; J. Giphart, trans.)

Transit time from Ternate to Batavia was about sixteen days. Wallace's letter and manuscript, mailed in Ternate on March 9, would have arrived in Batavia on March 25, 1858. The following official announcement from the post office in Batavia appeared in the newspaper *Java Bode* on March 24, 1858:

> —The Director of the Post Office calls herewith, those interested, to mind that the 2nd mail steamer in March will depart on Friday March 26, and that the packets of mail to be sent with this ship will be closed at the Post Office at Weltevreden on Thursday March 25:
> a/ at 8 o'clock P.M. for Europe, British India, China, etc., etc.
> b/ at 1 o'clock P.M. for Banka, Palembang, Billiton and Riouw.—
> (Translated by Dr. A. E. M. Ribberink)

On March 27 *Java Bode* reported that the *Banda* had departed on March 26 for Singapore.

From Singapore, of course, the P & O system carried the mails to London. The Hong Kong–Singapore–Ceylon packets, on a two-week schedule, visited Singapore twice in April 1858, on the seventh and the twenty-first. Dutch Indies mail transshipped from the *Banda* to the Calcutta–Ceylon–Suez packet presumably left Singapore on April 7 and reached Suez on May 4. Singapore mail leaving April 21 arrived in Suez on May 16.

An examination of records in the Central Headquarters/Record Room, Postal Headquarters, London, revealed a "Daily Packet Lists of 1858," which provided information (to the minute) of every step in the transit of incoming mail from Calcutta, Bombay, and Sydney (see fig. 11.3).

Table 1 extracts the information relevant to this study. It is evident that the Calcutta mail that arrived in Suez on May 4 was carried from Alexandria by the *Indus* to Malta, arriving on May 10. There the letters and heavy mail were divided. Letters (marked "via Marseilles") were transferred the same day to the *Euxine*, which left immediately (at 1:15 P.M.) for Marseilles, arriving on May 13. The packet arrived at 8:30 A.M.; by 10:00 A.M. the letters were on the train for Paris. They arrived in the General Post Office, London, on May 14, at 10:25 P.M. The heavy portion of the mail (marked "via Southampton") remained on the *Indus* and reached Southampton, and London, on May 20.

The mail from Singapore of April 21, arriving at Suez on May 16, had similar handling: carried by the *Pera* from Alexandria, it reached Malta on May 23. The letters were transferred to the *Valetta* for Marseilles and reached G.P.O. London on May 28. The heavy portion stayed aboard the *Pera*, reaching Southampton and G.P.O. London on June 2.

What, now, do we know of the fate of individual letters using this system? Unfortunately, as noted earlier, Wallace's letter and envelope are missing. Chief Archivist Ribberink, however, was able to provide dates for semiofficial letters from Buitenzorg, the seat of the Dutch colonial government, just south of Batavia to government offices in The Hague. The list he provided for all of 1858 demonstrated the regularity of this biweekly mail service. (Only one letter, late in the year, failed to arrive on schedule in The Hague.)

Sent Buitenzorg, Java (via Batavia)	Received The Hague, Netherlands
March 11	April 28
March 25	May 15
April 11	May 30

Packet despatched from	Date of Despatch: Day	Hour	Name of Packet	Date of Arrival at Suez Roadstead: Day	Hour	Date upon which Mails were handed over the side of the Packet: Day	Hour	Date upon which Mails were despatched from Packet Office at Suez — Bulk Mails: Day	Hour	Suez Mail and Small Parcels: Day	Hour	Date of Arrival of Mails at Railway Terminus at Alexandria: Day	Hour	Date upon which Marseilles portion of the Mails was put on board the Packet, according to the Time Bill: Day	Hour	Name of Packet	Date of Sailing: Day	Hour	Date upon which Southampton portion of the Mails was put on board the Packet: Day	Hour	Name of Packet
	1858.			1858.				1858.		1858.		1859.		1858.			1858.		1858.		
Calcutta "Extra Mail"	18 Mch	—	Bentinck	14 Apl	5.0 P.M.	—	—	14 Apl	8.15 P.M.	14 Apl	9.0 P.M.	17 Apl	2.0 A.M.	20 Apl	3.30 P.M.	Panther	20 Apl	4.10 P.M.			Colombo
Do	23 "	6.0 A.M.	Hindostan	18 "	1.0 P.M.	—	—	18 "	4.15 P.M.	18 "	4.50 P.M.	20 "	8.0 A.M.								
Sydney	11 "	Noon	Emeu	23 "	8.0 P.M.	—	—	24 "	2.30 A.M.	24 "	2.30 A.M.	25 "	8.30 P.M.								
Bombay	9 Apl	10.0 P.M.	Madras	25 "	0.03 A.M.	—	—	25 "	4.50 A.M.	25 "	5.10 A.M.	26 "	5.0 P.M.			Valetta	26 "	6.20 P.M.			Benares
Calcutta	10 "	6.0 A.M.	Bengal	4 May	4.25 P.M.	—	—	4 May	8.0 P.M.	4 May	8.30 P.M.	6 May	11.30 A.M.	6 May	—	Indus	6 May	6.15 P.M.	6 May	—	Indus
Bombay "Extra Mail"	12 "	9.0 P.M.	Punjaub	4 "	1.45 P.M.	—	—	4 "	8.0 P.M.	—	—										
Do	24 "	10.30 P.M.	Ottawa	9 "	3.30 A.M.	—	—	9 "	6.40 A.M.	9 "	7.10 A.M.	10 "	2.15 P.M.	11 "	3.30 P.M.	Panther	11 "	4.30 P.M.			Sultan
Calcutta	23 "	6.0 A.M.	Nubia	16 "	11.30 P.M.	—	—	17 "	9.0 A.M.	17 "	9.25 A.M.	18 "	4.15 P.M.	19 "	4.0 P.M.	Pera	19 "	4.50 P.M.	19 "	4.0 P.M.	Pera
Bombay	9 May	5.0 A.M.	Ganges	25 "	0.53 A.M.	—	—	25 "	4.35 A.M.	25 "	5.0 A.M.	26 "	6.0 A.M.	26 "	5.15 P.M.	Euxine	26 "	6.10 P.M.	26 "		Ripon
Calcutta	4 "	11.15 A.M.	Nemesis	3 June	0.20 A.M.	—	—	3 June	5.0 A.M.	3 June	5.30 A.M.	4 June	11.30 A.M.	4 June	5.15 P.M.	Colombo	5 June	5.0 A.M.	4 June	5.15 P.M.	Colombo
Sydney	11 Apl	9.0 A.M.	Victoria	6 "	3.15 P.M.	—	—	6 "	10.45 P.M.	6 "	11.30 P.M.	7 "	11.30 P.M.	"		Cambria	8 "	9.20 A.M.	"		Cambria
Bombay	19 May	11.0 P.M.	Bombay	6 "	4.45 P.M.	—	—	6 "	10.50 P.M.			8 "	2.0 P.M.	8 "		Valetta	8 "	6.20 P.M.	8 "		Valetta
Calcutta	18 "	5.50 A.M.	Alma	20 "	2.30 A.M.	—	—	20 "	8.30 A.M.	20 "	9.0 A.M.	21 "	9.30 A.M.	21 "	5.15 P.M.	Indus	21 "	6.05 P.M.	21 "	5.15 P.M.	Indus
Bombay	5 June	—	Madras	21 "	11.0 P.M.	—	—	22 "	2.40 A.M.	22 "	3.10 A.M.	23 "	1.0 P.M.	23 "	5.30 P.M.	Taurus Private Steamer	23 "	6.30 P.M.	23 "	5.30 P.M.	Taurus Private Steamer
Sydney	11 May	—	European	30 "	7.30 P.M.	—	—	1 July	0.20 A.M.	1 July	1.0 A.M.	2 July	4.0 A.M.	2 July		Teviot	2 July	Noon	2 July		Teviot
Calcutta	4 June	6.30 A.M.	Bentinck	6 July	1.0 A.M.	—	—	6 "	5.15 A.M.	6 "	6.05 A.M.	7 "	9.0 A.M.	7 "	3.30 P.M.	Vectis	7 "	4.30 P.M.	7 "	—	Northam
Bombay	20 "	0.30 P.M.	Ottawa	7 "	6.10 P.M.	—	—	7 "	10.10 P.M.	7 "	10.45 P.M.	9 "	4.0 P.M.	10 "	5.30 P.M.	Euxine	10 "	6.30 P.M.	10 "	—	Ripon
Calcutta	19 "	10.30 A.M.	Candia	17 "	6.15 A.M.	—	—	17 "	10.45 A.M.	17 "	11.50 A.M.	18 "	7.15 P.M.	18 "	—	Pera	19 "	5.0 A.M.	18 "	—	Pera
Bombay	4 July	6.15 A.M.	Bombay	23 "	6.20 A.M.	—	—	23 "	9.35 A.M.	23 "	10.15 A.M.	24 "	6.0 P.M.	25 "	0.35 P.M.	Vectis	25 "	1.06 P.M.	"		Sultan
Sydney	11 June	Noon	Australasian	30 "	9.0 P.M.	—	—	31 "	3.0 A.M.	31 "	3.30 A.M.	1 Aug	4.0 A.M.	1 Aug	—	Cambria	1 Aug	[illegible]	[illegible]	[illegible]	Cambria

Date of Sailing: Day	Hour	Date of Arrival at Malta of Packet with Marseilles portion of Mails: Day	Hour	Date of Arrival at Malta of Packet with Southampton portion of Mails: Day	Hour	Date fixed for Sailing from Malta of Packet for Marseilles according to Telegram: Day	Hour	Actual Date of Sailing: Day	Hour	Telegram received at General Post Office, London: Day	Hour	Date of Sailing from Malta of Packet for Southampton: Day	Hour	Date of Arrival of Packet at Marseilles: Day	Hour	Telegram received at General Post Office, London: Day	Hour	Mails despatched from Marseilles: Day	Day	Mails reached General Post Office, London: Day	Hour	Date of Arrival of Packet at Southampton: Day	Hour	Mails despatched from Southampton: Day	Hour	Mails reached General Post Office, London: Day	Hour
1858.		1858.		1858.		1858.		1858.		1858.		1858.		1858.		1858.		1858.		1858.		1858.		1858.		1858.	
20 Apl	4.15 P.M.	23 Apl	11.15 P.M.	23 Apl	6.10 P.M.	24 Apl	2.0 A.M.	24 Apl	4.30 A.M.	24 Apl	6.55 A.M.	24 Apl [illegible] 23 "	4.30 A.M. [illegible] 2.20 A.M.	26 Apl	8.0 P.M.	27 Apl	1.30 A.M.	26 Apl	10.30 P.M.	28 Apl	8.10 A.M.	10 May	2.30 A.M.			10 May	10.15 A.M.
27 "	5.10 P.M.	29 "	9.15 P.M.	1 May	2.15 A.M.			30 "	2.20 A.M.			1 May	11.0 A.M.	2 May	10.35 A.M.			2 May	Noon S.T.	2 May	10.30 P.M.	11 "	7.0 P.M.	11 "	9.30 P.M. S.T.	12 "	0.45 A.M.
6 May	6.15 P.M.	10 May	10.08 A.M.	10 "	10.08 A.M.	10 May	4.20 P.M.	10 May [illegible]	1.15 P.M.	10 May	1.0 P.M.	10 "	4.35 P.M.	13 "	8.30 A.M.	13 "	1.25 P.M.	13 "	10.0 A.M.	14 "	10.35 P.M.	20 "	4.50 P.M.	20 "	7.10 P.M.	20 "	10.30 P.M.
10 "	6.25 P.M.	15 "	7.0 A.M.	15 "	11.55 A.M.	15 "	Noon	15 "	1.0 P.M.	15 "	10.15 P.M.	15 "	0.35 P.M.	18 "	4.30 A.M.	18 "	0.05 P.M.	18 "	10.0 A.M.	19 "	10.10 P.M.	25 "	0.20 P.M.	25 "	8.00 P.M.	25 "	6.25 P.M.
19 "	4.50 P.M.	23 "	Noon	23 "	Noon	23 "	3.0 P.M.	23 " Valetta	3.05 P.M.	23 "	7.0 P.M.	23 "	6.0 P.M.	26 "	11.45 P.M.	27 "	0.25 P.M.	27 "	10.0 A.M.	28 "	10.20 P.M.	2 June	0.45 P.M.	2 June	3.0 P.M.	2 June	6.30 P.M.
26 "	6.0 P.M.	30 "	7.30 A.M.	30 "	10.50 A.M.	30 "	1.0 P.M.	30 "	1.0 P.M.	30 "	9.15 P.M.	30 "	4.40 P.M.	2 June	8.30 A.M.	2 June	8.0 A.M.	2 June	10.0 A.M.	3 June	10.15 P.M.	10 "	10.0 A.M.	10 "	11.30 A.M.	10 "	3.10 P.M.
5 June	5.0 A.M.	8 June	6.0 A.M.	8 June	6.0 A.M.	8 June	9.0 A.M.	8 June Panther	9.15 A.M.	8 June	6.23 P.M.	8 June	Noon	10 "	7.15 P.M.	11 "	1.15 A.M.	10 "	10.30 P.M.	12 "	8.15 A.M.	16 "	9.0 P.M.	17 "	1.30 A.M.	17 "	5.35 P.M.
8 "	9.20 A.M.	11 "	3.0 P.M.	11 "	3.0 P.M.	11 "	6.0 P.M.	11 "	6.0 P.M.	12 "	1.10 A.M.	11 "	11.30 P.M.	14 "		14 "	4.12 P.M.	14 "	1.30 P.M. S.T.	16 "	5.25 A.M.	20 "	5.30 P.M.	20 "	6.0 P.M.	20 "	9.30 P.M.
8 "	6.20 P.M.	11 "	5.10 P.M.	11 "	5.10 P.M.							11 "	11.50 P.M.									21 "	3.30 P.M.	21 "	5.0 P.M.	21 "	7.45 P.M.
21 "	6.05 P.M.	25 "	0.30 P.M.	25 "	0.30 P.M.	25 "	3.0 P.M.	25 "	3.20 P.M.	25 "	4.55 P.M.	25 "	7.0 P.M.	28 "	6.30 A.M.	28 "	1.20 P.M.	28 "	10.0 A.M.	29 "	10.20 P.M.	6 July	10.0 A.M.	6 July	11.30 A.M.	6 July	3.15 P.M.
23 "	6.30 P.M.	27 "	7.45 P.M.	27 "	7.45 P.M.	29 "	8.0 A.M.	29 "	8.10 A.M.	29 "	9.0 P.M.	28 " "Salsette"				2 July	0.50 P.M.	2 July	10.0 A.M.	3 July	10.30 P.M.	7 "	7.30 P.M.	8 "	1.30 A.M.	8 "	5.10 A.M.
2 July	Noon	6 July	5.15 P.M.	6 July	5.15 P.M.	6 July	7.0 P.M.	6 July		6 July	10.10 P.M.	6 July	11.30 P.M.	9 "		10 "	1.05 A.M.	9 "	10.30 P.M.	11 "	11.45 A.M.	18 "	Noon	18 "	1.45 P.M. S.T.	18 "	4.05 P.M.
7 "	5.0 P.M.	10 "	3.0 P.M.	10 "	5.30 P.M.	10 "	8.0 P.M.	10 "	8.20 P.M.	11 "	0.52 A.M.	10 "	11.30 P.M.	13 "	7.30 A.M.	13 "	0.30 P.M.	13 "	10.0 A.M.	14 "	10.30 P.M.	19 "	2.15 A.M.	19 "	7.0 A.M.	19 "	10.30 [illegible]
10 "	6.30 P.M.	14 "	7.45 A.M.	14 "	Noon	14 "	3.0 P.M.	14 "	3.30 P.M.	15 "	1.25 A.M.	14 "	5.30 P.M.	17 "	4.45 A.M.	17 "	0.25 P.M.	17 "	10.0 A.M.	18 "	10.20 P.M.	25 "	11.0 A.M.	25 "	6.0 P.M.	25 "	9.45 [illegible]
19 "	5.0 A.M.	22 "	0.45 P.M.	22 "	0.45 P.M.	22 "	4.0 P.M.	22 "	4.0 P.M.	22 "	7.32 P.M.	22 "	6.10 P.M.	25 "	1.0 P.M.	25 "	10.0 P.M.	25 "	4.0 P.M. S.T.	27 "	4.50 A.M.	31 "	0.15 P.M.	31 "	3.0 P.M.	31 "	6.30 P.M.
25 "	9.15 A.M.	28 "	7.0 P.M.	31 "	5.26 A.M.	28 "	9.0 P.M.	28 "	10.35 P.M.	29 "	7.40 A.M.					1 Aug	2.35 A.M.	31 "	10.0 A.M.	2 Aug	8.10 A.M.			12 Aug	3.0 P.M.	12 Aug	6.0 [illegible]
1 Aug	11.50 A.M.	4 Aug	10.50 P.M.	4 Aug	10.50 P.M.	5 Aug	1.0 A.M.	5 Aug		5 [illegible]	1.0 A.M.	5	[illegible]			8 "	1.20 A.M.	7 Aug	1.30 P.M.	9 "	8.24 A.M.	14 "	7.30 A.M.	14 "	[illegible]	14 "	1.0 [illegible]

Figure 11.3. "Indian and Australian Mail Homewards, 1857–61," pages for 1858. (Post 45/156 CHQ/Record Room, Postal Headquarters, London.) See text.

Table 1. Synopsis from Schedules for Homeward Mail (1858) via P & O.
See *figure 11.3 for details.*

LV Singapore (to Calcutta packet)	*ARR* Suez	*LV* Alexandria	*LV* Malta		*LV* Marseilles (via train)	*ARR* Southampton	*ARR* London G.P.O.
Apr 7	May 4	May 6 (*Indus*)	May 10	letters (*Euxine*)	May 13		May 14
				"heavy" mail (*Indus*)		May 20	May 20
Apr 21	May 16	May 19 (*Pera*)	May 23	letters (*Valetta*)	May 27		May 28
				"heavy" mail (*Pera*)		June 2	June 2

In accordance with the normal schedule for the interisland service, Wallace's letter from Ternate should, as described above, have reached Batavia on March 25. According to P & O records, it should have arrived in London about the time that the official Dutch letter was received in The Hague (May 15). The London arrival date, as shown by Postal Headquarters records, was May 14.

May 14, 1858, fell on a Friday. A May 18 (Tuesday) date for arrival at Down House, a few miles outside London, seems a little late for the mail service of the day. At any rate, May 17–18 is the most likely time for Wallace's letter and manuscript to have reached Darwin's hands.

Also to be considered, however, is the time of arrival in England of another letter that Wallace wrote in Ternate. A letter written to Frederick Bates of Leicester, the younger brother of Wallace's friend Henry Walter Bates, was dated March 2, 1858. Presumably this also left Ternate on March 9, with the letter to Darwin. Fortunately, the Bates letter and its envelope are still in the possession of the Wallace family (McKinney 1972:140–41). McKinney has reproduced the envelope, marked "via Southampton," which bears an April cancellation (the date appears to be "21") in Singapore, and London and Leicester cancellations of June 3. Working backward in the P & O schedule (see table 1), one finds that this letter, if on a normal schedule, would have reached Suez on May 16; it would have arrived in Singapore from Batavia in time for the second April departure (April 21), two weeks later than would have been expected. If the letter to Darwin, presumably marked "via Marseilles," arrived at Suez on May 16, with the Bates letter, it would have reached Malta from Alexandria on the *Valetta* and G.P.O. London, via Marseilles and Paris, on May 28. Heavy mail (Bates's letter), on the *Pera,* reached G.P.O. London on June 2.

Although such a two-week delay is unexplained, we must regard May 28 (Friday) or May 29, 1858, as a possible time for the arrival of Wallace's manuscript at Down House. But either date is earlier than June 12, the date that Darwin recorded in his diary for finishing "Divergence" and corrections to chapter VI.

Although a decision between the dates cannot be made on the basis of the mailing schedules, I believe that the earlier date is the more likely, for two reasons. First, there is the tone of Darwin's "18th" letter to Lyell; it sounds honest and despairing (see epilogue). (A second letter, dated "Friday," leaves a quite different impression.) The second reason is the length of time required to make the long insertions into the "Natural Selection" chapter. In summary, the evidence indicates that Darwin must have received Wallace's manuscript on either of two dates in May. Receipt on May 18 would leave 25 days for completion of those folios by June 12; May 28–29 would leave scarcely two weeks. But it must be conceded that desperation will make the pen move quickly.

EPILOGUE
What Really Happened at Down House?

The question, of course, refers only to the happenings in response to Wallace's essays. The simple answer is that no one knows. The version of events generally given currency appears to derive from information offered in *The Life and Letters of Charles Darwin,* published in 1887, five years after his father's death, by Francis Darwin. The greater part of this work is devoted to the arrangement, more or less in chronological order, of Charles Darwin's then-known letters. Included was a short autobiographical sketch prepared by Charles in 1876, primarily for the benefit of his family.

In the sketch Charles Darwin wrote that in 1856 Lyell had urged him to publish his views on species "pretty fully." He began his extensive treatment (the title "Natural Selection" was not mentioned), and it was half completed when his "plans were overthrown, for early in the summer of 1858, Mr. Wallace, who was then in the Malay Archipelago sent me an essay . . . ; this essay contained exactly the same theory as mine" (F. Darwin 1887 1:69). For an account of subsequent events he referred his readers to the Lyell-Hooker introductory letter to the joint Darwin-Wallace papers in the *Linnean Society* journal; he thus sanctioned that version. Darwin referred to the publication of bits of his private papers along with Wallace's essay: "I was at first unwilling to consent, as I thought Mr. Wallace might consider my doing so unjustified, for I did not then know how generous and noble was his disposition." Francis Darwin, as we have noted earlier, stated without comment that Wallace's manuscript had been received in June of 1858. Since then Darwin scholars have retold this version, variously embellished, based on the pivotal June 18, 1858, dating.

I wish to sketch an alternative reconstruction of the influences of Wallace's essays—one published and one in manuscript—on Darwin's activities in regard to his own formulations. Evidence presented in chapters 10 and 11, and some now available in recently discovered notebooks of Charles Lyell, permits a reinterpretation of Darwin's correspondence of that period.

Darwin never mentioned that his beginning to write his species book in 1856 had any relation to the publication of Wallace's "law" paper the preceding September; that possibility was suggested by the following information. In his autobiography Darwin noted that Lyell had urged him to write in 1856; in a letter to Wallace he revealed that Lyell had called his attention to the Wallace 1855 paper; and in an 1858 letter to Lyell Darwin also recalled that Lyell had urged him to read Wallace's paper, and added, "Your words have come true with a vengeance—that I should be forestalled." But Darwin skirted an explicit revelation that Wallace's paper had been pivotal in his beginning to assemble his own views in 1856 after a decade of attention to barnacles. The recent research of Leonard Wilson into Charles Lyell's works, however, has produced clear evidence that such was indeed the case (Wilson 1970:xlvii). Wilson recently discovered a hitherto overlooked set of manuscript notebooks recording Lyell's interest in species transmutation. They were found in Kinnordy House, Scotland, the Lyell family residence. The first notebook, which begins with "Wallace," is dated November 28, 1855 (Wilson 1970:3). According to it, in April 1856 the Lyells had visited the Darwins at Down House, and Darwin, made aware of Lyell's interest in Wallace's paper, had revealed to Lyell something of his own views on natural selection. Lyell's notes for April 16, headed, "With Darwin: On the Formation of Species by Natural Selection—(Origin Query?)" comprise four short paragraphs, beginning: "Genera differ in the variability of the species, but all extensive genera have species in them which have a tendency to vary." They continue, stating that when conditions change, individuals vary to adapt themselves to the new conditions and thus "flourish & survive" while others die. The second paragraph notes that extinction is more likely due to organic than to inorganic causes, and the third is about the embryology of pigeons. These are obviously Darwin's outline of his theory. The final paragraph states, "The reason why Mr. Wallace introduction of species, most allied to those immediately preceding in Time . . . seems explained by the Natural Selection Theory" (Wilson 1970:54, 55).

Shortly after this meeting with Darwin at Down House, if not at that very meeting, when Lyell apparently first learned any details of Darwin's theory (McKinney 1967:162; Wilson 1970:xlv), Lyell urged Darwin to publish something on his theory immediately. A recently discovered letter from Lyell to Darwin, dated May 1, 1856, closes with "I wish you would publish some small fragment of your data, *pigeons* if you please to go out with the theory let it take date to be cited and understood." (Wilson 1970:xlvii) To this Darwin replied in a letter of May 3: "With respect to your suggestion of a sketch of my views, I hardly know what to think, but will reflect on it, but it goes against my prejudices. . . . I rather hate the idea of writing for priority, yet I certainly should be vexed if any one were to publish my doctrines before me" (F. Darwin 1887 1:426–27). In his diary, on May 14, 1856, Darwin entered, "Began by Lyell's advice writing species sketch" (DeBeer 1959:14), but by mid-June he had abandoned the idea of a short sketch and begun writing on a greatly expanded scale. By the middle of October his diary records that he had finished the second chapter on geographical distribution for the beginning of a long "Natural Selection" manuscript. A month later (November 10, 1856) he finally broke the news to Lyell: "I am working very steadily at my big book; I have found it quite impossible to publish any preliminary essay or sketch; but am doing my work as completely as my present materials allow without waiting to perfect them. And this much acceleration I owe to you" (F. Darwin 1887 1:443).

In chapter 11 I discussed probable influences of Wallace's work on the long manuscript; it would be interesting to know if the short sketch that Darwin began in May showed any such influences. The sketch itself is not known to exist, but a letter to Asa Gray (see below) in mid-July gives an obviously unsolicited précis of his ideas that may reflect that just-abandoned sketch. Darwin employs words and phrases reminiscent of Wallace's 1855 "law" paper (see ch. 5). For example, compare Darwin's "Test this hypothesis with . . . well-established propositions . . . in geographical distribution, geological history, affinities. . . ." with Wallace's "The following propositions in Organic Geography and Geology give the main facts on which the hypothesis is founded" (Wallace 1855c:185; see list at beginning of my synopsis in ch. 5). This interpretation is lent greater credence by a comparison with the language of a short statement of Darwin's views that his good friend Hooker had requested a year earlier. It is also of interest to note that this account of his hypothesis, sent to Gray a year before the famous one quoted in chapter 10, did not mention divergence. Recall that its inclusion of the statement of Darwin's principle of divergence was probably the primary reason for the inclusion of the 1857 Gray letter in the joint Darwin-Wallace paper read in July 1858 to the Linnean Society.

C. Darwin to Asa Gray

Down, July 20th [1856]

It is not a little egotistical, but I should like to tell you (and I do not *think* I have) how I view my work. Nineteen years (!) ago it occurred to me that whilst otherwise employed on Nat. Hist., I might perhaps do good if I noted any sort of facts bearing on the question of the origin of species, and this I have since been doing. Either species have been independently created, or they have descended from other species, like varieties from one species. I think it can be shown to be probable that man gets his most distinct varieties by preserving such as arise best worth keeping and destroying the others, but I should fill a quire if I were to go on. To be brief, I *assume* that species arise like our domestic varieties with *much* extinction; and then test this hypothesis by comparison with as many general and pretty well-established propositions as I can find made out,—in geographical distribution, geological history, affinities, &c., &c. And it seems to me that, *supposing* that such hypothesis were to explain such general propositions, we ought, in accordance with the common way of following all sciences, to admit it till some better hypothesis be found out.
(F. Darwin 1887 1:437)

C. Darwin to J. D. Hooker

Down, 18th [July, 1855]

You ask how far I go in attributing organisms to a common descent; I answer I know not; the way in which I intend treating the subject, is to show (*as far as I can*) the facts and arguments for and against the common descent of the species of the same genus; and then show how far the same

arguments tell for or against forms, more and more widely different: and when we come to forms of different orders and classes, there remain only such arguments as those which can perhaps be deduced from similar rudimentary structures, and very soon not an argument is left.
(F. Darwin 1887 1:245)

I think it can be concluded that Wallace's 1855 paper—and Lyell's various urgings in relation thereto—was fundamental in forcing Darwin to write.

Darwin had rejected Lyell's advice to publish a short account of his views so as to establish his priority. Two years later he regretted it, as the following letter, probably written May 18, 1858 (see chapter 11), states:

> Down, 18th
>
> My dear Lyell,
>
> Some year or two ago you recommended me to read a paper by Wallace in the "Annals," which had interested you, and, as I was writing to him, I knew this would please him much, so I told him. He has to-day sent me the enclosed, and asked me to forward it to you. It seems to me well worth reading. Your words have come true with a vengeance—that I should be forestalled. You said this, when I explained to you here very briefly my views of "Natural Selection" depending on the struggle for existence. I never saw a more striking coincidence; if Wallace had my MS sketch written out in 1842, he could not have made a better short abstract! Even his terms now stand as heads of my chapters. Please return me the MS., which he does not say he wishes me to publish, but I shall of course, at once write and offer to send to any journal. So all my originality, whatever it may amount to, will be smashed, though my book, if it will ever have any value, will not be deteriorated; as all the labour consists in the application of the theory.
>
> I hope you will approve of Wallace's sketch, that I may tell him what you say.
>
> My dear Lyell, yours most truly,
>
> C. Darwin

(F. Darwin 1887 1:473)

An honest letter from a chagrined man. It is my view, however, that Darwin did not mail the letter then. Probably after much soul-searching, he restudied Wallace's Ternate manuscript and, with recourse again to Wallace's 1855 paper, wrote the material on the forty-one folios (26*–26nn), which I have already analyzed, and inserted it into the text of his chapter on "Natural Selection."

On June 8, Darwin wrote to Hooker that he had finally resolved the problem of how species diverged in nature and that he had "a very great confidence" that his principle was now "sound." He went on to say that his principle of divergence, together with natural selection, "is the keystone of my book" (F. Darwin and Seward. 1903 1:109). Months later, in a letter to Murray, publisher of the *Origin of Species,* Darwin used the same word, referring to chapter IV, "Natural Selection," "as the key-stone of my arch" (letter of April 5, 1859, in F. Darwin 1887 1:511). To my mind, these near-identical characterizations by Darwin himself corroborate my conclusion that the core of the theory presented in chapter IV of the *Origin* is based on the material written into chapter VI of the "Natural Selection" manuscript during May–June 1858, when Darwin had Wallace's Ternate manuscript as well as his 1855 paper before him. Remember that there is not a single reference to Wallace anywhere in that crucial chapter IV of the *Origin.* But there is also no mention of Wallace in the material inserted into chapter VI of the "Natural Selection" manuscript. Thus, assertions that Darwin's insistence on referring to the *Origin of Species* as an "Abstract" justifies its almost total lack of references do not have much substance when one knows that the text being abstracted also lacked any reference to the obvious major source of its ideas.

Having completed that insertion and the twenty-odd new folios to replace the end of the original chapter VI (by June 12, according to his diary), Darwin mailed to Lyell, probably around June 18, the letter he had written in May—but not sent—together with Wallace's manuscript.

In response to Lyell's reply, Darwin wrote a letter quite different in tone from the first:

Down, Friday [June 25]

My dear Lyell,

    I am very sorry to trouble you, busy as you are, in so merely a personal an affair; but if you will give me your deliberate opinion, you will do me as great a service as ever man did, for I have entire confidence in your judgment and honour.

I should not have sent off your letter without further reflection, for I am at present quite upset, but write now to get subject for time out of mind. But I confess it never did occur to me, as it might, that Wallace could have made any use of your letter [Italics added.].

There is nothing in Wallace's sketch which is not written out much fuller in my sketch, copied out in 1844, and read by Hooker some dozen years ago. About a year ago I sent a short sketch, of which I have a copy, of my views (owing to correspondence on several points) to Asa Gray, so that I could most truly say and prove that I [''stole'' lined out in original] take nothing from Wallace. I should be extremely glad now [both emphases omitted in letter as published] to publish a sketch of my general views in about a dozen pages or so. But I cannot persuade myself that I can do. so honourably. Wallace says nothing about publication, and I enclose his letter. But as I had not intended to publish any sketch, can I do so honourably because Wallace has sent me an outline of his doctrine? I would far rather burn my whole book than that he or any man should think that I had behaved in a paltry spirit. Do you not think his having sent me this sketch ties my hands? *I do not in least believe that he originated his views from anything which I wrote to him.* [Italics added.] If I could honourably publish I would state that I was induced now to publish a sketch (or I should be very glad to be permitted to say, to follow your advice long ago given) from Wallace having sent me an outline of my general conclusions. We differ only, that I was led to my views from what artificial selection has done for domestic animals. I would send Wallace a copy of my letter to Asa Gray, to show him that I had not stolen his doctrine. But I cannot tell whether to publish now would not be base and paltry. This was my first impression, and I should have certainly acted on it had it not been for your letter.

This is a trumpery affair to trouble you with, but you cannot tell how much obliged I should be for your advice.

By the way, would you object to send this and your answer to Hooker to be forwarded to me, for then I shall have the opinion of my two best and kindest friends. This letter is miserably written, and I write it now, that I may for a time banish the whole subject; and I am worn out with musing.

I fear we have case of scarlet-fever in house with Baby. Etty is weak but is recovering. [Italics added.]

My good dear friend forgive me. This is a trumpery letter, influenced by trumpery feelings.

Yours most truly,

C. Darwin

I will never trouble you or Hooker on the subject again.

(Sentences in the original that were omitted by Francis Darwin [1887 1:474–75] from the published letter are italicized. Two other omissions from the original letter are noted in brackets.)

Lyell's letter is not known to exist, but the first sentences omitted from the published letter suggest that Lyell had raised the question of whether Wallace's views might have "originated" from something that Darwin had written to him. Darwin rejected this out of hand. But Lyell also must have implied that he himself might have revealed some of Darwin's views in a letter Lyell claimed to have written to Wallace. (It should be inserted here that there is no evidence that Lyell ever wrote to Wallace during these years.) Darwin himself seems to have been a little puzzled by Lyell's statement about a letter to Wallace. Lyell may also have reiterated his plea of two years earlier to write a short sketch for publication. That might explain Darwin's sentence "I should be extremely glad now to publish a sketch. . . . But I cannot persuade myself that I can do so honourably." The double emphasis on "now" might refer to "now" as opposed to 1856. That would have meaning for Lyell. But, taken in connection with Darwin's initial use of the word "stole" in the previous sentence, might we interpret the double emphasis on "now" as a reflection of Charles Darwin's relief at "now" being able to "sketch his general views," "now" that he had just completed his theory with the help of Wallace's essays?

As history records, Darwin's friends Lyell and Hooker did even more for him than he had hoped. They awarded priority to Darwin on the basis of two excerpts, one from an 1844 manuscript, the other from a year-old letter.

Hooker asked Darwin to supply a copy of the Gray letter. Darwin sent the requested copy, together with a copy of the "sketch of 1844, solely that you may see by your own hand-writing that you did read it." This material was sent on the evening of June 29, so Darwin said in a letter to Hooker written that day, by a servant who would bear it directly to Kew.

A mystery that we noted in chapter 10 with regard to the dating of this "sketch" is clarified by a comparison of Darwin's autograph copy of the "sketch" or "essay" of 1844 with the bound copy in a fair hand, which bears a few comments by Hooker). Both manuscripts are among the Darwin papers at the University Library, Cambridge. Lyell and Hooker assumed, as they were supposed to, having only the fair copy, that the 1844 manuscript was copied from a manuscript written five years earlier. For across the front of the table of contents of the bound fair copy is written in Charles Darwin's hand, "This was sketched in 1839 and copied out in full, as here written and read by you in 1844" (F. Darwin 1887, 1:372). Darwin directed Hooker's attention to this page in his letter of June 29, 1858, by saying in regard to the sketch: "The table of contents will show what it is" (F. Darwin 1887 1:476). But on the back of the table of contents of the autograph manuscript is written: "This was written and enlarged from a sketch in 37 pages in pencil (the latter written in summer of 1842 at Maer and Shrewsbury) in the beginning of 1844, and finished it in July; and finally corrected the copy by Mr. Fletcher in the last week of September." This is consistent with Darwin's words in the first paragraph of the introduction to the *Origin,* quoted in chapter 10.

Another puzzling aspect of the Darwin excerpts in the joint publication is the question, Who selected the "extract" from the sketch that was read at the meeting and ultimately published? One is left with the impression, since the fair copy had been sent to them, that Hooker, or possibly Lyell, was responsible for choosing the passage. But a subsequent exchange of letters revealed that precious few hours were available for Lyell or Hooker to study the document. I interpret a remark in a letter to Hooker, after the crucial event, to suggest that Darwin himself had written out the selection and sent it along with the bound copy of the 1844 sketch. He must have copied this at a most difficult time, for mortal disease had struck his family; on June 28, his infant son Charles had died of scarlet fever. The extract had to substitute for the promised sketch of his "general views" because he was too emotionally overwrought to compose one. This letter to Hooker, on July 13, ended with the words, "Pray thank Mrs. Hooker for her very kind note, and pray, say how truly obliged I am, and in truth ashamed to think that she should have had the trouble of copying my ugly MS." The two documents that Darwin noted having sent to Hooker were not in Darwin's handwriting. The copy of the sketch sent to Hooker and Lyell was the fair copy in the hand of Mr. Fletcher, the schoolmaster, because that was the one on which Hooker had written a few comments. "Ugly MS." could also not have referred to the copy of the Gray letter, because Francis Darwin referred in a footnote to the first publication of the complete text of that now-famous letter: "The extracts were printed from a duplicate undated copy in my father's possession, on which he had written, 'This was sent to Asa Gray 8 or 9 months ago, I think October 1857.'" This copy, in a clear hand, is now in the University Library, Cambridge (Box 6, Darwin Papers). I think there can be little doubt that Darwin chose this passage from his 1844 manuscript because it was the only passage he had written anywhere that paralleled a part of Wallace's essay.

Darwin did not attend an extraordinary—but, for Darwin and his friends, fortunately timed—meeting of the Linnean Society. But his faithful, supportive (and self-serving?) colleague, Hooker, soon wrote to him with the details of the meeting. In a reply dated July 5, Darwin said,

> Thank you much for your note, telling me that all had gone on prosperously at the Linnean Society. You must let me once again tell you how deeply I feel your generous kindness and Lyell's on this occasion. But in truth it shames me that you should have lost time on a mere point of priority. I shall be curious to see the proofs. I do not in the least understand whether my letter to Asa Gray is to be printed; I suppose not, only your note. . . .
>
> Lastly, you said you would write to Wallace; I certainly should much like this, as it would quite exonerate me: if you would send your note, sealed up, I would forward it with my own, as I know the address, &c.

And in a letter to Hooker dated July 13:

> My dear Hooker—Your letter to Wallace seems to me perfect, quite clear, and most courteous. I do not think it could be improved, and I have to day forwarded it with a letter of my own. I always thought it very possible that I might be forestalled, but I fancied that I had a grand enough soul not to care; but I found myself mistaken and punished. . . .
> (F. Darwin 1887 1:484)

Thus Wallace learned from the Hooker letter what had happened in London on July 1, 1858. But whatever Darwin wrote, one can be sure it was not about the previous happenings at Down House. Wallace was the last person to be told.

Relevant Chronology of
Alfred Russel Wallace (1823–1914)
and
Charles Robert Darwin (1809–1882)

	Wallace	*Darwin*
1844	Leaves surveying to be schoolmaster, Leicester, for one year; meets H. W. Bates	Manuscript "essay" on possibilities of organic change; read by Hooker alone.
1845	Anon. *Vestiges* awakens interest in possibility of organic change	Puts ms. aside
1846	Surveying business declines	Begins study of barnacles
1848	Departs for Amazon with Bates as professional collector	
1852	Returns from Amazon; most collections lost. Writes papers, books	
1854	Departs for Singapore; Borneo	Barnacle study completed
1855	Paper on "law" regulating introduction of new species	Reads Wallace's paper
1856	Bali, Celebes, Aru	Begins long species manuscript, "Natural Selection"
1858	Feb.—writes ms. "On the Tendency of Varieties to Depart Indefinitely from the Original Type"	May—receives Wallace's ms

July 1—Joint Darwin-Wallace paper read at meeting of Linnean Society, London

1859	Eastern islands of Malay Archipelago	*Origin of Species*
1862	Returns to England	

WORKS OF ALFRED RUSSEL WALLACE

NOTE: The following abbreviations are used in the text to refer to Wallace's manuscript documents:

RC Registry of Consignments. 1854. Record of material sent to S. Stevens, agent for Wallace and Bates. Library, Linnean Society, London.
SR Species Registry. 1854–1861. Field notebooks, 2 books. General Library, British Museum (Natural History). Ref. No. 89aW.
SN Species Notebook. 1855. Field notebook. Library, Linnean Society, London.
IC Daily Register of Insect Collections. 1855–1859. Field notebook. Library, Linnean Society, London.
FJ Field Journal. 1856–1862. Field notebooks, 4 books. Library, Linnean Society, London.

NOTE: Page numbers cited in text for Wallace's published works refer to the modern edition, where one exists.

1847. Capture of Trichius fasciatus near Neath. *Zoologist* 5:1676.
1849. Letter to S. Stevens, Oct. 23, 1848, from Pará. *Ann. Mag. Nat. Hist.,* 2d Ser. 3:74–75.
1850a. Letter to S. Stevens, Sept. 12, 1849, from Santarém. *Ann. Mag. Nat. Hist.,* 2d Ser. 5:156–57.
1850b. Letters to S. Stevens: Nov. 15, 1849, from Santarém; March 20, 1850, from Barra de Rio Negro. *Ann. Mag. Nat. Hist.,* 2d Ser. 6:494–96.
1850c. On the umbrella bird (*Cephalopterus ornatus*), "Ueramimbé" L. G. *Proc. Zool. Soc. London.* Part 18:206–7.
1852a. Letter, Oct. 19, 1852. *Zoologist:* 3641–43.

1852b. On the monkeys of the Amazon. *Proc. Zool. Soc. London.* Part 20:107–10.

1853a. On some fishes allied to *Gymnotus. Proc. Zool. Soc. London.* Part 20:75–76.

1853b. On the Rio Negro. *J. Royal Geogr. Soc.* 23:212–17.

1853c. Application to Royal Geogr. Soc. June 13, 1853 (ms.). See appendix I in McKinney 1972.

1853d. On the insects used for food by the Indians of the Amazon. *Trans. Ent. Soc. London* n.s. 2 (1852–1853):241–44.

1853e. On the habits of the butterflies of the Amazon Valley. *Trans. Ent. Soc. London* n.s. 2 (1852–1853):253–64.

1853f. *Palm Trees of the Amazon and Their Uses.* Rpt., H. L. McKinney, ed. Lawrence, Kansas: Coronado Press, 1971.

1853g. *A Narrative of Travels on the Amazon and Rio Negro.* Rpt. of 2d ed. (1889), H. L. McKinney, ed. New York: Dover, 1972.

1854a. Letter, May 9, 1854, from Singapore. *Zoologist* 12:4395–96.

1854b. The entomology of Malacca. *Zoologist* 13:4636–37.

1855a. On the ornithology of Malacca. *Ann. Mag. Nat. Hist.* 2d Ser. 15:95–99.

1855b. Description of a new species of Ornithoptera. *Trans. Ent. Soc. London* n.s. 3:104–5.

1855c. On the law which has regulated the introduction of new species. *Ann. Mag. Nat. Hist.* 2d Ser. 16:184–96. (1960 Facsimile Rpt. *Proc. Linn. Soc. London* 171:141–53, with introductory notes by C. F. A. Pantin and Wm. T. Stearn).

1856a. On the habits of the Orang-Utan of Borneo. *Ann. Mag. Nat. Hist.* 2d Ser. 18:26–32.

1856b. Letter of April 8, 1855, from Borneo. *Zoologist:* 5113–54.

1856c. Observations on the zoology of Borneo. *Zoologist:* 5116–17.

1856d. Attempts at a natural arrangement of birds. *Ann. Mag. Nat. Hist.* 2d Ser. 18:193–216.

1857a. Letter to S. Stevens, Aug. 21, 1856, from Lombock. *Zoologist:* 5414–15.

1857b. Letter to S. Stevens, Sept. 27, 1856, from Macassar. *Zoologist:* 5559–60.

1857c. Letter to S. Stevens, Dec. 1, 1856, from Macassar *Zoologist:* 5652–57.

1857d. Letters to S. Stevens, March 10 and May 15, 1857, from Aru. *Proc. Ent. Soc. London* (1856–58), 8:91–93.

1857e. On the great Bird of Paradise, *Paradisea apoda* Linn.; "Burong moti'' (Dead bird) of the Malays; "Fanéhan" of the Natives of Aru. *Ann. Mag. Nat. Hist.* 2d Ser. 20:411–16.

1857f. On the natural history of the Aru Islands. *Ann. Mag. Nat. Hist.* 2d Ser., Supplement to vol. 20:473–85.

1858a. Note on the theory of permanent and geographical varieties. *Zoologist:* 5887–88.

1858b. On the entomology of the Aru Islands. *Zoologist:* 5889–94.

1858c. On the habits and transformations of a species of *Ornithoptera,* allied to *O. Priamus,* inhabiting the Aru Islands, near New Guinea. *Trans. Ent. Soc. London* n.s. 4:272–73.

1858d. Letter to S. Stevens, Dec. 20, 1857, from Amboina. *Zoologist:* 6120–23.

1858e. On the tendency of varieties to depart indefinitely from the original type. In C. Darwin and A. R. Wallace, On the tendency of species to form varieties; and on the perpetuation of varieties and species by natural means of selection. *J. Proc. Linn. Soc. London, Zoology* 3:53–62.

1859. Letter to S. Stevens, Oct. 29, 1858 from Batchian, Moluccas. *Zoologist:* 6546–7.

1860. On the zoological geography of the Malay Archipelago. *J. Proc. Linn. Soc. London* 4:172–84.

1862. On the trade of the Eastern Archipelago with New Guinea and its islands. *J. Royal Geogr. Soc.* 33:127–36.

1863. On the physical geography of the Malay Archipelago. *J. Royal Geogr. Soc.* 33:217–34.

1865a. On the varieties of man in the Malay Archipelago. *Trans. Ethnol. Soc. London* n.s. 3:196–215.

1865b. On the phenomena of variation and geographical distribution as illustrated by the Papilionidae of the Malayan Region. *Trans. Linn. Soc. London,* 25(1):1–71.

1869. *Malay Archipelago.* London, Macmillan. Rpt. of 10th ed. (1890), New York, Dover, 1962.

1876. *The Geographical Distribution of Animals.* 2 vols. New York: Harpers.

1898. *The Wonderful Century.* New York: Dodd, Mead.

1903. The dawn of a great discovery. My relations with Darwin in reference to the theory of natural selection. *Black & White,* Jan. 17, 1903, pp. 78–79.

1905. *My Life.* 2 vols. London: Chapman & Hall.

Marchant, J., ed. 1916. *Alfred Russel Wallace: Letters and Reminiscences.* 2 vols. London: Cassell; New York: Harper.

LITERATURE CITED

Bates, H. W. 1850. Letter to Stevens, March 22, 1850, from Barra. *Zoologist* 1850:2940.

—— 1851. Letter to Stevens, December 23 and 31, 1850, from Ega. *Zoologist* 1851:3230–32.

—— 1852. Letter to Stevens, Jan. 8, 1852, from Santarém. *Zoologist* 1852:3449–50.

—— 1862. Contributions to an insect fauna of the Amazon Valley. Lepidoptera: Heliconidae. *Trans. Ent. Soc. London* 23:495–515.

—— 1892. *The Naturalist on the River Amazons.* Rpt. of unabridged ed. (1863) with a memoir of the author by Edw. Clodd. London: Murray.

Beddall, B. G. 1968. Wallace, Darwin, and the theory of natural selection. *J. Hist. Biol.* 1:261–324.

Boisduval, J. A. 1832. *Faune entomologique de l'Océan Pacifique.* Paris.

—— 1836. *Diurnes: Papilionides, pierides.* Espèces Générales des Lépidoptères. Histoire naturelle des insectes, vol. 1. Paris, Librarie Encyclopédique de Paret.

Bonaparte, C. L. J. L. 1850. *Conspectus Generum Avium.* Leyden.

Brackman, A. C. 1980. *A Delicate Arrangement.* New York: Times Books.

Brooks, J. L. 1969. Re-assessment of A. R. Wallace's contribution to the theory of organic evolution. *Yearbook, 1968.* Philadelphia: American Philosophical Society.

—— 1972. Extinction and the origin of organic diversity. In E. S. Deevey, ed., *Growth by Intussusception,* pp. 19–56. *Trans. Conn. Acad. Arts Sci.,* vol. 44.

Browne, J. 1980. Darwin's botanical arithmetic and the "principle of divergence," 1854–1858. *J. Hist. Biol.* 13 (1):53–89.

[Chambers, R.] 1844. *Vestiges of the Natural History of Creation.* Rpt. with introduction by G. De Beer. Leicester: Leicester University Press, Victorian Library, 1969. (Dist. New York: Humanities Press.)

D'Abreda, B. 1975. *Birdwing Butterflies of the World.* Melbourne: Lansdowne Press.

Dahlgren, B. E. 1936. *Index of American palms*. Field Mus. Nat. Hist. Botanical Ser. 14, Publication 355.

Darwin, C. 1839. *Journal of Researches into the Geology and Natural History of Various Countries Visited by H. M. S. Beagle*. London: Colburn.

—— 1844a. Sketch of species theory. Original manuscript. Darwin Papers No. 7. Handlist of Darwin Papers in University Library, Cambridge.

—— 1844b. Sketch of species theory. Fair copy of above. Darwin Papers No. 113. Handlist of Darwin Papers in University Library, Cambridge.

—— 1845. *Journal of Researches into the Natural History and Geology of the Countries Visited During the Voyage of H.M.S. Beagle*. 2d ed. London: Murray.

—— 1857. Natural Selection. Ch. VI of the *Origin of Species* as originally planned, before abstract for publication in 1859. Darwin Papers No. 10(i). Handlist of Darwin Papers in University Library, Cambridge. (See Stauffer 1975).

—— 1859. *On the Origin of Species by Means of Natural Selection*. Facsimile of first ed. with introduction by E. Mayr, Cambridge: Harvard University Press, 1964.

Darwin, C. and A. R. Wallace. 1858. On the tendency of species to form varieties; and on the perpetuation of varieties and species by natural means of selection. *J. Proc. Linn. Soc. London, Zoology* 3:53–62.

—— 1958. *Evolution by Natural Selection*. De Beer, G., ed. Cambridge: Cambridge University Press.

Darwin, F., ed. 1887. *Life and Letters of Charles Darwin, Including an Autobiographical Chapter*. 2 vols. New York: Appleton-Century-Crofts.

—— 1909. *Foundations of the Origin of Species*. Cambridge: Cambridge University Press. (Reprinted in Darwin and Wallace 1958.)

Darwin, F. and A. C. Seward, eds. 1903. *More Letters of Charles Darwin*. 2 vols. London: Murray.

De Beer, G., ed. 1959. Darwin's Journal. *Bull. Brit. Mus. (Nat. Hist.) Historical Ser.* 2:(1):1–21.

Edwards, W. H. 1847. *A Journey up the River Amazon*. London: Murray.

Forbes, E. 1854. Anniversary address of the president (delivered Feb. 17, 1854). *Quart. J. Geol. Soc. London* vol. 10, part 1: *Proc. Geol. Soc. London*, pp. xxii–xxxi.

General Post Office, Her Majesty's Government. Indian and Australian Mail Homewards, 1857–61. Ref. No. Post 45/156.

George, W. 1964. *Biologist Philosopher: A Study of the Life and Writings of Alfred Russel Wallace*. London: Abelard Schuman.

Gray, G. R. 1852. *Catalogue of Lepidopterous Insects in the Collection of the British Museum. Part I. Papilionidae.* London: British Museum.

Haugum, J. and A. M. Lowe. 1978. *A Monograph of Birdwing Butterflies.* Klanpenborg, Denmark: Scandinavian Science Press.

Humboldt, A. and A. Bonpland. 1827. *Personal Narrative of Travels.* London: Longman, Rees.

Knight, E., ed. 1854. *English Cyclopedia,* Natural History Division. London. (See also 1866 ed.)

—— ed. N.d. Supplement to *English Cyclopedia,* Natural History Division. London.

Kohn, D. 1980. Theories to work by: rejected theories, reproduction, and Darwin's path to natural selection. *Studies Hist. Biol.* 4:67–110.

Lamarck, J. B. 1914. *Zoological Philosophy.* Hugh Elliot, trans. Rpt. New York: Hafner, 1963.

Latham, R. G. 1850. *The Natural History of the Varieties of Man.* London: Van Voorst.

Lawrence, W. 1819. *Lectures on Physiology, Zoology, and the Natural History of Man, Delivered at the Royal College of Surgeons.* London.

Lesson, R. P. 1829. *Zoologie du voyage autour du monde, éxecuté . . . sur la corvette . . . La Coquille, 1822, 1821, et 1825.* Paris.

Lindley, J. 1847. *The Elements of Botany.* 5th ed. London.

Linnaeus, C. 1758. *Systema Naturae.* 10th ed. Stockholm: L. Salvii.

Lyell, C. 1830–1833. Principles of Geology: Being an Attempt to Explain the Former Changes of the Earth's Surface by Reference to Causes Now in Operation. 3 vols. London: Murray. Facsimile rpt. New York: Johnson Reprint, 1970.

—— 1842. Principles of Geology: or, the Modern Changes of the Earth and its Inhabitants, Considered as Illustrative of Geology. 3 vols. Rpt. of 6th English ed. Boston: Hilliard, Gray. (See Wilson 1972 for the complicated printing history of the *Principles.*)

McKinney, H. L. 1967. Alfred Russel Wallace and the discovery of natural selection. Ph.D. Dissertation, Cornell University.

—— 1972. *Wallace and Natural Selection.* New Haven and London: Yale University Press.

Malthus, T. R. 1798. *An Essay on the Principle of Population As it Affects the Future Improvement of Society.* 1872. 7th ed. with author's preface to 2d ed. (Some chapters omitted in bks. I–III; bk. IV complete. Both in G. Himmelfarb, ed., *On Population.* New York: Random House, Modern Library, 1960.

Marchant, J., ed. 1916. *Alfred Russel Wallace: Letters and Reminiscences.* 2 vols. London: Cassell; New York: Harper.

Moore, H. E. 1973. The major groups of palms and their distribution. *Gentes Herborum* 11(2):27–140.

Munroe, E. 1961. The classification of the Papilionidae (Lepidoptera). *Canadian Entomologist,* Supplement 17.

Napier, W. 1973. Lands of Spice and Treasure, Part 1 of *Pacific Voyages,* pp. 8–161. The Encyclopedia of Discovery and Exploration. Garden City, N.Y.: Doubleday.

Newman, E. 1854. President's Address for 1853. *Trans. Ent. Soc. London,* n.s. 2:142–54.

Prance, G. T., ed. 1982. *Biological Diversification in the Tropics.* New York, Columbia University Press.

Prichard, J. C. 1813. *Researches into the Physical History of Man.* Facsimile rpt. ed. with introductory essay by G. W. Stocking, Jr., Chicago and London: University of Chicago Press, 1973.

St. John, S. 1879. *The Life of Sir James Brooke, Rajah of Sarawak.* Edinburgh and London: Blackwood.

Smith, S. 1960. The origin of *The Origin. Adv. Sci.* 64:391–401.

[Spencer, H.] 1852a. The developmental hypothesis. The Haythorne Papers, No. 2. *The Leader* (London), March 20, 1852.

[———] 1852b. A theory of population deduced from the general law of animal fertility. *Westminster Review,* n.s. 1:468–501.

——— 1904. *An Autobiography.* 2 vols. New York: Appleton-Century-Crofts.

Spruce, R. 1871. Palmae Amazonicae, sive enumeratio palmarum in itinere sue per regiones Americae aequatoriales lectorum. *J. Linn. Soc., Botany,* 11:65–183.

——— 1908. *Notes of a Botanist on the Amazon and Andes.* Edited and Condensed by A. R. Wallace. 2 vols. London: Macmillan.

Stauffer, R. C. 1959. "On the Origin of Species": An unpublished version. *Science* 130(3387):1449–52.

——— ed. 1975. *Charles Darwin's Natural Selection, Being the Second Part of His Big Species Book, Written from 1856 to 1858.* London: Cambridge University Press.

Stephens, J. F. *A Manual of British Coleoptera, or Beetles.* London.

Strickland, H. E. 1840. On the true method of discovering the natural system in zoology and botany. *Ann. Mag. Nat. Hist.* 6:184–94.

Swainson, W. 1835. *A Treatise on the Geography and Classification of Animals.* London: Longmans, The Cabinet Cyclopedia.

Weber, R. E. J. 1966. Zee- en landtransport in het post verkeer met bet vinl. nederlands-indië. *Het PTT Denkbeelden-Methode-Onderzoekingen* 14(4):115–202.

Wilson, L. G., ed. 1970. *Sir Charles Lyell's Scientific Journals on the Species Question.* New Haven and London: Yale University Press.

Zeuner, F. E. 1943. Studies in the systematics of Troides Hübner (Lepidoptera Papilionidae) and its allies; Distribution and phylogeny in relation to the geological history of the Australasian Archipelago. *Trans. Zool. Soc. London* 25(3):107–84.

INDEX

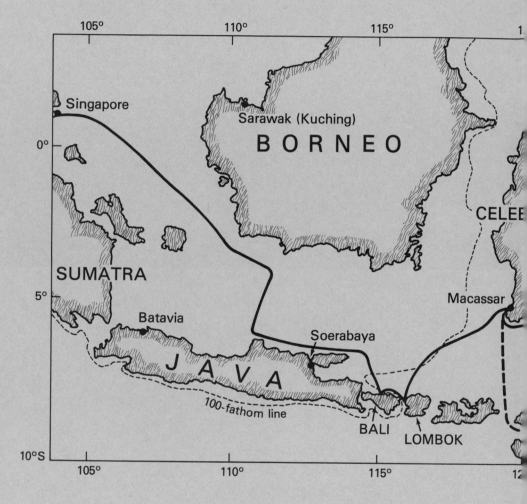

105°   110°   115°   1

Singapore

Sarawak (Kuching)

B O R N E O

0°

CELEE

SUMATRA

5°   Macassar

Batavia

Soerabaya

J A V A

100-fathom line

BALI

LOMBOK

10°S

105°   110°   115°   12